# AMERICA'S IMPASSE

# AMERICA'S IMPASSE

---

## The Rise and Fall of the Politics of Growth

---

### ALAN WOLFE

PANTHEON BOOKS    NEW YORK

All rights reserved under International and Pan-American Copyright Conventions. Published in the United States by Pantheon Books, a division of Random House, Inc., New York, and simultaneously in Canada by Random House of Canada Limited, Toronto.

Library of Congress Cataloging in Publication Data
Wolfe, Alan, 1942–     America's impasse.
Includes index.   1. United States—Economic policy—1971–
2. United States—Politics and government—1945–
I. Title.
HC106.7.W64      338.973      81–47216
ISBN 0–394–51012–7      AACR2

Manufactured in the United States of America

FIRST EDITION

To my parents,
Leon and Jean Wolfe

# Contents

# AMERICA'S IMPASSE

# I

# An Uncertain Mandate

IN 1980, Americans went to the polls and repudiated the Democratic party. Not only did an incumbent president, Jimmy Carter, go down to the most stunning defeat in modern American political history, but the U.S. Senate was reorganized under Republican leadership as a generation of Democratic liberals were sent scurrying from Washington. In a country not enamored of the British system of electoral mandates, a clear message was seemingly delivered. "The thing I get," said the then Democratic National Chairman John White as he surveyed the damage, "is that everybody thinks we ought to reassess some of the positions that we've taken."[1] Too late, one must add. Sensing that the American people were fed up with something, Ronald Reagan had already made that assessment and had been rewarded for it. Like the cowboy who organizes a posse to rid the town of sin and corruption, Reagan donned the white hat of rectitude and valor to cleanse the soul of a capital mired in the sins of excessive expenditure and national flabbiness.

The Republican victory in 1980 was immediately hailed as a turning point in American history. Certainly the victors thought so. "This could be the breakpoint election in bringing about a party realignment," Bill Brock, the Republican National Chairman, pointed out. "In this election we have brought together the elements of a new coalition."[2] Since 1932, according to a consensus among political scientists, the United States had been governed by an old coalition, based on the New Deal. The electoral elements of the coalition were blue-collar workers, blacks, urban political machines, and the traditionally Democratic South. To unify these elements, the coalition pursued the twin objectives of a welfare state at home and an active foreign policy abroad, financed by Keynesianism on the one hand and a global trading and currency system on the other. Save the presidential setbacks of the Eisenhower and Nixon years, the New Deal coalition was held to be the "natural" majority of the postwar period, the rule against which the exceptions were forced to define themselves.

Dominant political coalitions in America have a lifespan of thirty-two to thirty-six years. Beginning with the electoral revolution of 1800, which broke the power of the Federalists and brought Thomas Jefferson to power, the United States has gone through a series of party realignments with unnerving regularity: the Jacksonian ascendancy; the Lincoln coalition, followed by Reconstruction; the so-called system of 1896; and the New Deal. By the reckoning of that calendar, the United States was due for a realignment in 1968, a fact fully appreciated by the incoming Nixon administration. Yet Nixon's attempt to form a Republican majority, by adding to his strong base in the West blue-collar workers from the North and the Democrats of the South, did not take hold; and for some time thereafter, the United States kept searching for a missing realignment. The system had been primed for a change, yet the change did not take place, so that, as with a car that misses its tune-up, the contraption began to sputter and stall. Between 1968 and 1981, there were five different presidents, sharp policy reversals, and a general feeling that matters were out of control.

Ronald Reagan's impressive victory in 1980 offers the possibility that the long-lost party realignment has been found, that what Nixon began in the 1960s will be completed by Reagan in the 1980s. For once and for all, Republicans hope, the New Deal, whose demise has been reported any number of times, will be put to rest. What this means, if true, is that both the electoral coalition that made the New Deal possible, and the policies that were pursued by its representatives, will disappear as major forces in American politics.

Certainly there is good reason for the Republicans to be hopeful, for Jimmy Carter's disgrace could not have been more complete. Voters from every corner of the country sensed that the policies pursued by the Carter administration were ad hoc responses to unexpected developments. At home the administration could solve neither the problem of inflation nor the specter of unemployment. Its programs were too minimal to achieve their objectives, yet maximal enough to take their bite in taxes. Carter alienated traditional Democrats by adopting a Republican economic program premised on a balanced budget, but failed to win Republican support when he was unable to eliminate deficits. Overseas, the administration was its own best critic, staking out

policies only to repudiate them within months (in the case of a
U.N. resolution on Israel, within hours). Wandering off in different
directions at the same time and at the same speed, Carter pursued
foreign policy with neither rhyme nor reason. Duplicating his feat
at home, the president pleased almost no one, angering liberals
by increasing military spending, yet never gaining the support of
the conservatives he so determinedly courted. Sticking faithfully to
the middle of the road, Carter did not seem to understand, until
the day after the election, that the highway he had chosen was a
dead end.

America under Carter had reached an impasse, unable to move
forward, unwilling to move back. Sources of political energy dried
up as fast as oil reserves; as nonvoting increased, political aliena-
tion and cynicism took hold, and disgust with the candidates of
both major parties reached new heights. Jimmy Carter came to
symbolize an America unsure of itself, a country long enthralled
with a limitless horizon confronting an era of limits, a society used
to obtaining everything it wanted facing the possibility that the
pursuit of one goal necessarily meant sacrificing another. As if to
repudiate the mere suggestion that such an impasse existed, the
people turned to Reagan and voted into power a conservative
majority pledged to establish a new direction. It was not very clear
what the people wanted, but what they did not want was obvious—
no longer, the voters were saying, should we go on as we have
been. In the classic choreography of American politics, it was time
to throw the rascals out, in the hopes that a new group of rascals
would set things right.

Ronald Reagan and the Republicans, in short, have a mandate
to resolve the American impasse. They have been told that the
people crave action. Americans want a foreign policy that com-
mands the respect of the world, a domestic economy that creates
jobs while leaving prices stable, and an end to a sense of cultural
erosion and declining morality. As he pursues these goals, however,
Reagan will discover that his mandate, far from being clear, is an
ephemeral one, for it rests on shifting sands. Any new course
presupposes an understanding of the old one, yet there is reason to
believe, as I will argue in this book, that those who pledge to take
America in a new direction have misunderstood the departure
point. If the impasse that bedeviled the Democrats is incorrectly
mapped, then the Republican bypass will surely lead back to it.

## II

THE FIRST PLACE TO LOOK for an explanation of America's impasse is to the conservative consensus that propelled Ronald Reagan into office, for it was able to formulate an appeal to the majority that voted in 1980. In the years before Reagan's victory, American conservatism, once thought an exclusive property of the lunatic fringe, began a remarkable comeback among influential thinkers and publications. Great Society failures, disenchantment with affirmative action programs, impatience with the "Vietnam syndrome" (a reluctance to use force in defense of America's interests), and a sense that cultural changes in America were happening too rapidly and with too little reflection turned a number of former liberals into conservative Democrats or outright supporters of the Republican party. Old-line conservative publications like *National Review* were joined by *Commentary* and *The Public Interest* (and even by once liberal journals like *The New Republic*) as testing grounds for ideas that challenged the New Deal consensus. In short, by the time that Ronald Reagan was inaugurated, a conservative program had been formed that offered a diagnosis of America's impasse and a suggested cure.

One can turn to a number of sources for a statement of this conservative consensus: the Republican platform of 1980; President Reagan's budget speeches; the business press; a random issue of a host of new periodicals. The single best statement, in my opinion, was contained in two issues of *Business Week*. In a major cover story, later published in book form, *Business Week* addressed itself to *The Decline of American Power*. Then, in the summer of 1980, the magazine devoted a full issue to the causes of America's domestic troubles. Read together, these two issues establish the main points of the currently popular theory of what went wrong.

Scanning the domestic scene, *Business Week* lashes out at American complacency. Everyone is blamed, some businessmen among them. The thrust of the argument is that since World War II, government intervention—to protect business from competition, but also to protect ordinary people from economic collapse—has undermined the competitive position of the American economy. Workers are unproductive, management is complacent, government is inefficient. America is being deindustrialized, because other countries, more willing to take risks, are making goods cheaper and of better quality than Americans can. The situation is described as "drastic," requiring, in the words of the magazine, "a new social contract" for America. Everybody will have to change their ways, for "each social group will be measured by how it contributes to economic revitalization. . . . For government this means that all policies must be scrutinized and changed where needed in ways to promote rather than impede economic growth." There are a host of detailed recommendations, but they boil down to the single proposition that growth must become the yardstick for evaluating everything, including investment decisions, wage bargaining, and public policy.[3]

America's relations with the world are also subject to the magazine's harsh scrutiny. "The United States," we are told, "has failed to come to terms with its own role as the world's leading power." America entered the postwar period, according to *Business Week*, as the dominant power in the world. But unable to accept the responsibility that comes with power, the United States, especially in the course of the Vietnam War, became guilt-ridden, afraid to stand up to what it had to do. Americans allowed Middle Eastern oil producers to dictate terms to them, failed to keep ahead in international competition by putting ridiculous moralistic restraints on their multinational corporations, and allowed the dollar to decline because of inflation and unproductive activity at home. As America retreated, a power vacuum was created, one into which the Russians inevitably stepped. Other countries, no longer sure about America's resolve, turned elsewhere for help, and a vicious cycle was begun in which the failure to lead caused further failure. Once more the magazine has its policies to advance, and they are all variations on a single theme: America must put its guilt behind it. "The United States must redefine its global interests, state specifically to the world what they are, and go about protecting them."[4]

*Business Week's* analysis of the causes of America's problems adumbrates the sentiments that move the Reagan administration. One such sentiment is that there is something great about America, while another is that the sources of this greatness have been forgotten and need to be reclaimed. America performs best when it recognizes two verities: business is the source of growth and profit, and military power is the basis of the world's respect. During the postwar period, the conservatives hold, America lost sight of these truths. An understandable, if fundamentally misguided, idealism captured the American mind, producing the opposite of its intended effects. Government programs at home, designed to stabilize the economy and to correct social ills, led to stagflation and worsened social conditions. The same idealism applied to military and national security considerations, expected to bring about peace, simply encouraged Soviet expansion and therefore brought the country closer to war. The way out of the impasse, then, is to turn back to natural souces of strength, to rekindle the spirit of business enterprise, and to reawaken America's pride in itself as a world power. If the postwar period was dominated by a liberal belief in social reform and international cooperation, America must enter the *post*-postwar period, now dominated by business freedom and military might.

The program of the Reagan administration is oriented to achieve these twin objectives. At home, tax cuts are offered to stimulate economic growth, while deregulation and cuts in federal spending will encourage businessmen to invest. Rejecting Keynesianism, the Republicans offer "supply-side" economics, emphasizing the positive contribution that the private sector can make if only it is allowed to perform. Abroad, Reagan has called for a sharp increase in the military budget, a national refusal to allow the Soviets to obtain superiority over the United States, and an end to a policy of emphasizing human rights in the Third World. Growth in the economy and an expansion of American military power will right the wrongs, instill a sense of faith in the country's destiny, fight inflation and unemployment, and, as a result of the above, take America out of its impasse.

Will the conservative program succeed? Bill Brock, the Republican National Chairman who hopes for a new alignment in American politics, recognizes that one will come about only if the party finds a resolution to the impasse: "We've got to act with some urgency to deal with the problems on which people voted—unemployment and inflation."[5] Gary Hart, a Democratic senator from Colorado, put it more succinctly: "I give the Reagan administration about eighteen to twenty-four months to prove that it doesn't have any answers either."[6] Hart may well be right, for answers depend on asking the right questions, and the conservatives, Reagan included, are asking the wrong ones. Why did liberalism at home and idealism abroad fail? they ask. A more appropriate question: was liberalism and idealism ever really the guiding philosophy of postwar America? In this book I will argue that New Deal liberalism was already a spent force in America by 1948, and that the postwar experience was based on something else. Indeed, I will show in detail in the chapters that follow that the Democratic course so overwhelmingly rejected by the voters in 1980 was based on the same two propositions that the conservative consensus now offers: business freedom and military strength. America, in other words, was victimized by the program now being advanced to save it. The Reagan administration, and conservatives in general, offering to open America to an expansive future, will, if they have their way, chain it to a restrictive past.

## III

POLITICAL FAILURE in America was caused by economic success. Such, expressed in the briefest possible form, is the argument that follows.

The United States came out of World War II facing extremely important decisions about how it would organize its government and how it would relate to the world. For a variety of reasons, which I will discuss in the next chapter, neither the policies nor the constituencies of the New Deal were appropriate to the economic and political realities that faced Harry Truman. The conditions that had called for the New Deal having changed, the question facing postwar America was how to develop a new political formula for the organization and use of power.

Two possible courses seemed likely as the war came to an end. From the right end of the political spectrum, an anguished and bitter cry for a return to "normalcy" could be heard. Reflected in the Congress elected in 1946, conservative sentiment called for a return to business civilization; a holy, if inexpensive, crusade against communism; and a reassertion of once popular isolationist values. From the left a call was issued to carry the New Deal forward to its logical conclusion in some form of democratic socialism, American style (though, given the vocabulary of American politics, it could never be called that). Full employment, economic planning, national health insurance, and a commitment to peace organized through the United Nations—these would be the planks of a progressive program for America.

Whatever the differences between them, the right and left courses were both *political* options. Because neither was consensual, either would have required a popular mobilization and the building of new constituencies to support it. There was a sense of movement to both programs, one forward, the other back. Both implied struggle, dissent, controversy. Both were organized around an assertion of a particular vision and a sense of the means to achieve it. The key to understanding the formation of America's impasse, and the inability of both the Democrats and the Republicans to work their way out of it, lies in the fact that neither of these courses was chosen in 1946. Instead of making a political choice, America opted for an economic surrogate. A bipartisan coalition was formed to pursue economic expansion, at home through growth and overseas through empire. Once the rationale of the political system became the enhancement of growth, everything changed, including the role of political parties, the structure of political ideology, the nature of public policy, and the meaning of dissent. America embarked on a massive experiment. Politics would concern itself with the means—growth—and the ends, or purpose, of social life would take care of themselves.

Unlike political choice, economic growth offered a smooth and potentially harmonious future—instead of divisive, possible ugly, and certainly disruptive struggles over redistributional issues. Rapid economic growth, it was felt, could expand the pie sufficiently so that it would not have to be cut in a different way. And expansion overseas could create an imperial dividend, a periodic bounty from empire that would augment the sugar in the pie in the first place. Between them, economic growth and the imperial dividend created a whole new approach to government, one that would not so much exercise political power to make choices as it would manage expansion and empire to avoid choice. Growth, in other words, was transpolitical. While liberals blame conservatives for America's impasse and conservatives say that the fault lies with liberals, the truth is that growth allowed policies that substituted economic performance for political ideology. America sought, not what would create the best, but what would work the best. United behind a growth strategy, America expanded enormously in the postwar period, witnessing, some say, the greatest economic miracle in the modern world. So overwhelming was this growth that it created its own brand of politics, a compromise over policy so pleasing and rewarding that it would continue with unstoppable force long after the growth came to a halt, thereby worsening America's economic performance with the same determination with which it had once enhanced it.

The political costs of economic growth were not calculated for some time, and many refuse to examine them even now. Yet in retrospect it seems clear what happened. In the late 1940s, advocates of growth were believers in liberal ideals like economic planning, social welfare, international idealism, and foreign aid. But once the quest for growth became an all-consuming passion, those liberal objectives became dependent on conservative instruments. Growth at home could not take place without business confidence, and so liberals set out to win business support with favorable policies. Overseas expansion, to be made palatable to a generally isolationist America, had to be rationalized in terms of national security, encouraging a dependence on the military. With liberal objectives tied so firmly to conservative means, America developed a postwar political formula filled with contradictory language. Social justice would be pursued with all the vigor of profit maximization, while America would export to the world both humanitarianism and military power. Liberalism, in short, was submerged into the quest for growth; when its head popped up again, it was no longer liberalism. Without growth, the Democratic party, as Carter's presidency demonstrated, was a political organization without a political vision, something clearly recognized by the voters in 1980.

But if liberalism was seduced by its devotion to growth, so was conservatism. In the late 1940s, there was a genuine conservative tradition in the United States. Its faith was in economic competition, its roots in the farmers and small businessmen of the Middle West, its vision isolationist and even pacifist, and its conception of trade protectionist. An expanding economy at home, pushed forward by increasingly concentrated corporations and the benefits of overseas trade, dominated by multinational corporations and protected by a flourishing defense industry located in the South and West, transformed American conservatism as thoroughly as it did New Deal liberalism. Ronald Reagan bears as much resemblance to Robert Taft as Jimmy Carter does to Franklin Roosevelt. In the 1980s, the Republican party, as I will argue at much greater length in the concluding chapter, has become what the Democrats have rejected: the party of domestic economic growth and imperial expansion.

In their quest for respectability among business and the military, postwar liberals lost faith in their own objectives. Conservatives, whose links to business and some sectors of the military were strong, were incapable of becoming the majority party because they had given the world Herbert Hoover. For liberals, growth was a substitute for the respectability they lacked. For conservatives, growth became the key to the popularity they sought to gain. Just as liberals sublimated objectives like social justice into a quest for business and overseas expansion, conservatives would come to seek a balanced budget and stable prices through expanded profits and higher military spending. American liberalism lost its sense of purpose as it sought in expansion the resolution to its internal contradictions. With the arrival of the Reagan presidency, American conservatism promises to do exactly the same thing.

There are differences in the 1980s between liberals and conservatives, between the policies of Democrats like Carter and Republicans like Reagan. But they are not so much political differences as disagreements over how growth should be achieved in a no-growth economy. In order to understand why Jimmy Carter was defeated by the social and economic problems of the United States, and why the odds are so strong that the Republicans under Ronald Reagan will be as well, one must first uncover the reasons why the quest for growth achieved such a priority in postwar America. This book is about growth politics, its rise in the 1940s, its setbacks in the 1950s, its triumph in the 1960s, its collapse in the 1970s, and its rebirth, in the form of Reaganism, in the 1980s. America's impasse was caused by the fact that political traditions capable of organizing power in a coherent way were sidetracked to ensure that growth could take place in an unhampered fashion. The fantastic vitality of the economic system was dependent on an increasingly emaciated and contradictory political system. When the economy stopped growing, the shrunken political universe was revealed for what it was, and both Jimmy Carter's Democrats and Ronald Reagan's Republicans were stuck with it. America's impasse will remain until a coalition is able to come to power with a program that puts political vision, and not economic expansion, at the heart of its appeal.

# II

# The Rise and Fall
# of Growth Politics

AMERICA WAS FUNDAMENTALLY CHANGED by World War II, in every conceivable way. Economically, the war had a wondrous impact upon the gross national product (GNP). In 1929, the GNP stood at $103.4 billion, which then fell to $55.8 billion by 1933. Six years of New Deal policies saw the figure rise to $90.8 billion in 1939, still below the peak of ten years earlier. During the war, however, economic activity grew by leaps and bounds. The GNP reached $100 billion by 1940, $129.9 in 1941, $158.3 in 1942, $192 in 1943, and $210 in 1944.[1] At least this much can be said: war enabled production to take place once again.

But the need to turn out as many weapons as the economy was capable of generating was only a quantitative change, and there were important qualitative ones as well. Most noticeable was the growing role played by government. Public spending, $9 billion in 1940, increased tenfold to $98 billion in 1945.[2] The government offered the staggering sum of $175 billion in prime contracts between June 1940 and September 1944. Over one-third of all manufacturing structures and equipment existing in the United States during this period was constructed through the $17 billion worth of new plants financed by government to speed the war effort.[3] There could no longer be any doubt that government was capable of playing a positive role in economic stimulation.

In 1945, *Fortune* carried a Roper poll showing that only 41 percent of the American population thought that a postwar recession could be avoided.[4] It was generally assumed in America that periods of bust would follow periods of boom the way that thunder follows lightning. Yet the conditions of wartime production augured a transformation in the cyclical nature of American capitalism. First, the sheer size of the mobilization involved, much greater than in World War I, ensured that prewar conditions would not return in the same form; the sharply reduced military budget for fiscal year (FY) 1947, for example, was still $13 billion *higher* than the last prewar budget of 1940. Similarly, the number of civilian workers on federal payrolls after the war, and the number of women and men in uniform, was much higher than a decade earlier.[5] Second, vast savings by consumers, not spendable during the war, kept the economy afloat after the war had ended. Third, the Federal Reserve Board made a decision during the war to support the price of government securities at a predetermined rate, and this prevented tight-money advocates from constricting the economy in the late 1940s.[6] Finally, the war had created an effective system of wage-and-price controls, enabling expansion to take place without rapidly rising prices. Policymakers were thus able to prove that full employment and stable prices could coexist, so long as a political authority with appropriate power existed to ensure it.

Yet another qualitative change in the American economy brought about by the war was the freedom given to the United States by its strength in the world economy. Most countries at most times worry that trading rivals will increase their share of the world's output and threaten the advantages of domestic manufacturers. For the United States in the postwar period, the problem was the exact opposite of this. The U.S. economy was so much richer than those of war-devastated Europe that the latter were unable to absorb American surplus production; domestic unemployment would result unless the United States worked to *improve* the relative economic standing of its rivals. Some sense of the American advantage in the world economy is given by the fact that almost half of the world's manufactured goods in 1947 were made in the United States.[7] The dollar was far and away the world's strongest currency, especially since the collapse of the pound sterling. When the near U.S. monopoly on gold is considered—one estimate placed it as high as 72 percent of the world's supply in 1949[8]—America seemed in a position to benefit from economic changes in the world, not to be held down by them as it was during the Great Depression.

Nor was any other country in the world powerful enough to challenge the United States militarily. Germany and Japan, having been defeated, became the objects of an American effort to increase their productivity while keeping them under American political protection.[9] The so-called underdeveloped countries were as poor after the war as they had been before it, so there was no need to worry about them. Only from the Soviet Union could any possible challenge be forthcoming, and the Soviet Union had been an American ally during the war. In the late 1940s, and to the present day, there would be those who talked of a Soviet military threat to the United States, often with cataclysmic imagery. Certainly in the immediate postwar period these fears proved to be exaggerated. The Soviet Union had left its troops behind in Europe, but it had neither the weaponry nor the sophistication to challenge the United States at a time when policymakers allowed themselves to become haunted by a Soviet "threat."

Between them, domestic economic expansion, measured in the growth of the GNP, and the benefits to be obtained from unchallenged economic and military power combined to make the New Deal inappropriate to the situation of the late 1940s. New Deal measures had often been geared to doing—anything to get the economy out of its doldrums. But the postwar situation, with stimulation already in place, demanded something different. Two dominant points of view existed. There were a number of articulate economic activists who argued a fundamental restructuring of the economy in order to plan and direct the changes taking place. Domestic economic management, they claimed, must ensure full employment and the adequate use of all other resources, while America would join with the rest of the world in sponsoring global economic reforms to ensure greater prosperity. Opposed to these activists were businessmen and more orthodox economists, who held that, with the Depression over, the time had come to return to business as usual: a greater reliance on the private sector and international economic practices that increased American wealth, not the world's liquidity. In short, the fact that the economic situation of the late 1940s was different from that of the mid-1930s seemed to foreshadow a direction distinct from the ad hoc character of New Deal emergency measures.

Such a direction could only come from the political system, yet the politics of the late 1940s were as stagnant as the economy was dynamic. Shortly before America entered World War II, a political stalemate had emerged in the United States. The New Deal ran out of energy when its last major reform, a Wages and Hours Law, was passed in 1938. Conservative Democrats from the South and Republican isolationists from the West formed a coalition in Congress that was able to block Roosevelt from developing either a global foreign policy or a far-sighted domestic policy, yet the conservative bloc was still not strong enough to create an alternative governing strategy of its own. National unity produced by war overshadowed this deadlock for five years, but it would emerge again when the war was over. And when the war did end, Americans discovered that the conditions of wartime production, the rise in influence of the military, and the creation of a new political mood all deepened the political stalemate by strengthening the veto power of the conservative bloc.

Relations between business and government—touchy and suspicious during the Great Depression—went through two major changes during World War II. First, business began a political offensive designed to regain a positive image and to absolve itself as much as possible from any blame for the Depression. This offensive has to be rated a success. The large number of business executives who came to Washington "without compensation" to direct the war effort extracted major political concessions for their economic experience. The National Resources Planning Board, an agency that some New Dealers hoped to use to guide the economy in the postwar period, was abolished. Jesse Jones, Roosevelt's secretary of commerce, led the campaign from within to restore business influence. No-strike pledges kept labor subservient. In the guise of defeating Germany, businessmen were also defeating the New Deal, and they were determined to preserve their victory once the war ended. The more liberal New Dealers were in dismay. "I don't like to overuse the word 'fascist,'" Chester Bowles, head of the Office of Price Administration, wrote to Vice-President Henry Wallace in 1944, "but it does seem to me the only phrase that can be applied to the kind of thinking which I ran into among some groups in business."[10]

The political offensive of business during the war was facilitated by a second change in its relationship with government: business had, under the exigencies of wartime planning, become more monopolistic. The American economy in the twentieth century has been divided into a competitive and a monopolistic sector, the former dependent on the market, the latter trying to control the market. With government assuming the risks of entrepreneurship through cost-plus contracting, the monopoly sector of the economy was strengthened during the war. Thirty-three corporations received over one-half of the total prime contracts, while ten alone received over 30 percent.[11] Before the war there had been a significant element of antitrust sentiment in New Deal philosophy: Thurman Arnold, in charge of the antitrust division of the Justice Department, had tried to keep alive Louis Brandeis's faith in competition. This philosophy all but disappeared among liberals as the war brought concentration to a new peak and made competition seem somehow unpatriotic. With their power over markets more secure, monopoly-sector businessmen would be able to defeat, or at least to control, attempts to regulate them in the public interest. Indeed, a substantial portion of government intervention would become devoted to strengthening monopolization, not to curtailing it.

Besides a strengthened and revitalized business class, the war, not unexpectedly, had given rise to a powerful military apparatus, one closely connected to conservative Southern Democrats and Western Republicans. Before World War II, America had been an isolationist power, without a permanent standing army and without a substantial infrastructure in defense production. The creation of precisely such an infrastructure during the war raised the question of what would happen when peace returned. One does not need a conspiracy theory of history to suggest that military leaders and their supporters in the new defense industries would fight to preserve the privileges they had gained during the war. Spokesmen for the military sector were guilty of nothing more than the typically American pursuit of self-interest when they exaggerated military threats to the United States in order to enhance their economic and political power. The permanence of the new military sector, powerful in Congress due to the overrepresentation of the South, was a fact of life that made the political situation of the 1940s quite different from that of the 1930s.

Finally, war changed the nature of demagoguery in the United States. There has never been a time when America was without its advocates of simple-minded scapegoatism, but during the Depression the targets of the attack were often respectable elements, especially Wall Street. Even when anti-Semitic in nature, the demagoguery of the 1930s had a populistic tinge, enough to make established powers squirm. But if economic slowdowns unleash populistic themes, wars often give rise to reactionary ones. As early as the elections of 1944, the political coloration of the United States turned conservative. Right-wing appeals—anticommunism, racism, fear of modernity, antiurbanism—were gaining in strength day by day. Whoever could control the anger and frustration sparked by the war could ride to political power, and it became clear early on that business and the military were in a better position to channel this sentiment against the New Deal than the New Dealers were to use it to their own advantage. The objects of popular fury in the 1930s would become the beneficiaries of that fury in the 1940s.

As a result of these changes, the overwhelming political need to give direction to a set of economic transformations could not be met. Indeed, directions of all sorts seemed suspect. "A nation accustomed to the categorical yes or no, to war or peace and prosperity or depression," Eric Goldman wrote, "found itself in the nagging realm of the maybe. The liberals worried over the conservatives and the conservatives watched the liberals with an uneasiness akin to dread."[12] The stalemate that had been foreshadowed in 1938 returned, and with a vengeance. Conservatives had become a major force in Congress, but liberals still held the executive. America faced a political nightmare.

It was in this atmosphere of uncertainty that Harry Truman became president. Representing a border state, Truman existed geographically as well as politically in between the liberal cutting edge of the New Deal and the conservative opposition that had arisen to it. Confronted with a stalemate, both his personality and his location in the political structure of the time demanded that he extend it. Truman, in the perceptive analysis of Samuel Lubell, was "the man who bought time." "Far from seeking decision, he sought to put off any possible showdown, to perpetuate rather than break the prevailing political stalemate. . . . Truman's constant gamble was that the American public, when confronted with the unpleasant implications of decisive action, would prefer to continue with his policy of calculated drift."[13] The new president operated on both sides of the stalemate of 1938. Personally conservative, he surrounded himself with advisers who shared the emerging conservative sentiment as fully as any Republican. John Snyder, director of the Office of War Mobilization and Reconversion, a man with an "ideological fear"[14] of labor leader Walter Reuther, would use his powerful position to prevent any extensions of the New Deal. Truman appointed conservative friends to positions in the Reconstruction Finance Corporation (George Allen) and on the Federal Reserve System's board of governors (Jake Vardaman). But the most symbolic victory of the new conservatism was Truman's appointment of Edwin Pauley to be undersecretary of the navy in 1946. Not only was Pauley an archetypical monopoly-sector businessman and defense contractor—the John Connally of his day—his appointment also caused the resignation of Harold Ickes, the last New Deal progressive in Truman's cabinet. And, to complete the picture, Ickes was replaced by Julius Krug, who, in the words of Robert J. Donovan, "stood as high in the esteem of the business community as Ickes . . . stood with the liberals."[15]

Such appointments made it seem as if Truman would repeal the New Deal, and many liberals were aghast. "I see America destroying itself out of fear," I. F. Stone commented, "wasting its resources, betraying its past, moving toward a crime against humanity."[16] Yet a sharp shift to the right would have meant a way out of the stalemate, and that was not to be Truman's course. Especially as the election of 1948 came closer, the new president began to speak loudly in favor of the New Deal, which many of his key advisers disliked. The course that Truman decided to follow was brilliantly laid out in a memorandum drafted in November 1947 by Clark Clifford, Truman's most important political adviser. In this strategy memo—"based solely on an appraisal of the politically advantageous course to follow"[17]—Clifford developed a strategy that would produce Truman's reelection; lead to the creation of a new centrist coalition organized around economic growth; and set into motion the forces that would cause America's impasse a generation later.

One by one, like a Tammany Hall vote counter, Clifford ran down the roll call of domestic interest groups to see what they should be offered. Farmers, in his view, were having a good year; much rhetoric—though no promises of actual policy—should be directed to keep their loyalty. It was not a sure bet that workers would vote for Truman; they might not vote at all. Since "when they are well fed they are not interested," special steps would have to be taken to bring workers to the polls, for "they will probably be well fed in 1948." The black voter—"a cynical, hard-boiled trader," Clifford called him—might be susceptible to Republican appeal; Truman should deliver a major civil rights message to win him over, since the South would be unlikely to defect. (This is the only part of Clifford's memo that proved inaccurate.) The Catholic defection from the Democrats, which had begun in 1944, could be reversed with a heavy dose of anticommunism, since "the controlling element in this group . . . is the distrust and fear of communism." Italians, for some reason considered separately from the Catholics, were "volatile." Liberals could not be ignored for "the

'right' may have the money, but the 'left' has always had the pen."
The secret was to find the right combination of policies that could
fashion a winning coalition out of these elements.

Anticommunism was the key, and not just for Catholics. The
Soviet Union, in Clifford's view, wanted to see the Republican
party elected in 1948 and was therefore encouraging Henry Wallace, whom Clifford rightly foresaw as the left-wing challenger to
Truman. Although Clifford had been one of Truman's advisers who
had at one point downplayed the Soviet "threat" (see chapter 5),
he also saw "considerable political advantage to the Administration
in its battle with the Kremlin." Since "in times of crisis the American citizen tends to back up his president," Truman would profit
from the fact that "our poor relations with Russia will intensify."
The Republicans would be sure to attack Truman's record as soft,
but the president had fully covered himself. On the one hand, the
appointment of General Marshall as secretary of state was a "brilliant" move to prove how impeccably conservative the new president was in foreign affairs. And on the other, "The President
adroitly stole [the Republican party's] thunder by initiating his
own government employee loyalty investigation procedure." (Not
everyone viewed this act, which Arthur Garfield Hayes of the
American Civil Liberties Union called "the most outrageous, un-
democratic measure that could possibly be conceived,"[18] as adroit;
Clifford Durr of the Federal Communications Commission more
correctly noted that it would give "presidential sanction" to the
"very fears" that the right "was trying to create.")[19] But Clark
Clifford's point held in the short run; so long as the president did
not allow the right to appear more anticommunist than himself, he
was politically safe.

Finally, Clifford combined these moves to the right with a call
for the president to move sharply to the left—if only in rhetoric.
The real genius of Clifford's analysis was that he realized, unlike
the conservatives, how popular progressive goals still were. One
indication was the attachment of Western states to expensive government programs, including flood control and agriculture, which
the president could exploit to weaken the Republican hold on the
West. In addition, one simply could not deny the potential progressive appeal of Henry Wallace, for he "has a large following
throughout the country, particularly of the young voters who are
attracted by the idealism that he—and he alone—is talking and
who regard war as the one evil greater than any other." In trying

to win over this popular sentiment, Truman had one great advantage: Congress was controlled by the Republicans. Therefore the president could offer legislation that appealed to the common person and the idealist alike without seriously antagonizing his relationships with established centers of power, since none of this legislation would be in danger of passing. Truman could offer price controls, housing, and tax reform knowing that the battle over them would be symbolic only:

> . . . the Administration should select the issues upon which there will be conflict with the [Republican] majority in Congress. It can assume it will get no major part of its program approved. Its tactics must, therefore, be entirely different than if there were any real point to bargaining and compromise. Its recommendations—in the State of the Union message and elsewhere—must be tailored for the voter, not the Congressman; they must display a label which reads "no compromise."

What Clark Clifford offered Truman, perhaps without even realizing it himself, was a solution to the gap between economics and politics that had begun to emerge in the late 1940s. Clifford's strategy could hardly resolve the political stalemate; on the contrary, he would elect Truman by intensifying it, for his electoral strategy presupposed an unbridgeable gap between a conservative Congress and a liberal executive. Instead, Clifford foreshadowed, without actually articulating, the notion of using growth to render the political stalemate meaningless. Implicit in his memo was the notion that economic growth and an aggressive foreign policy could sublimate political choice.

For example, Clifford's electoral strategy was based upon interest group politics, which meant offering something to the workers, blacks, farmers, Jews, and Catholics whose votes were needed. So long as Congress was controlled by the Republicans, symbolic promises might do, but the general strategy ran the risk of being unworkable when and if the Democrats regained control over the legislative branch. At that point, rewarding workers and minorities through progressive legislation—guaranteeing full employment, for example, or eliminating racial segregation—would upset the conservatives whose support Truman was also courting. In other words, electoral considerations demanded that Truman be active while legislative politics prevented him from doing too much. Only one way out of this potential problem would be found to exist: rapid economic growth could work to expand the federal budget, rewarding voters without offending vested interests. Economic growth would become the invisible glue that would hold Clifford's strategy together. And since growth can only be obtained by offering concessions to businessmen in order to induce them to invest, Clifford's popular electoral base could be held together only by following policies advantageous to big business. Domestic policy under the Democrats in the postwar years would become a search for the proper way to win business confidence.

The foreign policy consequences implicit in Clifford's strategy were similarly unanticipated. Without a reform tradition to hold it together, the electoral coalition of the Democratic party could be unified around anticommunism. Furthermore, the creation of a *Pax Americana* rationalized through cold war policies would provide economic benefits in the form of an imperial dividend, just as a domestic growth strategy would expand the size of the pie. Finally, a move toward a global foreign policy and a domestic emphasis on anticommunism would, in Truman's words, "take the ball away from the right."[20] For all these reasons, the Democrats were forced, by the logic of a growth imperative, toward an anticommunist foreign policy, one that would provide immediate political rewards in the 1948 election. There were, however, long-term consequences. For one thing, the more Truman tried to steal the ball from the right, the stronger the right seemed to become. Moreover, just as a domestic growth strategy produced dependence on winning business confidence, an imperial foreign policy produced dependence on the military and its eventual industrial complex. Foreign policy under the Democrats in the postwar years would become a search for the proper way to win the confidence of the guardians of national security.

From Clifford's memo, in short, there followed the pursuit of economic growth and the expansion of empire as the two directions that could solve the problems of the political stalemate. Growth, both in the economy and in the empire, would get around the logjam by widening the river. To pursue that growth, a new coalition came to power in American politics. This coalition advocated an overall expansion of the economy through macroeconomic policies made acceptable to the monopoly sector of the economy. From the surplus generated through growth, it offered domestic policies to the poor and the minorities that would, it was hoped, enable them to take part in the reshaping of the cities and country-side that would follow from growth priorities. Based upon the rapid expansion of the economy, it developed a foreign policy that combined a reorganization of the world under American economic hegemony with military power to ensure American influence. Finally, it offered to incorporate the world's poor into the growth machine through foreign aid and developmental assistance. The tasks established by the growth coalition were herculean, but anything seemed possible in an expanding economy. America had never before seen anything like this coalition, and it may never see anything like it again. The uniqueness of the growth coalition can be established by ascertaining what it was not.

While Truman kept alive the spirit of the New Deal in his Fair Deal rhetoric, the growth coalition that stirred during his presidency was *not* the same as the domestic coalition organized by Franklin Delano Roosevelt to support the New Deal. There was little room on ship for liberal politicians who kept alive an aggressive and articulate concern with income redistribution, economic planning, or international idealism. Radicals who had risen to power in the 1930s based upon their ability to mobilize discontent from below were replaced by "pragmatic" liberals who were sympathetic to monopoly power and anticommunism. Those liberal politicians who could not forget the New Deal but did join the growth coalition, like Chester Bowles of Connecticut or Wilson Wyatt of Kentucky, would always be somewhat out of place. The growth-oriented liberalism of the times was determined to exclude, in Arthur Schlesinger, Jr.'s, marvelous phrase, the "Doughfaced,"[21] those who were not hard-headed or realistic enough to understand that growth and empire, unlike dissent and reform, meant concessions to established sources of power.

But if the coalition lopped off the left end of opinion, it also isolated itself from the right. Mr. Republican, Senator Robert Taft of Ohio, was the *bête noire* of the new coalition, for his tight-money financial policies and his isolationism had no place in a world oriented to expansion. Growth policies presupposed the use of government at home to enlarge the economy and the use of government abroad to enhance the empire. The whole venture would be expensive (though its advocates claimed that it would pay for itself). It would mean a confrontation with traditional American values of localism and private virtue. Looking backward to Lockean liberalism and nativistic isolationism was as ideologically repugnant to the growth coalition as looking forward to social democracy and economic planning.

The rise of the growth coalition was facilitated—some would say mandated—by the economic transformations taking place in America. The three most important were economic concentration, growing state intervention, and expansion overseas. All three created a new economic basis that became the core turf of the growth coalition.

Robert Taft's Republicanism had been based on an alliance between competitive-sector businessmen operating close to the margin and small-scale farmers concentrated in the Midwest. Both forces were becoming anachronistic in the economic atmosphere of the late 1940s. Monopoly-sector businessmen, protected by their control over prices from labor costs and overseas competition, could afford to be more liberal toward domestic innovations like the welfare state and toward free trade. The growth of monopolization, linked to multinational expansion and to the debt-encouraging practices of Wall Street banks and investment houses, made the rise of the growth coalition possible.

But growth also changed the traditional basis of New Deal support. Roosevelt's electoral majorities had been formed by mobilizing sentiment among the dispossessed, from tenant farmers to the working class. Growth politics, however, implied organized interest groups, not mobilization from below. The crucial constituencies of growth politics were unions not workers, civil rights organizations not blacks. The growth coalition could be held together so long as liberal monopoly-sector businessmen were willing to engage in an informal alliance with similarly monopolistic unions, together expanding productivity so that both could benefit. In that way, labor's almost instinctive protectionism could be modified to support free trade policies, while the threat that labor posed by its reformism could be channeled instead into cooperation with management. In other words, the social and economic basis of the growth coalition was an East Coast-based, European-oriented, financial and industrial elite located in large monopolistic corporations that had made its peace with conservative, anti-communist labor leaders and Democratic party interest groups that wanted urban growth and development.

The emergence of the growth coalition, then, was something new. Unlike conservative Republicanism, it favored state intervention at home and was opposed to isolationism abroad. But unlike the New Deal, it was not a reformist, mobilizing movement, and it sought free-trade policies toward the rest of the world. Sometimes called the "vital center"[22] and other times designated "cold war liberalism,"[23] the growth coalition should properly be character- ized by its dominant belief: the idea that growth at home and expansion abroad could unify the interests of the dominant sectors of the economy with an electoral base that would keep it in power so long as growth continued.

Domestically, the center of gravity of the growth coalition would become the Council of Economic Advisers, created by the Employment Act of 1946. From this forum, activists like Leon Keyserling, who because he became the most single-minded and determined advocate of economic growth also became one of the key policymakers of the late 1940s, began to put expansionist ideas into practice. Keyserling had like-minded associates both inside and outside government: Gerhard Colm and John D. Clark in the council; economists like Alvin Hansen and Seymour Harris; sena- tors like Paul Douglas (Ill.), Hubert Humphrey (Minn.), and Robert Wagner (N.Y.); legislative draftsmen like Wilbur Cohen (health care) and John Blandford (housing); advisers inside the White House like Clark Clifford; labor leaders such as Walter Reuther; intellectuals like Arthur Schlesinger, Jr., and other liberal anticommunists; maverick businessmen like Beardsley Ruml of the Committee for Economic Development; and Wall Street invest- ment bankers to be mentioned shortly. Joining with these individ- uals were organizations dedicated to the growth credo, such as the Committee for Economic Development and the National Planning Association. While these men and organizations did not win all the struggles in which they were engaged—Truman rebuffed Keyser- ling's plans for economic expansion, for example—they were successful at establishing a framework for a growth policy that would come to fruition in the early 1960s under John F. Kennedy.

Internationally, the growth coalition was dominated by that wing of the foreign policy establishment that had led the campaign against "isolationism." Dean Acheson, W. Averell Harriman, Thomas Finletter, George Ball, John McCloy—these were the most prominent names. All were associated with Wall Street financial institutions and with prominent organizations like the Council on Foreign Relations or the Rockefeller Foundation. They were adept at recruiting specialists: George Kennan, Charles Bohlen, and Paul Nitze, who were instrumental in shifting American foreign policy in a more aggressive direction, even though some, like Kennan, would later come to regret their participation. Unlike the domestic activists, the cold warriors had a number of immediate victories, the Truman Doctrine and the Marshall Plan being the most conspicuous. But they, too, would have to wait until the 1960s to see their dreams of empire realized.

By 1950, the growth coalition had defeated any serious opposition to its left. Henry Wallace and the Progressive party had been disgraced, and anticommunism had established itself as a permanent feature in American political life. There was still, however, a major problem on the right. The growth coalition was only half formed; it required a Republican administration to complete it.

## II

THE FORMATION of the growth coalition was a centrist alternative to the New Deal. Anticommunist and respectful of the organized power of big business, the chastened liberals who sponsored economic and imperial growth took pains to keep themselves free of any tinge of radicalism. Yet it was a sign of how conservative the times were that a coalition dedicated to the expansion of the economy and the empire was still viewed by the voters (and by many businessmen) as dangerously progressive. The growth coalition, barely in power, was voted out of power in 1952 in favor of a former general whose ideas about the economy and foreign policy were ambiguous at best. Growth policies, in short, would not come about automatically; a struggle would have to be fought to obtain them.

Eisenhower, at first, was a massive disappointment to the pro-growth liberals. Faced with a sputtering economy, the general did little to bring about perpetual prosperity. While no return to the conditions of the Great Depression came about, there were two relatively serious postwar recessions, one in the last quarter of 1948 and the other in 1953 as businessmen anticipated a decline in Korean War expenditures. (Recessions immediately after elections are a common feature of American politics.)[24] The first Eisenhower recession saw a sharp rise in unemployment (although not as high as the 7 percent at the end of 1949) and an equally sharp drop in investments for new plants and equipment.[25] Eisenhower, like Truman, concluded that the best method of dealing with these recessions was to avoid decisive action and to hope that the economy would return to normal with minimal intervention by government. Rapid economic growth stimulated through government action—the raison d'être of the growth coalition—was more hope than actuality.

Conditions became worse in Eisenhower's second term. Another, more serious recession took place in 1957. Not only was the recovery from it slower, but the recession was accompanied by disturbing signs of inflation. Eisenhower was extremely cautious in advocating stimulation in order to cure the recession, on the grounds that such activity would exacerbate inflation. The administration did little as the rate of unemployment rose to 7.6 percent in August 1958. Internally divided, the Council of Economic Advisers was unable to push through a tax cut to stimulate the economy and could only indulge in exhortations, both to restrain prices and to increase production. The picture did begin to brighten toward the end of the year, at which point the administration aimed at building a massive surplus for the 1960 campaign. Without any consistent macroeconomic policy, the economy grew, but not by leaps and bounds. The GNP, calculated in constant 1958 dollars, was $408.8 billion at the end of 1953, increasing only to $461.6 billion by 1958. What the figures indicated, could be ascertained by merely looking around. There was something of a boom—as the new suburban developments and the emergence of the "affluent society" testified—but it was a far cry from abundance.

Eisenhower's pursuit of empire was as ambiguous as his pursuit of expansion. On the one hand, the cold war had become an institutionalized feature of American politics, and the innovations of the late 1940s were everywhere judged a success: an international monetary and trading system was working; Europe was going through its economic miracle, bursting at the seams with growth; and, once the Korean War ended, U.S.–Soviet rivalry was intense without being overly belligerent. Still, something seemed wrong to the foreign policy activists. For one thing, the Eisenhower administration, for all its anticommunist bluster, seemed unwilling to take an active role in confronting Soviet power, both in Eastern Europe and in the Middle East. In addition, the administration appeared unconcerned about the gold drain and the balance of payments deficit, both of which, if not properly managed, could become impediments to rapid growth.[26] In short, to the pro-growth liberals, Eisenhower was as reluctant to take political and economic action in the international arena as he was in the domestic.

Yet, in spite of the frustration felt by the economic activists, the Eisenhower administration actually solidified the triumph of growth politics. After eight years of Republican rule, the old-fashioned Republican notions of laissez-faire monetarism and overseas isolationism could barely be heard. (Indeed, when the Republican right would make itself visible again, in 1964, it would bear little relationship to Taftism; from this time forward, the "right" would advocate more extreme cold war policies than the center and would base itself on a military sector that was heavily dependent on government spending.) Eisenhower legitimated growth by not abandoning it. His main domestic advisers, like Arthur Burns of the Council of Economic Advisers, were hardly economic activists on the order of Keyserling, but nor were they monetarists. The administration's specialists on defense and foreign policy—from Secretary of State John Foster Dulles to Admiral Arthur Radford to eventual Defense Secretary Thomas Gates—were holding down the military budget, but they surely were not isolationists. With Eisenhower, ideas about growth did not rush forward into the future, but neither did they slip backwards into the past.

During the 1950s, the political vocabulary of the United States underwent a major transformation. When the New Deal was the decisive frame of reference, debate was divided into two camps called liberal and conservative. Liberals were those who believed that the government should play a positive role in correcting the abuses of capitalism by promoting a concern with equality and social justice. Conservatives argued that business had made America great and that therefore as few reforms as possible should be passed that would undermine its privileges. While the terms liberal and conservative were retained in America, their meaning shifted as growth priorities were accepted by both parties. From now on, a liberal was one who believed that growth should happen rapidly and a conservative, one who believed that growth should happen in a more tempered fashion. There were other differences, of course. Liberals were willing to use government to bring about more rapid growth, and they also argued that growth could create a fiscal dividend out of which more welfare benefits could be financed. In addition, liberals combined their notions of economic expansion at home with a call for imperial expansion overseas; the creation of the national security state and an aggressive foreign policy were basically liberal inventions. Similarly, conservatives, though committed to growth, wished to see it occur through the private sector, with Washington acting like a rabid fan, cheering business on. Moreover, conservatives did not want growth to occur at such a fast pace that it would cause inflation; and, tied more closely to the protectionist and competitive sector of the economy, they were dubious about a zealous pursuit of overseas empire. But these were differences in emphasis, not in basic outlook. By the end of the Eisenhower period, words like liberal and conservative no longer meant what they did during the New Deal. A senator like Paul Douglas and a Republican like Nelson Rockefeller agreed on little else but spending huge sums to promote economic expansion, making them both "liberals." Arthur Burns had little in common with Everett Dirksen or Richard Russell, but they all urged caution in too rapid a commitment to expansion, making them all "conservatives."

Growth created its own particular politics. Liberal notions of growth were embodied in a constellation of forces: the executive branch of the Democratic party; Eastern Republicanism; unions, particularly in the monopoly sector; constituents of the New Deal voting coalition; the free-trade, monopolistic, financial wing of business; universities; and downtown redevelopment interests in the major cities. Conservative growth advocates settled in the Southern and congressional wing of the Democratic party, the Western wing of the Republican party, the military–industrial complex, the water–public works–Army Corps of Engineers network, agribusiness, protectionist and isolationist business concerns, and, ultimately, the aerospace, high technology industries of the 1960s. Neither wing of the growth network could govern by itself. Liberals, with a built-in electoral majority, needed to make their policies acceptable to business and the military in order to pass legislation. Conservatives, secure among the powerful, needed to liberalize their programs in order to win national elections. As each wing of the growth network lurched toward the center in search of what it did not have, a pattern of politics was created that would last for a generation. Here are the main features of what I will call *growth politics*:

1. Liberal advocates of growth would, in general, dominate the executive branch, while Congress would institutionalize the power of conservative ideas about growth. Thus, the passage of legislation in the postwar years often represented uneasy

compromises between contrasting conceptions of growth, as I will try to show in the following chapters.

2. Despite a later cynicism about the political parties, there were real differences between them, but the differences were not ideological ones. Democrats, at least most of them, saw domestic and overseas growth as a means of solving problems, while Republicans saw problems with domestic and overseas growth. The debates between the parties were real, but they concerned how fast and at what cost growth should be achieved.

3. In spite of these differences in approach, the parties often became indistinguishable in practice. For in order to carry out their notions, liberals had to win the confidence of business and the military and therefore they made their notions more conservative, while conservatives, distrusted by the voters, expanded their ideas to make them more liberal.

4. Since growth was the agreed-upon goal, politics in America would no longer be divided along even minimal class lines, as it was becoming during the New Deal, and would no longer be encumbered by discussions of "issues." Debates would concern means, not ends. Major questions of public policy were simply removed from debate. Growth, in short, presupposed the suppression of fundamental political choice. The purpose of campaigns and elections was to ratify technical decisions about how expeditiously growth was occurring, not to mandate radical departures in policy.

5. As a result of all the preceding, neither wing of the growth coalition would seek to mobilize discontent from below, to tap new sources of support among underrepresented groups, or to encourage whatever popular protest existed in society. Liberal growth advocates connected themselves to interests like unions, not to passions like the labor movement. Conservatives needed popular support to come to power, but discovered a preference for demagogic themes ("Had enough?" "law and order") as an alternative to building a mass base. There would be few new sources of political energy forthcoming. "Politics" would come to mean a discussion among interest groups, not an attempt to develop a vision of a better society.

6. Finally, each wing of the growth coalition would discover, over time, that it had more in common with the other than it did with the base out of which it had emerged. Liberal growth

advocates found themselves to be more comfortable with the conservative wing of the growth coalition than they did with old-fashioned progressives and unreconstructed New Dealers, while conservative growth advocates could talk more easily to hard-headed economic activists than they could to extremists on the radical right. The two wings of the growth coalition deeply needed each other, and while they would engage in political combat in public, they would often arrange harmonious compromises in private.

The consolidation of this growth-oriented pattern of politics under Eisenhower was the most important consequence of the Republican interregnum of the 1950s. Not only did it imply a containment of the isolationist and laissez-faire right, it also curtailed the last stirrings of the New Deal left. Deprived of the presidency during the Eisenhower years, the Democrats had created the Democratic Advisory Council (DAC) as an institution to aid in formulating policies and proposals. Within the DAC, the committee on economic policy was headed by John Kenneth Galbraith, and he still retained some old-fashioned liberal ideas that grew out of the New Deal. Galbraith argued, as he had in his best-selling book *The Affluent Society*, that government must take the lead in providing resources to the neglected areas of society. Rather than the conspicuous consumption of tail fins, he thought that money should be spent on activities like education, health, and housing, implying a moderate form of income redistribution. These were not especially radical ideas, but they encountered substantial opposition within the modernized liberal wing of the growth coalition, due to their implicit suggestion that the private sector had failed. Leon Keyserling, who was as committed to growth as Galbraith, argued within the DAC that a rapid expansion of the private sector, instigated through a tax cut, was preferable to Galbraith's plan and more likely to win support.[27] It was Keyserling's position, not Galbraith's, that would become the basis for the growth coalition after 1960.

Similarly, debates over foreign policy during the eight years of Democratic exile reflected the consolidation of the growth coalition. Those who dissented from the dominant hawkish attitude within the coalition, like Chester Bowles or G. Mennen Williams of Michigan, were treated with a certain disdain. The official position of the Democratic party during the 1950s was to criticize Eisenhower for not being expansionist enough in his pursuit of imperial goals. Men like Paul Nitze became important advisers within the party, while George Ball and Thomas Finletter were active in writing speeches for Adlai Stevenson. The latter, who embodied the ideological stance of the Democratic party in these years, attacked Eisenhower for weakening America's resolve, even as he endorsed plans to curtail nuclear weapons. During the 1950s, the Democratic party had become the home for those who believed in an expansion, not only of the military budget, but also of the *Pax Americana.*

By 1960, expectations of growth had become such an institutionalized feature of American politics that, the next time the liberal wing of the coalition came to power, it would not find itself hampered as it was under Truman. The transformation that had come over the American political system was apparent within a year after John F. Kennedy assumed office.

# III

DURING THE 1960s, the economic changes that had begun to reveal themselves as World War II came to an end reached their full flower. Those changes, it may be recalled, included the growth of government, the increasing concentration brought about by monopolization, and the dominant role played by the American economy in the world. By every measure, an era of permanent boom seemed to have been created.

The intensification of economic concentration, worrisome to old-fashioned liberals and believers in antitrust, was warmly welcomed by the "new" liberals, like Adolf Berle, who swore by the virtues of growth. In almost every industry of consequence in America, the control over the market exercised by a handful of dominant firms increased. Not only did important industries like steel and rubber become more monopolistic, but between 1947 and 1967 the rate of concentration, according to John M. Blair, increased in greeting cards (70 to 86 percent), floor coverings (80 to 89 percent), and chewing gum (70 to 86 percent). The percentage of total manufacturing assets held by the 200 largest corporations increased from 45 percent in 1947 to 60.4 percent in 1968.[28] During the 1960s, a brand-new wave of concentration began, reflected in the growth of conglomerates like ITT, Gulf & Western, and Ling-Temco-Vought, which were also anxious to expand abroad. Monopolization was penetrating formerly unorganized sectors of the domestic economy just as it was penetrating the world.

Economic concentration was both facilitated and accompanied by the increasing role of government in the economy. Government expenditure as a percentage of the gross national product, which had been 12.4 percent in 1940, rose to 24.6 percent a decade later due to wartime needs. Over the course of the postwar period, however, the proportion of the GNP occupied by government continued to increase, up to 27.8 percent in 1955, then to 28.1 percent in 1960, and to 30 percent in 1965.[29] (It would continue to increase into the 1980s.) Spending by government, especially on military production, generally works to the advantage of monopolistic firms, and it also makes the question of who controls the government that much more important to private business. By the middle of the 1960s, the twin forces of increasing concentration and greater public spending were laying the groundwork for the further consolidation of the growth coalition.

These trends were also enhanced by the worldwide activities of U.S. corporations. When manufacturing was primarily domestic in nature, businessmen tended to be protectionist and suspicious of domestic government intervention. As firms expanded abroad both to find cheaper sources of labor and to sell goods, a greater sensitivity to the need to expand the empire developed among the industrial elite. To be sure, there were still nationalistic firms that were suspicious of rapid growth and international trade, but the dominant trend produced by the rise of multinational corporations in the 1960s was toward the kind of pro-growth policies first advocated during the Truman administration. As business became more multinational, businessmen became more willing to consider the kinds of pro-growth policies advocated by the liberal wing of the growth coalition.

All of these economic forces came together to make possible the triumph of growth policies under the Kennedy administration. The 1960s would represent the peak of the growth cycle, the period in which expansion at home and abroad would become the unquestioned first priority of the American political system. And the growth that was produced was, in fact, astonishing. Measured in constant 1958 dollars, the GNP increased far more dramatically than it had under Eisenhower, from $511.7 billion in 1961 to $636.6 in 1965, to $716.5 in 1968. Industrial production came close to doubling during the decade, new construction jumped, and investment in plant and equipment more than doubled. Even more remarkable, these gains took place with low unemployment and stable prices. The unemployment rate, which had been 5.7 percent in 1963, fell to 4.5 percent in 1965 and then to 3.8 percent in 1966. Inflation was negligible between 1961 and 1963, and even when it began to increase, it was at minimal rates: 2 percent through 1965, increasing to only 3.8 percent in 1966. The federal deficit dropped while the stock market rose. "To accuse Mr. Kennedy of being anti-business," one Wall Street columnist wrote, "is almost akin to accusing Senator Barry Goldwater of being pro-communist."[30] The same could be said for Lyndon Johnson. Economic growth was proving to be exactly the cornucopia that had been promised.

Not only did the economy expand during the early 1960s, so did the empire. Kennedy's administration represented the high-point of the *Pax Americana*. During his three years in office, a distinct remilitarization of the society took place, reflected in sharp increases in the military budget and a rise in the number of foreign interventions. Even the tone of the period, with its emphasis on physical fitness and civil defense, harkened back to earlier imperial figures like Cecil Rhodes and Theodore Roosevelt. This was an administration preoccupied with America's role in the world, determined to improve relations with Europe, to expand America's influence in the Third World, and to stand up to what it perceived as a major challenge from the Soviet Union. Of course the net result of this more aggressive foreign policy would be the undermining of the *Pax* with a genuine war, but few perceived that problem at the time. Foreign expansion, like economic growth, was presumed to have so many benefits that doubting Thomases were simply ignored.

Kennedy's administration bridged the gap between two generations of pro-growth liberals. Many of the advisers from the Truman period, like Keyserling, Clifford, and particularly Nitze, were around to influence the new administration. At the same time, a younger generation of liberal intellectuals had matured, and Kennedy was willing to listen to them. For economic advice the president turned to men like Walter Heller and James Tobin, advocates of what was then called the "new economics." (See chapter 3.) The president also forged links with a growth coalition in the cities, where reform mayors like Richard Lee in New Haven and J. Richardson Dilworth in Philadelphia were advocating urban policies premised upon economic expansion. (See chapter 4.)

Allied with the mayors were specialists in urban renewal, like Robert Moses and Edward Logue, both activist city planners. Crack academic experts in social policy—typified by Joseph Califano, who would become Jimmy Carter's secretary of health, education, and welfare—were important in the 1960s, as were pragmatic intellectuals like Arthur Schlesinger, Jr., and Richard Goodwin. Whatever the differences among them, all of these men shared the vision of stimulating economic growth at home through vigorous government action.

The influence of a new generation of pro-growth intellectuals was even more deeply felt in foreign policy. Some of the older men, like John McCloy, Robert A. Lovett, and Averell Harriman, retained influence. But the new president, who did not have as strong a reputation on defense as challengers like Henry Jackson or Stuart Symington, went out of his way to recruit men who would be seen as "tough." For strategic ideas Kennedy was influenced by rebellious generals like Maxwell Taylor, who objected to Eisenhower's complacency about the state of the empire. He also raided the Harvard–MIT complex for men like McGeorge Bundy, Walt Rostow, Carl Kaysen, and Lincoln Gordon, all of whom would become instrumental in reviving a concern with the Third World. Financial advice came from a politically sensitive Wall Street: C. Douglas Dillon and Robert Roosa were two of the liberal bankers whom Kennedy recruited into his administration. Every one of these men had in common a desire to strengthen America's role in the world, both by increasing the military power of the United States and by more vigorously asserting its economic interests. If anything, the second generation of pro-growth internationalists seemed slightly more aggressive in their foreign policy intentions than the first.

By 1964, the political success of the growth coalition had become complete. Financial capital and multinational enterprises allied themselves more firmly with the Democratic party than ever before, and when Barry Goldwater received the Republican party nomination, monopoly-sector businessmen deserted the Republican party in droves. Economic growth, moreover, was predicated on contracts with organized labor that provided for cost-of-living allowances in return for increased productivity, firming up union support for the liberal wing of the growth coalition. It seemed for a time as if everything big—business, labor, defense contractors, universities, ideas—had united behind the growth coalition, the only opposition being a fanatical Republican party that had lost touch with economic reality. A one-party state seemed in the making, as businessmen, bankers, cold warriors, intellectuals, urban activists, and labor leaders all supported the growth coalition. Johnson's massive electoral margin in 1964 was the icing on the cake. Having brought about the expansion of both the economy and the empire, the growth coalition was rewarded with what seemed like total political hegemony.

Yet Johnson's victory would disappear in only four years. Underneath the euphoria were signs that would have proved disturbing to the liberals in the growth coalition if they had noticed them. For one thing, the conservative wing of the growth coalition grew in strength in the Republican party with the defeat of Goldwater. In order to keep themselves in power, growth-oriented liberals needed to win business confidence and to prove their cold war proclivities, and both imperatives tended to strengthen the right. The economic growth desperately needed by liberals to keep the support of working-class and minority constituents had an unexpected consequence. To win business confidence, liberals allowed industry the freedom to expand as it pleased, and it pleased to expand, not in the industrial heartland of the Midwest and Northeast, but in the South and West, where Republicans were strong. Ironically, the macroeconomic programs of the liberal Democrats strengthened the political base of the right. Meanwhile, the anticommunist foreign policies of Kennedy and Johnson, instead of silencing the right, gave credence to the right-wing notion that communism was a deadly enemy and contributed to the charge that liberals and communists were cut from the same cloth, no matter how hard the liberals tried to prove otherwise. In short, the greater the success of the liberal wing of the growth coalition, the greater the potential strength of the conservative wing. Thus, it became possible for Nixon to win in 1968 when he could not in 1960; the liberals of the Kennedy and Johnson administrations paved the way for the Republicans to elect their first indigenous president since 1928. The pro-growth liberals, who had developed their strategy to contain Dewey, wound up helping to elect Nixon.

Even more surprising was the fact that the success of the pro-growth coalition gave rise to a left that had not existed since the defeat of Henry Wallace. Cities erupted, forcing Johnson to make his domestic program more ambitious, and therefore less consensual and growth-oriented. An apparently new kind of protest emerged, one based on prosperity, raising issues to which the political system—given its emphasis on pragmatism—could not respond. A war was dividing the country, when the empire was supposed to unify all around a common glory. Economic growth and the expansion of empire had achieved their major goal—they had displaced controversy from the political system. But they did so only by placing it in the streets. America was in turmoil, and at the very time that its future was supposed to be brightest. It had taken eight years for the liberals of the growth coalition to come to power. It took them exactly the same amount of time to discredit themselves. By 1968, a new political alignment seemed to be just around the corner.

## IV

THE STORY of the Nixon and Carter administrations is the story of two attempts to reorganize the American political system, both of which failed. Between 1968 and 1980, two trends had become clear. One was that the pattern of rapid economic growth had come to an end. Indeed, the three main economic transformations that had contributed to growth in the postwar period—monopolistic concentration, the increasing role of the government, and overseas empire—were all exacerbating the economic difficulties they once overcame. Second, it was obvious that without economic growth a political coalition based upon its existence could hardly be secure; in short, the political stalemate that had first emerged in 1938 returned, more severe for being in its second time around. America's impasse deepened, characterized by a political system dependent upon economic growth coexisting with an economic system that could no longer provide it.

Both the Nixon and the Carter administrations recognized the problem. Both tried, at first, to develop a new political coalition that would be in tune with the new economic realities. Both attempts aroused intense opposition, and both presidents backed off when the going got rough. Nixon, after shifting radically from a rejection of the liberal coalition's ideas to an acceptance of some of its key notions, ultimately fell back on the safest course for an incumbent Republican: a conservative strategy roughly like Eisenhower's. Carter, after rejecting in his first two years some of the features of growth politics, found the political price too steep and lost his reelection campaign even though reverting to a traditional growth strategy. Both presidents knew that the old rules were bankrupt, but neither was in a position to change them. Consequently, the net effect of their two presidencies was to intensify America's impasse even further.

Almost overnight, the American economy was transformed from a smoothly running growth machine into a spurting, stalling clunker. Productivity was slowly up as early as 1965. Sometime between 1967 and 1969 the postwar longwave of economic growth peaked and began to descend. In the years between 1947 and 1965, for example, the annual compound percentage growth of industrial output for the United States averaged 5 percent, but over the next ten years, from 1966 to 1975, it averaged only 1.9 percent.[31] In 1967 and 1968, for the first time since a brief flurry during the Eisenhower period, the rates of inflation and unemployment went up together, heralding the possibility of permanent stagflation. The early 1970s were marked by an unprecedented trade deficit, which combined with speculation in the Eurodollar market to necessitate drastic action, ultimately taking the United States out of the arrangements established at Bretton Woods in 1944. (See chapter 6.) By the time that Nixon became president, these economic transformations were compounded by such worldwide structural problems as the drying up of ready energy reserves in the West and a population increase in the Third World that was outstripping agricultural production.[32] The postwar boom had come to a rapid end, and Nixon would be the first president who would have to begin his administration under a new set of realities.

Evidence of the transformation of economic conditions did not take long to manifest itself. Almost as soon as Nixon took office, the unemployment rate began to increase, and it did so, with only one downturn, during the entire Republican period. Recessionary conditions often prevailed, and even the periods of "recovery" were slack. The administration seemed desperate to find some way of improving economic performance, for the state of the economy was having negative effects on Republican political fortunes. But a fear of inflation stood firm against decisive action, resulting in a series of "stop-and-go" measures that left the economy in a shambles. These uncertainties combined with sharp policy reversals—like the August 1971 imposition of wage-and-price controls—to give the Nixon administration the impression of floundering. During Nixon's presidency there began what George Perry called "the longest and deepest postwar recession,"[33] cresting in 1975 with the highest postwar unemployment rates on record, over 8 percent. This was becoming worse than no growth; it was an actual reversal.

The downspin of the economy, to complicate matters further, did not bring about restraint on prices—the one advantage, in orthodox theory, of a recession. Stagflation seemed to be permanent; and, while there was a decrease in the rate of inflation in the early 1970s, by the end of 1974 inflation rates were actually outstripping unemployment rates in their severity. The only growth in the economy was the growth of negative indicators; yet, as detestable as inflation was to the conservative coalition, little could be done about it. For under Nixon the final nail in the coffin of economic troubles became obvious; the economy was failing because of the very forces that had once made it work: economic concentration, state intervention, and the expansion of empire.

So long as the economy is booming, concentration seems to bring benefits, expanding profits and providing higher wages that stimulate consumption (the monopoly sector of the economy traditionally pays higher wages than the competitive sector). But when the economy slowed down in the late 1960s and early 1970s, concentration caused as many problems as it solved. Protected from competition, monopolistic firms engaged in less research and development, leading to lower rates of productivity. The tendency for management to become complacent was reenforced by the gains made by labor in the monopolistic sector, for, as Samuel Bowles and Herbert Gintis have shown, the relative share of the surplus going to labor increased during this period, cutting into profits.[34] Profit decreases, offset only by "paper" profits that grew out of increased acquisitions, had little multiplier effect, and in that sense were unable to counter the recessionary conditions imported from the slowdown in the world economy. Moreover, concentration interfered with the ability of government to improve economic performance. Over the postwar period administrations attempted to increase employment by providing incentives for corporations to grow, but since the monopoly sector was far less labor-intensive than the competitive sector, such policies did not automatically produce new jobs. Similarly, postwar economic policy had been based on fighting inflation by inducing recession, yet corporate control over pricing guaranteed that prices would not fall as fast as economic conditions. The entire pro-growth coalition had been based on an expansion of the monopoly sector of the economy, yet that very expansion made it more difficult for the growth coalition to govern in a changed economic environment.

State intervention, once a stimulator of growth, was becoming a drain on the economy. Huge sums were needed to pursue an imperial foreign policy while simultaneously expanding the economy at home, yet taxpayer resistance was a fact of life from the beginning. Seeking a way to finance government expenditures while minimizing the tax burden, administrations allowed the money supply to expand, and thereby contributed to rapid inflation. Between 1960 and 1972, the gap between governmental revenues and governmental expenditures increased in every year except 1969–70, producing a fiscal crisis of the state. The money supply increased every year from 1965 to 1973, sometimes by annual rates as high as 13 percent. The inflationary consequences of this expansion of the public sector (without an expansion of the willingness to tax) were reenforced by the growth in private debt. The total U.S. debt increased from $400 billion in 1946 to $2.5 trillion in 1974; while it took the decade and a half between 1945 and 1960 for the debt to double, it doubled again in only ten years between 1960 and 1970.[35] It did not take a political genius to realize that the particular pattern of state intervention that had smoothed the path for the pro-growth coalition had come to an end.

Finally, the costs of empire had clearly begun to outweigh the benefits. Expansion overseas in the postwar years had taken two basic forms: a military presence and economic penetration. Both had begun to undermine domestic economic performance by the early 1970s. Not only was the war in Vietnam a major drain on the American economy (and a drain as well on the legitimacy of America's leaders), it reflected the increased costs of maintaining a military apparatus in a time of economic trouble. Troops and equipment overseas contributed to negative payments balances, exacerbated inflation at home, and intensified investment in nonproductive, capital-intensive industry. The expansion of the military sector had been a major objective of the liberal wing of the growth coalition, yet, while military spending could have a stimulating effect during the upswing of a growth cycle, it seemed less beneficial when the economy turned downward. Nonetheless, powerful interest groups organized to keep military spending high would still clamor for more, no matter how serious the overall negative impacts on the economy.

While the United States increased its military presence abroad, American multinational corporations found overseas investments to be more profitable than investments at home. U.S. corporations received $1 billion in profits from overseas investments in 1945, compared to $8 billion–$10 billion in 1970. The rate at which export-oriented firms expanded profits abroad increased rapidly between 1966 and 1970 according to a Commerce Department study. The percentage of new corporate investments abroad was 21 percent in 1960, 25 percent in 1966, and 40 percent in 1970. When combined with the expanded overseas activities of American banks, which increased from 30 percent of deposits in 1965 to 70 percent in 1972, there was a serious drain on the domestic economy.[36] Not only was unemployment at home increased by greater profits abroad, but the ability of American manufacturers to remain competitive in world markets was undermined as investors looked elsewhere. Whatever the domestic fallout, little could be done about the growth of American multinational enterprise, for, as I will discuss in chapter 6, overseas investment was one of the products of growth politics that could not be reversed when the growth no longer took place. An American public that had once received an imperial dividend was now being asked to pay an imperial price.

Richard Nixon was astute enough to recognize that these altered economic circumstances required an alternative political coalition. A substantial amount of energy was devoted to building one. Breaking with the core of the liberal wing of the growth coalition—the free-trade-oriented bankers and multinationals of the East Coast—Nixon turned to the protectionist and nationalistic manufacturers of the competitive sector: the traditional home of the conservative half of the growth network. But by turning protectionist, Nixon discovered the problem that conservatives have always had: how does one build a mass base for pro-business economic policies? The administration's answer was thorough: Nixon would sponsor a complete realignment of the American political system.

When the growth coalition came together under Harry Truman, it was tied by Clark Clifford's strategy of aggregating as many domestic voting blocs as could be assembled. Clifford's secret was to find a way to keep the South and the West in the Democratic fold while holding on to the votes of workers and minorities in the North and East. Nixon was one of the first to understand that Clifford's electoral alliance had broken down under the impact

of worsening economic conditions. Every one of the domestic voting blocs that supported a liberal growth strategy was disaffected:
Catholics were attracted to George Wallace and could be induced
to vote Republican; Jews were unhappy about both U.S. policy
toward Israel and affirmative action and were in the process of
shifting away from automatic liberalism; labor could be had—or at
least neutralized—because of its conservatism on "social issues";
and even blacks might be won over with a few strategic appointments. At the same time, new policies, such as a halt to civil rights
progress or wheat sales to the Russians, could break the South and
West away from the Democrats and swing them over to the Republicans. Clifford's approach had worked for twenty years, surely
a remarkable record, but it no longer made either economic or
political sense.

Thus, Nixon's attempt to form an alternative to the liberal
growth coalition was based on two changes: a new electoral
strategy and a new base in the dominant sectors of the society.
Yet neither would be completed. Democratic voters, after a brief
fling with Nixon, went back to a concern with growth and
supported policies to foster it, thereby returning the Republican party to minority status for another eight years. And protectionist businessmen found that multinationals had become so
powerful that major opposition would exist to any movements
away from tested policies of overseas expansion. George Meany,
the symbol of the domestic wing of the growth coalition, grew increasingly suspicious of Nixon; and David Rockefeller, representative of imperial dreams, was unhappy about John Connally.
Substantial opposition to the directions that Nixon was taking sur-
faced. It is impossible to know what would have happened had
Watergate not intervened, but it is possible to conclude that once
it did, the East Coast "Establishment," as Spiro Agnew called the
liberal wing of the growth coalition, used the scandal to contain
Nixon. By the time that Gerald Ford became president, any
thoughts of a major shift to the right had been dropped, and Ford
came to rely on the usual conservative practice of helping business
to profit and hoping that everyone else would accept it. Everyone
did not, and Ford retired to Palm Springs.

Because he was perceptive enough to understand the limits to
growth politics but not powerful enough to go beyond them, Nixon's policies were highly contradictory in both domestic and foreign affairs. From time to time, he seemed to move in a "pro-

gressive" direction, as in his early support of a family assistance plan that would circumvent the welfare bureaucracy. At other times the moves were just as clearly "conservative"—for example, the presidential assault on the Office of Economic Opportunity. A president who could praise the free market and also impose wage-and-price controls was a president caught between a set of assumptions based upon growth and a set of realities rooted in austerity.

Nixon was equally contradictory in foreign policy. Recognizing that overseas expansion through military means was costly and counterproductive, Nixon tried to contain anticommunism. Détente, wheat deals with the Russians, a Strategic Arms Limitation Treaty with the Soviets, and an opening to China were all premised upon assumptions strikingly different from the pro-growth, cold war policies of the Truman period. Some of the president's advisers, especially Henry Kissinger, repudiated their earlier support for traditional cold war policies. (Kissinger would later repudiate his repudiation.) Yet, while Nixon seemed to reject the activist, interventionist foreign policy that had characterized previous Democratic administrations, he also shifted to the "right" in his approach to Latin America and in his attempt to develop a strategic superiority in nuclear weapons. The times were simply too contradictory for the growth-at-any-cost foreign policies of an earlier period.

Richard Nixon (and then Gerald Ford) left office with the economy in disarray and without having brought about a new political coalition capable of restoring it. Without the glue of economic growth, political unity in the United States disintegrated. Voters seemed to want social programs, but they also did not want to pay for them. Americans were retreating to an earlier isolationism, yet they also had not given up the idea of unquestioned military superiority. Right-wing ideas were becoming more popular, even if somewhat suspect. At the same time, established sectors of the society were in disarray. The military was in shock from its defeat in Vietnam, while businessmen were increasingly divided into protectionists and free traders. Organizations like the Council on Foreign Relations seemed unsure of what they wanted to advocate; and, in the vacuum created, newer organizations like the Trilateral Commission arose, only to find themselves internally divided as well. There was a widely recognized need for a post-growth approach to domestic policy and a less ambitious imperial strategy, but few were sure how to develop one. A unified and articulate elite—one that possessed so much self-confidence and self-importance during the 1960s—was nowhere in evidence. The growth coalition had collapsed, and it was unclear what would replace it.

## V

UNDER DIVIDED, querulous, and bitter circumstances, Jimmy Carter was elected president in 1976. The new administration pledged itself to morality and unity after the Watergate scandal, but the problem was deeper than the misbehavior of one ex-president. Carter was the heir to a political coalition organized only for economic growth, yet the economy was, and gave every indication of continuing to be, in a no-growth state. If the new president tried to develop policies in line with economic conditions, he would win almost no political support and would find himself nonelectable. If, on the other hand, he sought to win political support, he would quickly worsen economic conditions. After a brief attempt to develop a post-growth, post-imperial perspective, the new president quickly retreated, thereby guaranteeing both the perpetuation of the political stalemate that had undergirded American politics since 1938 and an early retirement.

Jimmy Carter, unlike Truman or Kennedy, did not have a unified elite from which to pick advisers who would develop his policies. It was necessary for him to choose between the traditional advocates of liberal growth strategies and those who were urging a break with the politics of the past. In both domestic and foreign policy, Carter at first seemed willing to make the break. In Keyserling's position as chairman of the Council of Economic Advisers, for example, Carter placed Charles Schultze, a man who repudiated "spend more, grow more" policies in favor of a greater reliance on marketlike incentives.[37] Other domestic advisers, like Stuart Eizenstat or Alfred Kahn, were more loyal to Carter's re-election efforts than to the traditions of the growth coalition and would advocate whatever was in the president's interest. A shift to the right on domestic policy was hardly a step forward, but at least it indicated some intellectual understanding on the part of the new administration that the policies pursued by the liberal growth network had become bankrupt.

The effort to break with the past was even more pronounced in foreign affairs, where Carter initially turned to the Trilateral Commission for advice. The Trilateralists were a motley bunch, but nearly all of them agreed that the whole thrust of postwar national security policy needed reevaluation in the light of Vietnam. Some of the Trilateralists, like Cyrus Vance and Paul Warnke, were former advocates of cold war policies who had gone through a political conversion. Others constituted a new generation of chastened empire builders, seeking post-imperial solutions to America's foreign affairs: men like Leslie Gelb, J. Fred Bergsten, and Richard Cooper. Still others—Harold Brown, Zbigniew Brzezinski—were men who had not changed their ideas at all but were looking for a new route to power. Examining Carter's initial appointments, one would have thought that a post-expansionist foreign policy would be coming into existence.[38]

A political coalition that had been as successful as the growth network does not roll over and play dead merely because the economy turns downward, however. While Carter may have understood the need to move in a new direction, there existed sufficient obstacles in the form of residues from the era of unreconstructed economic growth to prevent him from understanding it too well. Organizations like the Coalition for a Democratic Majority in domestic policy and the Committee on the Present Danger in foreign policy kept alive growth politics as usual. Politicians like Henry Jackson and Daniel Patrick Moynihan warned of the dangers that would follow if pro-growth policies were ignored. In the rapidly changing political environment of the late 1970s, the liberal advocates of growth had moved to the right, but they were still influential enough to block changes while not powerful enough to dominate the executive branch. The stalemate that had once existed between the two parties came home to rest within the Democratic party. The differences between Carter and Senator Edward Kennedy, for example, became as sharp as the differences between Harry Truman and Thomas E. Dewey.

Carter's one term began with an attempt to develop post-growth, post-imperial policies. (See chapter 8.) Vetoing water projects—one of the keys to Clark Clifford's 1947 strategy—the new president seemed decidedly willing to challenge expensive domestic boondoggles. Similarly, Carter announced during the 1976 campaign his willingness to cut military spending and portrayed himself, shortly after election, as no longer obsessed with "an inordinate fear of communism." Both kinds of acts showed considerable political courage, arousing, as they did, intense opposition from vested interests determined to pursue growth strategies whatever their cost to the overall economy. When the depth of the opposition became clear, Carter rapidly retreated. Within two years, the president had proposed an expensive, inflationary, and growth-oriented Energy Mobilization Board and had announced his support for rapid and permanent increases in the military budget, cushioned by his discovery of the political potential of cold war themes during the Democratic primaries of 1980. By the time he faced reelection, Carter had given up completely on governing, gearing nearly every aspect of his domestic and foreign policy to his own (unsuccessful) campaign. He had become the Nixon of the Democratic party, recognizing what needed to be done, but too much a product of growth politics to do anything about it.

As Carter abdicated his role of policymaker in favor of the longest and least successful reelection campaign in American political history, the economy, informed that no action would be forthcoming to alter it, went into a deteriorating tailspin. The rate of inflation, for example, reached its highest postwar peak in the spring of 1980, as the prime rate hit a 20 percent ceiling that had once been thought unthinkable. Under the impetus of inflation, the housing industry came to a standstill, while key manufacturing industries like steel and autos began to lay off workers. A long anticipated recession finally arrived in 1980; and even though (statistically) it lifted before the presidential election, Carter suffered from the perception that he was unable to manage the economy. Carter was a victim of America's impasse: in order to win respectability, he had to leave the economy alone, yet leaving the economy alone enabled inflation and unemployment to undermine his popularity. The heir to a growth strategy at a time when growth was not taking place, Jimmy Carter was—literally—in a no-win situation.

# VI

RONALD REAGAN came into office under high hopes that he would be able to manage the economy in a more convincing manner than his predecessor. Lift the restrictions on business and protect America's security, he proclaimed during his campaign, and the normal world you knew a generation ago will be restored. No temporizer, Reagan began immediately to pursue his plans for economic revitalization. In his highly publicized February 1981 speech to both houses of Congress, the president, saying that the United States could no longer procrastinate, asked for budget cuts totaling $41.4 billion and called on Congress to support a 30 percent reduction in federal taxes spread out over three years. Seeming to reverse the course of American history, Reagan not only endorsed "supply-side economics," but offered an indirect repudiation of nearly forty years of political philosophy: "Spending by government must be limited to those functions which are the proper province of government. We can no longer afford things simply because we think of them."[39] Congress was inclined to agree.

Reagan's first six months in office indicate that he is aware of America's impasse and the need to resolve it. Cutting taxes, even while tolerating an unbalanced budget, is a fairly radical proposal for a Republican to make. Both Reagan himself, and his domestic advisers David Stockman and Martin Anderson, have questioned whether Americans are entitled to government programs, also something of a revolutionary notion. Massive increases in military spending, furthermore, seem to mark a sharp break with the recent past, when the "Vietnam syndrome" operated as a check on the exercise of American power abroad. One may or may not like what Reagan is trying to do, but both his defenders on the right and his critics on the left can agree that he is trying to do something. Surely the image of an impasse does not apply to a program so unorthodox and far-reaching.

Time will tell whether Reagan's program will work, but a realistic look at both his party and his platform indicates that the Republicans after 1980 face much the same dilemma as the Democrats before 1980, if in a different form. Jimmy Carter could not govern because his politics required growth and his economics could not induce it. The Republican party's impasse is caused by the fact that its economics demands growth, but its politics will be unable to generate it.

During the upswing of the postwar growth wave, the Republican party was dominated by men who were suspicious of too rapid growth and called instead for monetarist restraints. To check inflation, men like William Simon and Alan Greenspan advocated high interest rates to "wring out" the economy, combined with balanced budgets to reassure investors. Had Reagan run on such a program in 1980, he would never have become president. The key to Reagan's victory was that the new president picked up the

growth mantle discarded by the Democrats. By basing himself on
the expansionary economics of Stockman, Congressman Jack Kemp,
and supply-side theorists Arthur Laffer and Jude Wanniski, Reagan
was able to win working-class votes, overcoming his party's
minority status.

Jimmy Carter's presidency also began with an understanding
of the need to resolve America's impasse. Carter attempted to cut
back growth projects, only to backtrack once he felt the need to win
political popularity. Reagan's course will be the exact opposite.
The new president begins with a program for stimulating the
economy that has wide popular support, but if he carries it forward,
he will alienate all those bankers and businessmen whose primal
instinct is caution. Carter, in short, began with austerity and moved
toward growth, ending his presidency in an unhappy middle.
Reagan will begin with growth and end in austerity, finding himself very much a symbol of, rather than a resolution to, an impasse
that he cannot control.

Nothing will illustrate Reagan's version of the American impasse better than inflation. If the new president remains committed
to economic expansion through tax cuts, he will, supply-side theory
to the contrary, exacerbate inflation. By decontrolling oil prices,
while slashing funds for mass transit, the administration will oversee a price rise in one basic factor in the inflationary spiral; and
Reagan's blank check to business will raise other prices across the
board. Moreover, because Reagan specifically exempted the military from his budget-cutting schemes, he will be unlikely to eliminate the federal deficit, as conservative senators have already
begun to realize. Reagan will learn what Democrats have already
learned: all popular courses are, *ipso facto*, inflationary courses.

Once prices refuse to come down, or even show a sticky tendency to go up, the Republicans in the future, like the Democrats
in the past, will become the party of inflation. Seeking to avoid
such a political kiss of death, Republican conservatives, again mimicking Democratic liberals, will verge back toward recession and
traditional Republican constraints last adapted by Jimmy Carter.
Reagan may seem like a radical, venturing into uncharted seas, but
in reality he faces the same impasse that brought him to power in
the first place: politics demands growth, the economy cannot
provide it. Neither Reagan's popularity nor even an assassin's
attempt on his life can reverse the course of postwar economic and
political development.

# III

# Counter-Keynesianism

W HEN JOHN F. KENNEDY was organizing his administration in late 1960, he called James Tobin to offer the Yale economics professor a position as one of the three members of the Council of Economic Advisers. "I am afraid that I am only an ivory-tower economist," said Tobin, resisting the offer. "That is the best kind," Kennedy replied. "I am only an ivory-tower president."[1]

Such is the stuff around which the Kennedy legend has been built, but, like most of the legend, there is a substantial amount of self-delusion in the interchange. Kennedy was anything but an ivory-tower president—the whole term, in fact, is absurd. Nor was Tobin an ivory-tower economist, for, at least among the elite of his profession, few such creatures existed. Economists, unlike Marx's philosophers, not only wanted to understand the world, they desired to change it as well. The thin line between analysis and policy had become even thinner as economists moved back and forth from the Ivy League and the Big Ten to Washington. Economists would try to succeed where capitalists in the past had failed; they were going to make the system work. Armed equally with mathematical models and exuberent self-confidence, economists dared the state: allow us to work for you, and we will stabilize the economy so that the future of American prosperity will be assured.

Government did not disappoint the economists, welcoming them into the policymaking process with an open checkbook. But the economists failed the government, for they were unable to deliver on their promises. The success of an economy can generally be evaluated by two criteria. First, it should generate sufficient productive capacity that work is available to everyone who wants it. Second, it should grow steadily, so that the value of money remains stable and people can make plans. Economists differ among themselves about which goal is to be preferred, half of them willing to sacrifice the former to achieve the latter and half of them the opposite. (By 1981, the ratio had shifted toward the former position.) The important point is that judging from *both* criteria, something has gone wrong with the American economy. Not only are unemployment rates, especially among minority youth, as high as a civilized society can tolerate, but prices are rising at their highest postwar pace. Stagflation— simultaneous unemployment and inflation—has become the number-one symbol of the American impasse. Nothing in the American experience has prepared the American people for the coexistence of rising prices and high unemployment. No political system can hope to survive prolonged stagflation unscathed.

Why has the economy failed so badly? In the business and conservative press the answer is obvious—this is what happens when government, in the words of Reginald Jones of General Electric, goes about "clogging the streams of investment."[2] Even among liberal economists, the sentiment is now strong that government overregulated and that incentives for investment and selective deregulation are the answers. An emerging consensus, strongly represented among the economic advisers to the Reagan administration, holds that postwar economic policy has been a failure. Since the economists who streamed to Washington were, to one degree or another, believers in the ideas of John Maynard Keynes, Keynesianism is judged to be the culprit of the economic collapse. Stagflation is held to be proof-positive that Keynesianism was doomed to fail.

There is only one thing wrong with the view that Keynesianism failed: it was never really tried. Economic activists were doing many things in Washington, but one thing they were conspicuously *not* doing was using the public sector to influence and plan decisions made in the private sector. Indeed, the actual policies followed in the postwar years were, in many crucial respects, so hostile to the implications of Keynes's thought that they can only be described as counter-Keynesian. There was a failure, to be sure, but it was the failure of a growth coalition, not of a Keynesian coalition.

Keynes was a great thinker, and like all great thinkers he left an intellectual legacy subject to multiple interpretations. I do not claim to have the last word on what Keynes "really" meant, but it does seem to me obvious that his purpose was to use government to save capitalism from itself. Keynes was certainly no socialist. "No obvious case," he wrote, is made out for a system of State Socialism which would embrace most of the economic life of the community. It is not the ownership of the means of production which it is important for the state to assume. *If* the state is able to determine the aggregate amount of resources devoted to augmenting the instruments and the basic rate of reward for those who own them, it will have accomplished all that is necessary.[3]

Although not socialist, Keynes's reforms were premised upon the existence of a political coalition that could force upon the state reforms, giving it some say in determining "the aggregate amount of resources. . . ." In countries where a strong labor movement or Social Democratic party existed, such as Sweden, such a coalition existed. Thus, Keynesianism, designed to save capitalism from the capitalists, could exist only when a socialist or social democratic tradition was strong enough to force it upon the political agenda. This was decidedly not the case in the United States.[4] Emerging out of the political stalemate of 1938 with renewed power and legitimacy, American businessmen and conservatives were able to block legislation that would give government the power to impose Keynesian reforms. At the same time, American liberals were both unwilling and unable to wage a political struggle from below to override the conservative veto. Keynesianism may have made economic sense but, in America, it was a political impossibility. The "if" in the cited passage from Keynes was a major qualifier.

## II

"THE OUTSTANDING FAULTS of the economic society in which we live," Keynes wrote at the end of his masterpiece, "are its failures to provide full employment and its arbitrary and inequitable distribution of wealth." Full employment was the precondition for any other reform. An economy committed to full employment would necessarily redistribute income, for economic stimulation would rebound to the advantage of all. Moreover, the preference of bankers for high interest rates to discourage inflation would be undermined by an emphasis on full employment. Keynes advocated lower interest rates to stimulate investment, reducing the rewards to holders of capital, and bringing about "the euthanasia of the rentier, and, consequently, the euthanasia of the cumulative power of the capitalist to exploit the scarcity-value of capital. . . ."[5] Finally, a full employment policy suggested some controls on free trade, so that the domestic planning capacity of the state would not be undermined by international resource movements. ("I sympathize, therefore, with those who would minimize, rather than those who would maximize, economic entanglement among nations. . . . Let goods be homespun whenever it is reasonably and conveniently possible, and above all, let finance be primarily national."[6])

When an act to offer full employment to the American people was introduced into Congress as one of the first items on the postwar agenda, a test case was at hand that would indicate the applicability of Keynesian ideas in the American context. (New Deal economics were not deliberately Keynesian, and some of the New Dealers were rather hostile.) Understanding how crucial full employment was to the Keynesian program, a group of liberal economists, believing that "it is still up to us to prove that capitalism is not but a passing phase in the historical process from feudalism to socialism,"[7] argued for a program of conscious economic planning. Such men, among them Seymour Harris, Leon Keyserling, George Soule, and Alvin Hansen, suggested that a program of full employment and social justice could provide the economic base for a revitalized liberal wing of the Democratic party.

The Full Employment Bill posed the question that was at the heart of Keynesian doctrine: was it possible to use government to ensure that full employment would produce economic growth, or should one accept the position of business that economic growth could ensure full employment? As originally conceived, the bill was in line with Keynes's thought: it contained a guarantee of jobs for all and created a government planning mechanism to help ensure that full employment would be brought about. For this reason, the bill aroused furious resistance from businessmen and conservatives, who denounced it as socialistic, fearing its impact on inflation, wage costs, profits, and business prerogatives. In the amending process, as Stephen Kemp Bailey's masterful history of the legislation recounts, conservatives managed to strip the act of its teeth and to turn it into a commitment to full employment that was, at best, only symbolic. Given the strength of the conservative bloc in Congress, American Keynesians could fight to maintain their commitment to theory and lose, or agree to support a flawed bill in order to obtain something. Arguing that a symbolic victory was preferable to a principled defeat, most of them agreed to support the final version.

The issues in the debate over the Employment Act (the word "full" now deleted) established the main features of macroeconomic policy in the postwar period. Which was true: that "every American able to work and willing to work has the right to a useful and remunerative job . . . ," as the original version of the bill stated; or that "it is the policy of the United States to foster free competitive enterprise . . . ," as the final version proclaimed?[8] Would America, in other words, move beyond the New Deal into planning for full employment or would it go back to the days of unhampered business influence? The answer was neither. The compromise fashioned over the Employment Act gave business its commitment to profits, and economic activists the rhetoric of full employment. Seemingly contradictory, both objectives could be combined on the assumption of economic growth. A dynamic economy would create jobs and profits at the same time, subsuming questions of planning and equity into a quest for growth. Without realizing it, supporters of the Employment Act were taking the first step in the formation of growth politics.

When the Employment Act passed, liberal economists felt that they had won a major victory, for an agency charged with economic planning—the Council of Economic Advisers—had come into existence. Moreover, the agency itself would be dominated by the very activists who had called for full employment legislation in the first place; Leon Keyserling was one of the first three members of the council and would be its second chairman. Yet the agency that Keynesians were so proud to have established was one that had been deprived of its ability to bring about Keynesianism. For one thing, the 1946 law could be read as a repudiation of the right to full employment, for, if sufficient growth were not around to provide it, there would be no effective government guarantees to ensure it. Without jobs for all who want them, little else in Keynesianism makes sense; the most fundamental star in the Keynesian galaxy was extinguished from the beginning. An even more important consequence of the compromise over growth would also soon become apparent. Seeking full employment through an expansion of the private sector would completely transform the dynamics of macroeconomic policy in America and, with it, the whole pattern of postwar politics.

By making employment dependent on the expansion of the

private sector, American Keynesians turned into their opposite. The key to obtaining a program that would win the support of workers became a policy designed to help business to invest. Businessmen, by nature, do nothing without charging a price, and the price that they demanded in return for expanding the economy was a weakening of the ability of government to plan. Ironically, then, American Keynesians could ensure their political power only by sacrificing their economic power. They could occupy positions of political authority only if they promised not to use their economic theory. The more power they obtained, in short, the less power they had. An emphasis upon growth, at least the kind of growth stimulated through the expansion of the private sector, was incompatible with an emphasis on planning, at least the kind of planning directed by the public sector. The success of a growth coalition meant the defeat of a Keynesian coalition, even though the same economists belonged to both. If Keynesianism implies the use of government to influence and direct decisions made in the private sector, then postwar macroeconomic planning could only be defined as counter-Keynesian: the use of the private sector to influence the scope and activities of government. For the only way that liberals could hope to reward their working-class and minority constituents with jobs and public programs, once they had deprived themselves of economic management, was by generating an expansion of the economy sufficient to provide a fiscal surplus. Desperate to win "business confidence," pro-growth liberals would find themselves pursuing a course in striking contrast to the ideas of their mentor.

The Employment Act of 1946 was an indication that Keynesians had come to power in America, but Keynesianism had not. In order to obtain the support of businessmen for expansion, economic reformers found themselves in the awkward position of promising *not* to use the mechanisms that they knew could work to improve economic performance. In at least five areas, American Keynesians repudiated their own tools of economic management in order to win business confidence. These tools include government intervention on the "supply-side" of economic activity; coordinated monetary and fiscal policy; the incorporation of labor into government planning; insulation from the world economy; and a choice of government spending techniques that were redistributive in nature. In one area after another, the pattern begun by the Employment Act was continued: economic planners had no choice but to sacrifice their economic understanding in return for political acceptability.

## III

IT IS 1950, and hearings are being held before the Joint Congressional Committee on the Economic Report (later called the Joint Economic Committee). Testifying before the committee was J. Cameron Thomson, president of the Northwest Bancorporation of Minneapolis and chairman of the subcommittee on monetary and fiscal policy of the Committee for Economic Development (CED). Thomson was an unusual businessman, for he was arguing in favor of government policy to stimulate investment. (Most businessmen denounce government policy as inflationary, wasteful, and an interference in a realm reserved for themselves.) Thomson's testimony was strongly welcomed by one of the members of the committee, Senator Paul Douglas, a well-known economist and an enthusiastic advocate of economic expansion. Douglas's report for the Joint Congressional Committee concluded that demand management was compatible with the "maintenance of our democratic system and with the fostering and promotion of free competitive enterprise." Such methods

> do not involve the Government in detailed control of the particulars of the economy; they do not require the Government to intervene in individual transactions between buyer and seller, in dealings between employer and employee, and in the determination or the prices and production of particular commodities. These millions of intricate decisions are left to the operation of the market mechanisms while general monetary, credit, and fiscal policies work toward stabilization by influencing the total supply and cost of money income at the disposal of the private sectors of the economy. There is every difference between the effects of general overall monetary, credit, and fiscal policies which indirectly influence the economy toward stabilization and the effects of an elaborate system of direct controls.[9]

In order to understand the harmony between a banker like Thomson and an economic liberal (and former socialist) like

Douglas, it is necessary to use the distinction that economists make between intervention on the supply-side versus policies on the demand-side. Supply-side activity involves direct measures by government to influence production, like establishing how much steel should be produced by the steel industry or by favoring one industrial sector (oil) over another (coal). (Supply-side intervention should not be confused with the supply-side economics that have become popular among Republicans in the 1980s. They are opposites. The former seeks intervention into the private sector to control it, while the latter is calling for the freedom of the private sector to escape regulation. Both, however, agree on the central importance of the supply-side.) The National Recovery Administration of the New Deal, which established production codes for specific industries, was one example of supply-side intervention, and was also an example of how unpopular such direct controls over business are in the United States. (A more current example is the program of an organization called Consumers Opposed to Inflation in the Necessities, which seeks to curtail price increases in energy, housing, food, and medical care.) In contrast, demand-side intervention refers to attempts by government to influence the amount of money available in the society to purchase goods and services. Lowering interest rates in order to stimulate borrowing is an example of demand-side intervention, as is raising taxes to discourage investment. Both monetary and fiscal policy exist on the demand-side; monetary policy refers to attempts to influence the total amount of money in the society (generally by changing the interest rate), while fiscal policy concerns itself with government revenues (taxes) or government expenditures (appropriations).

Supply-side intervention, especially when disaggregated, is precise and effective, for it is capable of targeting bottlenecks in production and resolving them. Economically powerful, such intervention on the supply-side is also politically precarious, for it directly confronts what Charles Lindblom calls "the privileged position of business,"[10] and therefore is generally denounced as socialistic, a serious disadvantage in the American context. Demand-side intervention is also distrusted by most businessmen, for few in the private sector are willing to grant that any actions by government are tolerable. Yet, if there is to be intervention of any sort, and depression and war seemed to guarantee that there would be, some businessmen, particularly from the monopoly sector of the economy, could be induced to support it, so long as it was intervention not into the conditions of supply but concerning the aggregate amount of demand.

Keynes himself argued for demand-side management; far-reaching alterations in the capitalist mode of production were not his intention. Yet Keynes's preference for enhancing aggregate demand was forged by the European situation, where some forms of planning and incomes policy were already accepted by business elites. In the United States, demand-side reforms would take on a different meaning, for American businessmen had so much more freedom of action compared to their European counterparts that a policy of avoiding intervention on the supply-side would simply reenforce the independence of business from the state. In this context, the agreement fashioned between J. Cameron Thomson and Paul Douglas was indicative of the emergence of a new coalition in the United States, one that would spur economic growth through demand-side intervention while at the same time pledging never to interfere with the conditions of production on the supply-side.

An emerging consensus that government intervention should avoid "detailed control of the particulars of the economy," as Douglas put it, placed the growth advocates squarely in the center of the political spectrum. Farmers and competitive-sector business-men, dominated by fantasies of a free market, were opposed to any economic management at all. Social Democrats and economic activists hoped to see government intervene wherever necessary to correct the defects of the private sector. Unlike both of these positions, a consensus over demand-inspired growth was a meeting of the minds of "realistic" Keynesians, who were willing to move to the right by dropping their emphasis on direct planning, and monopoly-sector businessmen, who were willing to move to the left by supporting government intervention, even if the most minimal sort.

With demand-side intervention established, a second question facing economic policymakers needed to be addressed: should government be streamlined and coordinated or fractured and decentralized? During the New Deal, radicals and liberal activists had argued for a centralized economic policy on the grounds that planning could take place only if a public agency had sufficient authority to match the power of big corporations. Men like Harold Ickes, for example, were ardent advocates, not only of executive supremacy over Congress, but of the more centralized parts of the executive branch over the more pluralistic. On the other hand, conservatives in America have traditionally favored fractured public authority, often in order to enhance the exercise of private power.[11]

The question of governmental authority was fought out over the issue of monetary versus fiscal policy. In the United States, the Federal Reserve System determines the money supply; and conservatives, strong believers in the virtues of monetary policy over fiscal policy, want to see the Federal Reserve be "independent," autonomous from other agencies of government. Monetary policy has the advantage of seeming to be beyond the control of men, thereby reenforcing the conservative belief in the "natural" workings of the market. As Joan Robinson has written, "There is in some quarters a great affection for credit policy because it seems the least selective and somehow lives up to the ideal of a single overall neutral regulation of the economy. The enormous ideological attraction of the Quantity Theory of Money . . . is due to the fact that it conceals the problem of political choice under an apparently impersonal mechanism."[12] In order to guarantee that impersonality, most businessmen prefer to see the Federal Reserve have the authority to make monetary policy on its own, whatever the rest of the government is doing.

Keynesians, no longer able to count on intervention on the supply-side, should have fallen back on a strong fiscal policy as an alternative. Something like the World War II situation constituted a model. Then an independent Federal Reserve was considered anathema in the face of the need to centralize decision making for wartime purposes. The Federal Reserve was forced to act in accordance with government policy by purchasing treasury bonds on the open market as a way of keeping interest rates low and thereby financing the war debt. After the war, conservatives and businessmen attacked this procedure, while the Federal Reserve asked Truman for the authority to end its support of the bond market and pegged interest rates. If granted, bankers would be able to fight inflation by raising interest rates. In that case, attempts by economic activists to create full employment by encouraging growth in one part of government could be counterbalanced by restrictive and deflationary monetary policies in another part of the government. As senseless economically as it was to have fiscal and monetary policy contradicting each other—one spurring the economy forward to create jobs, the other slowing it up to fight inflation—such a compromise made eminent political sense, and Truman approved it. "The liberation of monetary policy," as Herbert Stein called it, strengthened the centrist coalition over growth, but in a precarious way.[13] Economic activists won support from business for the right of government to make economic policy, but the government that was making it was so fractured and decentralized that one part of it could negate what the other was doing.

A third question over which there were sharp debates in the late 1940s concerned the proper role to be played by labor unions. Keynesianism was sympathetic to unions, given its attitude toward full employment. Moreover, by de-emphasizing profits, credits, and costs, Keynesianism softened the impact of those who sought to discipline labor by forcing workers to live more closely to the subsistence margin. Labor's role was very much on the political agenda of 1946. The United Automobile Workers (UAW) struck General Motors (GM), demanding a peek at the company's books, interpreted by GM as an attack on capitalism itself. Such uncharacteristic militance was both cause and effect of a hardening of the antilabor position in America at the time, such as the restrictions on organized labor contained in the Taft-Hartley Act (1947). The emotionally charged issue of whether to advance or limit the freedom of action for labor unions put the growth coalition into a difficult position. Its economic analysis led to an expansion of labor's power, but the political mood was calling for limits. Fortuitously, economic growth made a precise answer to the question unnecessary.

At the shop-floor level, economic growth offered a compromise by which workers would be encouraged to produce more, thereby increasing their wages but at the same time augmenting company profits. A vivid contrast existed between the bitter GM strike of 1946 and the harmonious settlement reached in 1948. In the latter year, GM and the UAW made a deal: increased productivity in return for a cost-of-living allowance. Workers would produce more for a given unit of time, thereby increasing profit, but in return, the company would protect the workers against inflation by guaranteeing wage increases tied to the cost of living. Productivity would generate economic growth, and economic growth would keep labor relations peaceful.[14] The 1948 settlement, premised upon the existence of a perpetual growth machine, became the basis of the postwar social contract between management and labor.

Growth operated as a similar panacea in terms of governmental policy toward labor. If the economy is stagnant, then demands from the working class for more can be met only by taking from

someone else, like business. But if the economy grows, then the
total social wage going to labor can increase, even if the relative
proportion does not. (The social wage refers to all those goods and
services provided by government that would have to be paid for
out of wages if the government did not provide them, such as
social security, unemployment compensation, etc.) No wonder that
the stimulation of economic growth became the number-one priority of economic policymakers, with controversy being confined
generally to the means. When the first postwar recession struck in
1948–49, Council of Economic Advisers members Leon Keyserling
and John D. Clark proposed an "Economic Stability Act" designed
to ensure continued production. The act would have given the
president the power to control prices and to allocate commodities,
as well as to stimulate new productive capacity where business was
unwilling. The economic expansion bill, as it was called, was too
much for business; even the CED joined the condemnation of such
blatant supply-side intervention. When the bill was withdrawn, it
had become clear that as important as economic growth was, some
indirect means would have to be found to stimulate it.

By the 1950s, no clear-cut solution to the problem of what to do
about organized labor had yet been reached. The growth coalition
desired an overall expansion of the economy, but it was unable to
win support for a direct program to do so. Later on, in 1962, a
more acceptable method of achieving growth through tax cuts
would be discovered, and then, it was hoped, labor could continue
to be rewarded without interfering with, but conceivably expanding, the prerogatives of business.

The relationship between the United States and the world
economy constituted a fourth area in which ideas basic to the
theory of Keynesianism would be compromised in order to allow
the growth coalition to come to power. Keynes's own inclinations
varied from time to time, and he was more internationalistic on
international monetary affairs than he tended to be on trade policy.
His major concern was the stimulation of full employment, and if
overseas economic activity could stimulate growth to bring it
about, he was sympathetic, whereas if vulnerability to the world
economy undermined an ability to plan, he was suspicious. Effective economic management, Keynes argued toward the end of his
life, presupposed, for most countries, a certain protection from the
ability of another country to disrupt high employment rates by
keeping wage costs down. On this issue, Keynes's tolerance of

protectionism was one of his characteristic departures from conventional economic wisdom. (Most economists thought that the Great Depression, let alone World War I, was caused by tariff barriers.)

Labor tended to be protectionist, as did the competitive sector of the economy. But protectionist sentiments were held to contradict an emphasis on growth, for, growth theorists argued, less efficient and productive industries should not be kept in business for essentially political reasons. A position emerged that claimed that worldwide economic growth would make Keynesian concerns with stable full employment unnecessary, since jobs would be produced as other countries expanded to buy American products. The appeal of growth made it possible for economic planners to put aside their protectionist inclinations and to join a free-trade bandwagon. The debate between open and closed economies seemed so trivial in the late 1940s because, as I will argue in chapter 6, the U.S. domination of the world economy was so overwhelming. So long as the U.S. economy and the world economy were virtually the same, America could have both full employment and overseas economic expansion. Thus, the growth coalition linked itself to an open world economy, but at the same time was able to claim the major advantage of a closed economy: national control over economic events. The resulting compromise smoothed over the controversy between free trade and protectionism, but the planners who accepted the compromise were stepping into a trap. If the world economy and the U.S. economy were to diverge, and it did not take much vision to realize that at some point they might, then the openness of the U.S. economy to the world might rebound to the disadvantage of full employment, exporting jobs rather than creating them at home. This the growth coalition would later learn, when it was prevented from increasing employment at home because of the commitments it had made to the world economy.

A fifth and final compromise that shaped the form of the growth coalition was the support given by domestic liberals to military spending. Unhappy at losing the economic expansion bill of 1949, expansionists like Keyserling were anxious to discover some other method of stimulating growth through federal spending policies. Government spending can either be structured to redistribute income, transferring money from the wealthy to the poor, or it can operate as a subsidy to the already well-off, thereby stimulating profits. Keynes at one point suggested that it did not matter, that augmenting aggregate demand was the key, and he claimed that putting gold in holes and then digging it up again would be sufficient. But it is also true that redistributional spending has a multiplier effect, for, as the poor receive more, they can spend it and thereby increase the rate at which the economy expands. Radical Keynesians no doubt preferred federal spending that brought about greater equality, and for the same reasons that businessmen and conservatives opposed redistribution. This makes Keyserling's decision to chip in his support for military spending a crucial choice, for military spending is among the least redistributive forms that federal spending can take and is also the most popular among conservative elites. In 1951, Keyserling urged that the military budget be used as a stimulant, a notion still too radical for President Truman, who opted to "stretch" it out over time. The president, according to Barton Bernstein, was "primarily interested in stability, not growth."[15] Never fully converted to pro-growth doctrines, Truman worried about the inflationary impact of an increase in spending for Korea, giving the economically orthodox a strong ally in the White House.

Nonetheless, Keyserling's position, not Truman's, was the future. Anticommunism was becoming a consensus in the United States, and many domestic liberals did not want to be left out. Feeling vulnerable to the charge that the Democratic party was "soft" on communism, they became advocates of a strong military posture in order to counter the charge, and thereby found a convincing rationale for pro-growth federal spending. A new world view came into being, one that linked an active national security state with a domestic emphasis on economic expansion. "Yet," as Daniel Yergin has written, "it was a world view living beyond its means. It lacked the requisite budget."[16] Growth would provide the budget, and the linking of federally induced growth with a cold war foreign policy solidified the political position of the growth coalition.

The emerging national security consensus had its own economics. First, in direct contrast to the position that had dominated economic thinking for some time, the growth network argued that the U.S. economy would not be damaged by a huge increase in military spending. "We must not hobble ourselves," the Committee for Economic Development remarked, "by the notion that there is some arbitrary limit on what we can spend for defense, now within reach, that we can exceed only with disastrous consequences to the economy."[17] Second, an increase in the military budget would foster economic expansion and would not interfere with business profits, seemingly a miracle. Finally, rearmament and foreign military aid could replace the Marshall Plan in providing a stimulant for other countries, thereby boosting U.S. exports. This would keep employment high in the United States (for greater exports means the preservation of high production levels) and would consequently ease the pressure on government to guarantee full employment. Fred Block has described this package as "a brilliant solution to the major problems of the U.S. economy," which it was.[18] But it also tied the U.S. economy to a form of stimulation that would in retrospect prove inflexible, inflationary, wasteful, and damaging to the balance of payments.

Support for military spending was one more initiation rite for the growth coalition, another way of showing that if it had to choose between a Keynesian emphasis on planning and an expansionist emphasis on growth, it would choose the latter. As was the case with each of the other features of the compromise, methods used to win political respectability among business and the military would eventually prove to be economically troublesome.

And so, by 1952, American Keynesians had won unexpectedly strong political support. By lowering the vision and by softening the reformist implications of Keynes's thought, American Keynesians delivered the United States out of the hands of conservative economics. They did not, however, deliver it into the hands of Keynesian economics, stopping halfway between at a pro-growth compromise. Winning allies among monopoly-sector businessmen, labor leaders, social planners, anticommunists, and pro-growth intellectuals, a bipartisan growth coalition came to dominate the economic policymaking process in the postwar period. Herbert Stein has well described the major features of the consensus that was hammered out:

> By the end of 1949 the country had reached a consensus on fiscal policy which was a long way from traditional ideas of annual budget balance and from the early post-Keynesian ideas of compensatory finance. We would not try to balance recession budgets by raising taxes or by cutting expenditures. In recessions of some exceptional degree of severity we would do more than accept the automatically resulting deficit and take affirmative steps to enlarge the deficit. In contrast to earlier thinking

about deficit spending, these steps were more likely to be on the revenue side of the budget than on the expenditure side. And we would in general look to some version of balancing the budget in prosperous conditions as a norm. We would not expect positive fiscal measures to respond to and counteract every actual or forecast departure from the high employment target, but would accept the principle that in fiscal policy, as in many other things, striving for the best may be the enemy of achieving the good. Also in contrast to earlier "new economics," we would give a considerable role to monetary policy as the partner of fiscal policy.[19]

Stein describes this triumph as a fiscal revolution. It was a triumph, but hardly a revolutionary one. The creation of the growth coalition was a victory of the center, a break with the past, to be sure, but not a thrust into the future.

Now in power, American Keynesians found themselves bereft of most of the major tools that would enable them to manage capitalism as they had promised. They could not intervene into conditions of production; coordinate fiscal policy through the executive branch unhampered by monetarist deflations; count on labor to mobilize from below in support of reforms; protect jobs against inroads made by the world economy; or redistribute income to generate increased aggregate demand. Left without these tools, they were in a bind, for they had offered to the traditional constituents of the Democratic party an ideology that emphasized social welfare and a better life for all. In order to deliver on this promise, economic activists had only one tool left—economic growth—but it was a tool that made them dependent on businessmen, the only class that could provide it. As a result, American Keynesians were forced to structure their policies so as to win business confidence. Rather than managing the economy, they became reluctant advocates of counter-Keynesianism: expanding the private sector in order to enhance the surplus of government. In the name of a man who urged that the public sector be used to stimulate the private, the growth coalition followed policies that used the private sector to stimulate the public.

## IV

COUNTER-KEYNESIANISM would finally come to power during the Kennedy administration, but before that would happen the centrist position of the growth coalition would be strengthened under Eisenhower.

Eisenhower himself had little or no sympathy for Keynesian ideas, and his appointment of Arthur Burns to chair the Council of Economic Advisers turned that body over to a prominent critic of the Keynesian program. But even though Burns was unsympathetic to Keynesianism, he was not unsympathetic to growth. Under his leadership, macroeconomic policy during the Eisenhower years attempted to walk a fine line between minimal state management and action necessary to prevent a recession. Thus, Eisenhower, through Burns, did contribute to a solidification of the growth network, but in a generally negative way. First, he did not roll back the federal budget, recognizing that, Republican rhetoric to the contrary, there was precious little "fat" to be trimmed. Second, he did not repudiate the use of countercyclical measures to offset recession. Finally, the administration also did not oppose a plan developed by Republicans in the House to cut back excise taxes (at the risk of unbalancing the budget), a politically popular idea aimed at the 1954 election.

Without any overweening desire to expand the economy, Burns and Eisenhower were pragmatic enough not to want to contract it either. By taking minimal actions to prevent recession, they demonstrated the importance that notions about growth had achieved when compared to, say, the Hoover period. The main difference between Burns and his critics was over how to achieve growth, with Burns preferring a conservative strategy of helping business and using government's negative powers to prevent recession. Thus, while not fully supporting the more extreme notions about growth, Eisenhower did not really oppose them either. Like the hero of Joseph Heller's *Good as Gold*, who was opposed to segregation but also opposed to integration, Eisenhower neither set back nor advanced the growth coalition.

Neutrality, however, was not enough for the growth-oriented activists. They had made their compromises with Keynes's original doctrine in order to hold power, and under Eisenhower they did not. Thus, during the 1950s, an attack from academic exile was launched against Eisenhower's macroeconomic policy. One battleground of the war was the Joint Economic Committee, from which men like Senator Paul Douglas ridiculed Eisenhower's passivity. Pro-growth advocates came and testified, such as Paul Samuelson, who expressed the coalition's beliefs perfectly when he argued that "with proper fiscal and monetary policy, our economy can have full employment and whatever rate of capital formation and growth it wants."[20] From New Haven and Cambridge, studies flowed forth, arguing that inflation, the great fear of the Eisenhower administration, need not be a major concern, so long as macroeconomic stimulation contributed to rapid growth. Like their compatriots in the national security establishment, whose story I will recount in chapter 5, the economic activists at once attacked Eisenhower for inaction and also promised that action need not interfere with the prerogatives of the powerful. They would have a chance to prove this hypothesis once they took power.

The body of ideas through which the activists criticized Eisenhower and Burns came to be called the "new economics." As formulated by men like Paul Samuelson and Walter Heller, the new economics argued that deficit spending and governmental "fine-tuning" could abolish recessions. Unlike earlier Keynesian notions, the new economics did not call for overall governmental coordination of the economy, but took the less controversial position that tax cuts could enable private firms to expand and thereby increase growth. As opposed to Keynes's personal emphasis on full employment, the new economics sought a balance between fiscal and monetary policy that would trade off a small amount of unemployment in return for price stability. In short, the new economics represented the form that counter-Keynesianism had taken by 1960; it was concerned much more with running the economy efficiently than it was with social justice or income redistribution. Keynesianism had been an ideology of reform; the new economics was a technocratic procedure. Thus, for all the vehemence with which advocates of the new economics criticized Eisenhower, they were not criticizing the goals of the Eisenhower adminsitration, just the means used to reach them.

Giving credence to the position of the new economics was the uncertain performance of the American economy in the 1950s. John Kennedy took office after campaigning against sluggish economic performance, and it was expected that his economic managers would quickly try to stimulate more growth. Yet Kennedy discovered almost immediately that the political stalemate that confronted Truman still existed; the conservative bloc in Congress was powerful enough to prevent the adoption of any reforms that it did not like, and conservatives were worried that too much growth would disrupt the overseas position of the United States, drive up wages, and intensify inflation. The reflex activism of Kennedy's advisers came face-to-face with corporate and congressional leaders who were unsympathetic even to the modified and defanged ideas of counter-Keynesianism. Thus, Kennedy found that in order to expand the economy, he had to take a watered-down program of economic growth and water it down even further. A package already designed to win the support of business and the military would have to be redesigned one more time.

Although Kennedy took on the steel industry in a 1961 quarrel over a price hike, the experience left him shattered. The administration, as Arthur Schlesinger, Jr., later wrote, "simply did not want another major fight with business."[21] It did not get one. Kennedy went about as far as he could, given his support among labor and working people, to win business backing for his macroeconomic policies. Kennedy became the first president to squarely face the issues involved in the triumph of counter-Keynesianism, for the only way that he could keep alive his commitment to Democratic party voting constituencies was by offering concessions to business to induce investment. As the president said in a 1961 press conference:

> This country cannot prosper unless business prospers. This country cannot meet its obligations and tax obligations and all the rest unless business is doing well. Business will not do well and we [will not] have full employment unless they feel there is a chance to make a profit. So there is no long-run hostility between business and government. There cannot be. We cannot succeed unless they succeed.[22]

Kennedy's words betrayed the irony of his position. His administration was a triumph for the economists, the first administration dominated by men who called themselves Keynesians. Yet, because of the compromises necessary to bring ·the growth coalition to power, these men could do little but plead with business to help them out of their fix. The impotence of Kennedy's economists was reflected in the tactics used to combat recession. Keynesian theory proposed two methods of stimulating aggregate demand: government expenditures can be increased in order to create a deficit or taxes can be reduced in order to put more money in the hands of business and consumers. Planners and activists generally preferred the former; deficit spending was largely a code word for increased public expenditure, which would centralize investment, make the economy more controllable, and work to redistribute income, since the government could determine the allocation of the new resources. But deficits can also be created by cutting taxes while holding spending constant (or even decreasing it, depending on the size of the tax cut). This method is less compatible with planning, for one cannot know in advance where the new investment will take place, whether income will be redistributed, and when the extra expenditure will occur. For obvious reasons, however, a tax cut is preferable to business, and can also be framed to win general political support. Firms that would automatically repudiate deficit spending if it occurred through increased federal spending might be induced to support it if it came from a cut in taxes. (Ironically, Republican party economic theorists came to support the idea of a general tax cut, and it became the favored economic scheme of the Reagan administration, whose economists were pleased to quote John Kennedy on the advantages to be gained.)

Kennedy, recalling the debates in the 1950s within the Democratic Advisory Council between John Kenneth Galbraith and Leon Keyserling (see chapter 2), concluded that the most "realistic" alternative, given the political stalemate, was to cut taxes, not to increase spending; and by June 1962, the president had made his choice.[23] There followed his speech to the Economic Club of New York, about as Republican and conservative a body as Kennedy could find. The audience was enthused, for what they heard was, in Galbraith's words, "the most Republican speech since McKinley."[24] The tax cut of 1964, which followed from Kennedy's decision, was one more nail in the coffin of economic planning directed by government.

Almost as significant as the tax cut was Kennedy's decision to offer special breaks to business. Although Eisenhower had toyed with the notion of an investment tax credit before dropping the idea, Kennedy picked up on this essentially Republican notion and brought it to legislative fruition. (Business, for reasons that only it can understand, actually fought Kennedy's idea of giving it a special deal, although later it would learn and reverse its position.) The investment tax credit of 1962 was regressive; it shifted money from the poor to the rich. It was also a giveaway to business, one that by 1975 constituted the second most costly tax subsidy in the United States. In addition, as recent studies have shown, it subsidized the larger and more monopolistic corporations at the expense of the competitive sector.[25] In short, investment tax credits have little to do with Keynesianism; they are a counter-Keynesian mechanism of supporting the private sector in order to encourage growth in the state. In making an investment tax credit a crucial part of his macroeconomic policy, Kennedy proved himself more willing to make concessions to business than Eisenhower had been. (Jimmy Carter would pick up this idea and make a promise to extend the investment tax credit to 90 percent of new investment, instead of the 50 percent of an earlier period.)

Decisions like the tax cut and the investment tax credit were not the product of Kennedy's personal political attitudes toward business but grew out of the political pattern that had been established by the rise of the growth coalition. Republicans, as it turned out, did not need to be as solicitous of business support as Democrats. Because the conservative wing of the growth network does not offer general promises of an expansion of the welfare state and campaigns against inflation, it need not rely on economic growth to expand the public budget (the fiscal dividend, as Walter Heller would call it). But the liberal growth advocates, lacking tools to manage the economy because of the compromises they made to come to power, were in desperate need of economic growth and therefore had to mortgage their future to business confidence. The economists upon whom Kennedy relied for advice, Keynesian in their self-image, had no choice but to advocate policies counter to some of Keynes's more cherished ideas in order to remain in power.

Interestingly enough, counter-Keynesianism worked. Tax credits and reductions did stimulate the economy, also pushed along by the military production associated with the war in Vietnam. Through the first two years of the Johnson administration, the economy went through its longest sustained upswing in the postwar period. Economists, who took the boom as evidence that the new economics was a scientific breakthrough equivalent to the double helix, jumped for joy. Infected with utopianism, the Council of Economic Advisers reported in 1965 that "both our increased understanding of the effectiveness of fiscal policy and the continued improvement of . . . our economic information, strengthen the conviction that recessions can be increasingly avoided and ultimately wiped out."[26] Lyndon Johnson told the American people that he "did not believe that recessions were inevitable."[27] Not only that, prosperity could be achieved without inflation. Walter Heller, chairman of the Council of Economic Advisers, claimed that fine-tuning permitted expansion without rising prices, even though, by the time Heller's comments were published, an upsurge in prices had begun (one that has yet to stop).

Actually, the peak of economic performance in the mid-1960s was also the point at which counter-Keynesianism began to fail. Economists had come to put their faith in something called the Phillips curve. This diagram was a shorthand way of expressing a key relationship in the new economics between inflation and unemployment. According to the theory, any rise in unemployment would lead to diminished production, which would slow down the rate of growth and therefore reduce inflation. As prices came down, attempts would be made to take advantage of cheaper costs, leading to increased production and therefore to higher rates of employment. In other words, counter-Keynesianism suggested that it was impossible for rising inflation and rising unemployment to happen together, at least for any extended period of time. Permanent stagflation was, according to the theory, impossible, no more an option than water's running uphill.

Yet stagflation came about nonetheless. By the late 1960s, prices seemed to be increasing at the same rate that jobs were disappearing. The diagram below indicates how serious this problem had become by the end of the Johnson administration.[28] The point at which the two lines in the diagram converge was the moment of truth for counter-Keynesianism. From then on, both the economics and the politics of the growth coalition became much more problematic.

Economically, advocates of growth argued that unemployment could be reduced by expanding aggregate demand through tax cuts, while inflation could be counterbalanced by reducing government spending. Yet, by 1967, neither was happening. Demand-side intervention, attempting to influence economic events indirectly through the tax system, had reached its limits. Some economists, like Galbraith, began to argue for wage-and-price controls as a way of dealing with inflation, but such controls are a form of intervention on the supply-side, for they legislate decisions typically made in the private sector, and as a result considerable opposition to controls existed. "Controls," said Arthur Okun of the Johnson Council of Economic Advisers, "were never seriously considered in the Johnson administration." The CEA was suspicious of them for the same reason that Paul Douglas had objected to supply-side intervention during the Truman years:

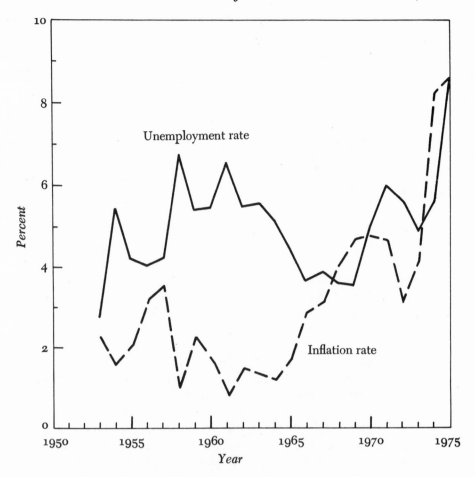

... Mandatory controls on prices and wages ... distort resource allocation; they require reliance either on necessarily clumsy and arbitrary rules or the inevitably imperfect decisions of Government officials; they offer countless temptations to evasion or violation; they require a vast administrative apparatus. All of these reasons make them repugnant.[29]

This language is instructive; the Johnson council was opposed to supply-side intervention, not because it might be a burden on the working class, but because it would interfere with the ability of the market to offer the correct signals. So closely tied had the liberal wing of the growth coalition become to counter-Keynesianism that it was prohibited from considering at least one mechanism that might have brought inflation under control, especially in its initial stages.

Prevented from attacking inflation, the growth coalition also found itself unable to do much about rising unemployment. As international economic conditions, the switch to capital-intensive equipment, higher productivity, and increased economic concentration produced fewer jobs, counter-Keynesians, having relinquished their ability to manage the economy, found themselves without a job-creating strategy. Unable to eliminate unemployment, they chose to redefine it. Warren Smith, for example, offered the following conceptualization:

> Full employment may be defined as the lowest level of unemployment that can be achieved without encountering significant inflationary pressure—or, somewhat more generally, as that level of unemployment beyond which, in the opinion of responsible officials . . . the social benefits of a further reduction in unemployment are not worth the social costs of the inflation associated therewith.[30]

These words describe what actually became the employment strategy of the growth coalition. The rate of "acceptable" unemployment rose from 4 percent to 5 percent to 6.5 percent, as each new administration found the problem more intractable.[31] (In June 1980, President Carter, faced with an unemployment rate of 7.8 percent, announced that improved conditions were just around the corner.) One interesting aspect of this new policy toward redefining full employment is that there may be periods where it becomes necessary to throw people out of work in order to achieve "full" employment, for if the inflation rate is deemed by "responsible officials" to be too high, then too many people are working, even if the unemployment rate reaches 8 percent. What began in 1946 as a commitment on the part of the growth coalition to full employment ended, during the Carter administration, as a policy of deliberately throwing people out of work in order to hold down prices.

Losing the battle against both unemployment and inflation, the growth coalition found itself also losing its political base. The beauty of counter-Keynesianism was that it gave both wings of the growth coalition something to take home. Liberal Democrats could carry out a war on unemployment at the exact same time that conservative Republicans were battling inflation. Both economic activists and businessmen had a friend in Washington at the same time. For all the talk of controversy between right and left in the early 1960s, there was actually little tension and controversy over economic policymaking. But as stagflation digs itself in deep, suppressed political choices reemerge. Liberals find that they must be true to their promise of full employment and social welfare or risk losing working-class votes, while Republican conservatives must make good their promise to hold down inflation or risk becoming a minority party of businessmen. Stagflation was a challenge to the whole bipartisan strategy of relying on economic growth as an alternative to resolving the political stalemate that had existed since 1938.

The Democrats faced the problem first. Unable to formulate a program that could lower either prices or joblessness, Hubert Humphrey ran for president in 1968 with no particularly attractive domestic program. Speaking for a cold war that the United States was not winning and a growth strategy that was obviously failing, it is a miracle (or a commentary on Nixon) that Humphrey came as close to winning as he did. He lost at a time when macroeconomic policy was in disarray. So politically tame had American Keynesians become that the likes of Milton Friedman and Richard Nixon could proclaim that everyone was now a Keynesian. Yet Friedman had not changed his ideas, while the liberals had altered theirs. That should have been a clue. Conservatives had not become believers in the state so much as believers in the state had become conservative. Counter-Keynesianism, the intellectual baggage that the economists brought with them on the train to Washington, was simply too expedient and eclectic a set of ideas to work for very long.

## V

"I've ALWAYS THOUGHT this country could run itself domestically, without a president," Richard Nixon told Theodore White after the 1972 election. "All you need is a competent cabinet to run the country at home. You need a president for foreign policy."[32]

Nixon's words were probably never true, but they were true least of all after the failure of the growth coalition to develop a workable form of counter-Keynesianism. For 200 years economists have been involved in a never-ending feud about whether markets or the state should lead the economy. Counter-Keynesianism offered the worst of both. On the one hand, the solution adopted by Kennedy and Johnson was not free-enterprise capitalism, for state intervention on the demand-side was essential. Having used government, the growth coalition exposed itself to criticism from the right for not relying on the private sector. At the same time, state intervention was tame, indirect, and passive, opening up criticism from the left for not using the public sector effectively. At one time, the centrist location of the growth coalition was a major political advantage; by 1968, the center had become an uncomfortable place to rest.

As he scanned the horizon for an alternative to counter-Keynesianism, Richard Nixon came up with a brilliant idea. He unconsciously rediscovered Keynes. Although one would have thought that Nixon's position in the conservative wing of the Republican party would have led him to a reliance on the market, the pattern of politics established by the success of the growth coalition indicated otherwise. Liberal advocates of growth, needing to expand the state's surplus, become dependent on business; Nixon, a man of the right, was freed from that need and as a result was in a better position to use the state to control the private sector. In all five areas in which the counter-Keynesians compromised their doctrine save one (organized labor), Nixon showed himself more willing to confront the shibboleths of conservative and business opinion than the Democrats had been. Ultimately, his ambition and his need for revenge colored his policies, and he failed to develop a coherent program for managing either the economy or the state. Nonetheless, the fact that he was drawn to some of Keynes's original ideas is the next-to-the-last installment in the story of counter-Keynesianism's failure. (The last installment, Carter's, will be discussed in chapter 8.)

The first important aspect of the counter-Keynesian compromise was the failure to consider intervention on the supply-side, particularly controls on wages and prices. Such opposition was dropped on August 15, 1971, when Nixon announced an elaborate plan for controlling both. (At the same press conference, he also took the United States off the gold standard established at Bretton Woods and reverted to protectionism, but more on that later.) Nixon, by his acts, seemed to suggest that counter-Keynesianism had failed, an impression endorsed when Arthur Burns, politically revivified under Nixon, proclaimed that "the rules of economics are not working quite the way they used to."[33] (Burns's honesty, however, aroused Nixon to a burst of presidential fury.)[34] It took a Republican president and a moderately conservative economist to realize that the problems facing the American economy were beyond the point where indirect tinkering on the demand-side would cure them. (Postwar patterns would be reestablished when Jimmy Carter, a Democrat, would refuse under any circumstances to consider wage-and-price controls.)

Although Nixon was courageous enough to counter the counter-Keynesians on the question of supply-side intervention—just as he would soften Democratic cold war hostility to Russia and China—he allowed his sense of cronyism to stand in the way of an effective incomes policy. A Wage and Price Council was established, but its interventions were minimal and were not used to bring about effective state planning. Indeed, the probusiness orientation of wage-and-price controls under Nixon was blatant. C. Jackson Grayson, director of the council, asked and answered his own question on these matters: "Have we taken the big stride toward the perfectly planned economy? I hope not."[35] Nixon's personal ties to business interests gave him something of a short-sighted view on these matters, in direct contrast to his more long-term political vision. Having had the sense to create a possibly effective mechanism for dealing with inflation, he then stripped it of its powers. As a result, both inflation and unemployment would continue to rise under his presidency, and he would leave office with stagflation as much of a problem as it had been when he entered.

Nixon's downfall was brought about because of his clumsy attempt to centralize power in the White House. Yet, as I have tried to show in this chapter, centralization of political power has been an idea associated with activist liberals. In this area, ironically, Nixon's penchant for authority brought him closer to the original Keynesian vision of a coordinated and effective public agency for economic planning than anything tried by Kennedy or Johnson.[36] To Nixon belongs the credit for the following innovations in executive centralization: the coordination of the Office of Management and Budget in an attempt to unify federal spending programs (under the Democrats it had been called the Bureau of the Budget, deemphasizing its management function); the creation of a domestic council responsible for the overall coordination of domestic policy; a resurgence of impoundment as a device to bring federal spending into a consistent pattern (impoundment in the past had been advocated by Democrats and repudiated by Republicans); the birth of a National Goals Research Staff that tinkered with social engineering; and his support of wage-and-price controls. All of these innovations were compatible with Keynesian thought, for each of them enhanced the planning capacity of the state. Previous Democratic administrations had shied away from implementing plans like these for fear of arousing conservative sentiment. (Conservatives have denounced most plans for centralized state power since the New Deal as dictatorial.) Nixon's moves on these matters thus represented an outflanking of his opposition party, an attempt to steal their ideas, as was his trip to China. He would consider Keynesianism in a way that the Keynesians could not.

But once more Nixon's own ambivalence prevented the success of his political move. Keynesians favored centralized planning for a reason: it was more compatible with a reliance on fiscal policy over monetary policy. Although Nixon was willing to adopt the apparatus, he was too much a monetarist at heart to use it. And so he remained traditionally Republican in his notions about the independence of the Federal Reserve and a tight money supply. Without a rationale for tighter control, his innovations in this area were increasingly used to coordinate his personal power, not to make policy.

The one area in which Nixon failed to follow the logic of Keynesian priorities was in his attitude toward organized labor. He did try to reach out to the working class, bringing a labor leader into his cabinet and reaching out to Democrats like Daniel Patrick Moynihan for advice. Nixon's "new majority" featured a strong appeal to blue-collar workers, but more on the basis of the "social issue" (opposition to integration and cultural concerns) than of higher wages. These steps were limited and symbolic ones only, however. Unemployment was becoming worse, and to do something about it, policymakers would have to be far more radical.

If the years of the Korean and Vietnam wars are omitted, and if unemployment is measured at successive business cycle peaks, then the history of the postwar period is the history of rising unemployment. Every five-year subperiod, excepting war years, had a higher unemployment rate than its predecessor from 1945 to 1976. And since the official unemployment rate does not measure underemployment or discouraged workers, it taps the surface of the more general failure of the U.S. economy to create jobs for its labor force. Government seemed incapable of doing anything to stem the tide, for, in truth, economists did not have any remedies for rising unemployment except to stimulate an economy that was no longer open to rapid stimulation. This became a problem far too intractable for any administration; Nixon, after a flurry of words, backed off from any serious attempt to do something favorable toward labor. He had little choice but to try and impose the burdens of recessions upon the poor and hope for the best.

Nixon's inaction on the labor front must be judged against his position on free trade. Counter-Keynesianism, as we have seen, accepted free trade even though there was a strong protectionist current in Keynes's original formulations. Nixon's attempts to reconstitute a protectionist agenda, while denounced by Democrats as short-sighted and parochial, was more in line with the capacity for economic planning than the Trilateral notions that would flourish under Jimmy Carter. I will more fully examine Nixon's policies in chapter 6. These include his repudiation of the Bretton Woods agreements; his tolerance for mandatory controls on the export of capital (Democrats had made them voluntary, as they sometimes do with wage-and-price controls); his program of "national self-sufficiency" in energy; his preference for currency schemes designed to relieve pressure on the dollar; his suspicion of Japanese and European imports, expressed through his militantly protectionist Treasury Secretary John Connally; and his policy of détente, which resulted in lower military spending and therefore an attempt to reduce the outflow of U.S. funds.

While Nixon understood the need to engage in long-range international economic planning, his personal ties to *nouveau riche* businessmen and his instinctive nationalism prevented him from taking all the necessary steps. As he did in domestic policy, Nixon never made full use of the tools that were available to him. But the fact that he made the tools available brought him closer to Keynes than the liberal growth advocates who refused to hold the tools in their hands.

Finally, counter-Keynesianism had sought to win support for government stimulation of the economy by relying on military spending as an alternative to redistributional policies. Nixon, a conservative, was hardly likely to promote equality in social policy; and, an anticommunist, was not about to become a peace candidate. But his administration did eliminate the draft, reduce U.S. troops abroad, and rely on strategic weapons that brought down the relative share of the military budget. Under Nixon, military

spending decreased, relative to the gross national product, from its
Vietnam peak. In 1967, spending for national defense was 8.98
percent of the GNP, decreasing every single year thereafter until
1974, when it was only 5.45 percent.[37] (Again, the pattern of
postwar politics would reestablish itself when Jimmy Carter, a
Democrat, would do everything in his power to raise the rate of
military spending.) Nixon, without ever declaring it as policy,
blunted yet another aspect of the counter-Keynesian compromise,
although he did not put anything in its place.

In sum, Nixon's approach to macroeconomic policy confused
matters even more than did the non-Keynesian Keynesians'. The
new administration firmly rejected the approach of the liberal wing
of the growth coalition, which had been to soften the planning
capacity of Keynesianism in return for a promise from business to
invest. Searching for a substitute, Nixon discovered the original
Keynesian doctrine, but when he tried to apply it he backed off
because of his personal conservatism and lack of interest in domestic affairs. Deprived of an alternative to counter-Keynesianism,
Nixon slowly retreated to the traditional conservative strategy of
relying on tighter money and stop-and-go economic policies. The
similarities to the Eisenhower period increased the longer Nixon
was president, culminating when the president was forced to resign. For, as Otis L. Graham, Jr., noted, "Richard Nixon's most
negative single contribution to the search for a different political
economy, adequate to the needs of America's future, was his decision to appoint Gerald Ford as vice president."[38] If Nixon had a
confused vision, Ford had none. During his few years, Ford made
Eisenhower-like swipes at policy, as he simply tried to hold on
until the next election.

By 1976, not only had counter-Keynesianism been thoroughly
discredited, but so had Keynesianism. The private sector was
clearly not working, and the public sector just as clearly could not
make it work. In the realm of macroeconomic policy, America's
impasse was complete. The only significant debate was over which
was worse: a badly functioning economy or an impotent state. If
policy is defined as a conscious and deliberate attempt to improve
economic performance, one must conclude that no policy was taking place. A major reason for the impasse was the fact that the
growth coalition had followed policies that were as politically brilliant as they were economically disastrous. Counter-Keynesianism
fashioned a broad approach to growth (in the center of the political

spectrum) that gave it respectability in conservative circles, but the price that it paid for its acceptability was impotence. American Keynesians had made a Faustian pact with economic growth. They relinquished their ability to manage the economy in return for a perpetually youthful fascination with economic expansion. So long as the expansion took place, their life and outlook were carefree and gay. But when reality hit home, as it must, then, like Goethe's hero, they had nothing to look forward to except a reckoning.

# IV

## Reform Without Reform

THE WELFARE STATE, like Keynesianism, has been tried and found guilty, and by much the same jury. Facing an economic downturn in the early 1980s, policymakers instinctively turned conservative, while a harried public looked suspiciously at extensions of government programs. Republicans who had denounced efforts to achieve equality through government action in the past felt vindicated in their critique, while Democrats who once supported the idea wondered aloud whether the costs of achieving equality might exceed the benefits to be gained.[1] Ronald Reagan's victory in 1980 symbolized the new feeling. Government, the new president stated early in his tenure, would no longer even try to pretend, as it once expended considerable energy doing, that equality could be achieved. On questions of welfare and social justice, benign neglect was once again in fashion.

America's failure to contemplate, let alone redress, social injustice and inequality is another indication of its impasse, a backhand confession that social ills are beyond the reach of human action to remedy them. For a "can do" culture, such an intimation of impotence was found relatively easy to accept. America under Reagan seems prepared to deal with the poor by pretending that they do not exist.

Before the funeral oration for the welfare state is delivered, it might be pointed out that, while domestic policy in the postwar period did indeed often fail to reach its goals, equality was not one of them. From Truman to Carter, most social policy has been aimed, not at a direct attempt to improve the lives of the poor, but instead at an indirect attempt to stimulate economic growth so that all, including the poor, would benefit. The liberalism that came to power in postwar America did have a vision of a better world, but it was a complacent vision, one that sought its goals without threatening the prerogatives of the wealthy and the powerful. It offered social justice without pain, a better life without mobilizing the energy to achieve it. Liberal goals like better housing and improved health care, unable to be passed through a conservative Congress, were transformed into a bipartisan, centrist, and non-ideological crusade to expand the economy through massive expenditures on public works. Housing for the poor became urban renewal, while a concern for better health produced the construction of hospitals and medical complexes. The major role played by poor people in this saga is that they were called upon to take the blame when policies that overwhelmingly worked to benefit the better-off were discovered to be inflationary, cumbersome, and unworkable.

## II

THE NEW DEAL CONTAINED a strong rhetorical commitment to equality and social justice, and at least some of its programs—such as the Wagner Act or the creation of the Farm Security Administration—were premised upon mobilizing oppressed groups to demand structural changes in the organization of government. (Much of the New Deal was also a conservative response to an economic crisis.) The legislative majorities that supported reform in the early 1930s had disappeared by the late 1940s, but the inequalities and injustices that demanded reform had not. America's postwar political stalemate played havoc with an effective domestic policy. On the one hand, popular support for New Deal-type policies still existed; on the other, conservatives in Congress were capable of vetoing such policies or at least transforming them into ad hoc compromises. What emerged from the blocked character of the American political system was an approach to reform that represented neither a liberal crusade against injustice nor a stand-pat preference for the status quo. Housing and health care are illustrative of the new approach that emerged, the former because Hoovervilles and shantytowns were the most visible symbols of the Great Depression and the latter because access to health services was the one major policy area left virtually untouched by the New Deal.

By the late 1940s, planners and housing specialists knew enough to ascertain the preconditions for an effective housing policy in the United States. First, a strong and unambiguous commitment to the ideal of decent housing for all would have to be made by the federal government as a declaration of national policy, similar to a declaration of the need for full employment. Second, an administrative apparatus charged with this responsibility would have to be created, and the head of the agency would need considerable power to overcome the obstructive tactics of vested interests that would oppose a national housing policy. Third, power to enforce the goal should be lodged in the federal government, for turning the matter over to states, cities, or special districts would in effect allow the real-estate industry—which controlled local governments to a much greater degree—to subvert the policy. Fourth, sufficient funds appropriate to the task would have to be forthcoming. Finally, a housing policy implied a planning capacity, one that could coordinate different sectors of both the economy and the government around a unified approach to substandard living arrangements.

While each of these goals had been met from time to time in the past, the housing and real-estate industries were determined to fight every one of them in the late 1940s. Words fail in describing the politics of the housing industry. Many businessmen approach the political arena with a short-sighted and selfish point of view, but at the top of the list for sheer venality would have to be the real-estate and building lobby. In 1940, when Congress passed the Lanham Act to provide 700,000 units of government housing for defense workers, the industry inserted a clause that the units would either be sold or destroyed when the war ended. Developers wanted to tear down buildings, at a time of severe housing shortage, rather than accept the notion that the public sector should provide housing. A Philadelphia realtor expressed the industry's *Weltanschauung* well when he said: "If I had to choose between seeing every old city in the country as an ash heap and seeing the government become landlord to its own citizens, I should prefer to see the ash heap."[2]

In the tactics it used to oppose public housing, the real-estate complex lost all touch with propriety. Between 1946 and 1949, its lobbyists denounced various housing bills—each of which had been thoroughly modified to win conservative support—as "European socialism in its most insidious form," "the cutting edge of the Communist front," and "the first step in the socialization of our country."[3] When the Housing Act of 1949 was being debated, *Headlines*, the newsletter of the real-estate lobby, called on every realtor to become a "Fanatic for Freedom" in defeating the bill.[4] And it was a strange conception of freedom for which the lobby fought.

Herbert U. Nelson, chief lobbyist for the National Association of
Real Estate Boards (NAREB), a most influential figure in postwar
housing debates and the man who will go down in history for
having called Senator Robert Taft a communist, defined freedom
in this way:

> I do not believe in democracy. I think it stinks. I believe in a
> republic operated by elected representatives who are permitted
> to do the job, as the board of directors should. I don't think
> anybody except direct taxpayers should be allowed to vote.[5]

Such was the approach of the industry that had a stake in any
public policy toward the poor. Spoiled, petulant, and extremist, the
real-estate lobby had a position as clear as a political position can
be—it would do anything in its power to defeat an attempt to have
government provide housing for poor people.

Thus was opinion polarized in 1946: housing reformers knew
how ambitious any program had to be to succeed, and opponents
of housing reform were geared for an all-out war to prevent it.
Some indication of what would happen as a result was foreshadowed in 1946 when Harry Truman appointed Wilson Wyatt as his
housing expediter. The former mayor of Louisville and a Southern
progressive, Wyatt understood the elementary truth that reform in
housing would come only over the undying opposition of the real-
estate industry. His tactic was to use a continuation of wartime
price controls as a way of fighting off the industry while attacking
the postwar housing shortage with zeal.[6] (At its 1946 convention,
the American Legion called for a ten-year halt on immigration as
*its* policy for the housing shortage.)[7] Wyatt's strategy might have
worked but he needed strong support from Truman, and the president was being urged by businessmen and conservatives to lift
price controls immediately. Caught between Wyatt and his conservative Treasury Secretary John Snyder, the president opted to
lift the controls, and Wyatt's ambitious program was doomed.
Construction did boom with the "free market" restored, but precious little went into housing; instead, there appeared, in Wyatt's
words, "a rash of race tracks, mansions, summer resorts, bowling
alleys, stores, and cocktail bars."[8] Wyatt had attempted to meet just
one of the five conditions of an effective housing policy—strong
leadership—and for that he was fired. His replacement, Raymond
M. Foley, was exactly the kind of man that NAREB wanted. Self-

effacing, weak, a front man for the private sector, Foley used all his efforts to ensure that reforms would not interfere with profits. The housing shortage continued.

The real test for housing would come over a long-stalled bill supported by progressive reformers that would commit the federal government to a national housing policy. In the years since Leon Keyserling had written the 1937 housing act, progressive reformers had put their faith in public housing and in the provisions that guaranteed relocation for slum residents removed by urban development. As the postwar shortage intensified, activists like Alvin Hansen, the Keynesian economist, housing administrator John Blandford, and Senators Robert Wagner and Paul Douglas led the fight for a federal housing policy. The strength of the opposition, however, was enormous. Supported by a huge fund-raising campaign, the real-estate lobby was also bolstered by the conservative composition of Congress that had emerged from the political stalemate of 1938, and it could also take courage from Truman's failure to stand up to it in 1946. No compromise seemed possible between a militantly right-wing opposition to a federal housing policy and the existence of an articulate tradition of progressive reform.

As it happened, a compromise was fashioned; Congress passed the Wagner-Ellender-Taft bill, the Housing Act of 1949. This act literally transformed America. Title I laid out the whole postwar approach to urban housing and became the basis of massive urban renewal programs. Title II redesigned the suburbs, creating insured government mortgages to purchasers of new homes in the Levittowns that were beginning to appear. The Housing Act of 1949 was a masterpiece of political juggling. Senator Robert Wagner was an urban liberal and outspoken progressive reformer. Senator Allen Ellender was a Southern segregationist and fiscal conservative. Senator Robert Taft was an opponent of the welfare state and an intensely partisan Republican. For these men to have dinner together, let alone co-sponsor a piece of legislation, was a political breakthrough. How, one might ask, given the intense controversy between the real-estate lobby and its critics, could an attempt to create a federal housing policy win such broad support? The answer was that it was not an attempt to create a federal housing policy. The Housing Act of 1949 was the growth coalition's answer to the domestic political stalemate.

Speaking about his successful efforts to pass the housing act,

Senator Burnet Maybank of South Carolina, chairman of the Senate Banking and Currency Committee, said, "We wanted to get the politics out of it."[9] That is exactly what occurred. The question of whether the government should create public housing for the poor—which reformers answered positively and the real-estate industry answered negatively—was a political question. To take the politics out of a proposed policy is to confess that it is not a policy at all. In order to steer through America's political stalemate, the Housing Act of 1949 promised something to everyone. It guaranteed public housing, for example, but then immediately retracted the guarantee. It called for a federal policy toward housing, but then turned effective power over to newly created urban renewal districts at the local level. Noting the existence of a housing *shortage*, it called for slum clearance. Recognizing that housing problems were caused by the failure of private enterprise —or why have a law at all?—it proclaimed that "private enterprise shall be encouraged to serve as large a part of the vital need as it can." Sold as a continuation of the New Deal, the 1949 act eliminated the New Deal's commitment to the principle of equivalent elimination—i.e., guaranteeing one unit of public housing for every housing unit demolished by urban renewal. The law was considered a planner's manifesto, but it backed away from making any comprehensive statement of an urban policy. In short, broad support for the legislation was achieved by depriving the act of a guiding policy, substituting instead a series of policies, each of which contradicted the others. The law did not choose between one course and another; it combined all courses into one.

Rather than making a political choice, the housing act fashioned a new coalition organized around economic growth. Premising itself on the hypothesis that social injustice was not caused by the search for profit, it offered the alternative notion that the goals of progressive reformers could be combined with those of private industry so long as sufficient growth created political harmony. Domestic policy, therefore, should be devoted to promoting growth, in this case by a massive public works campaign. Both the industry and the reformers changed their ideologies and agreed to a growth program. The main political difference between them was no longer whether the government should spend money to stimulate economic expansion; it became instead a difference over the proper recipients of the funds.

For all its denunciation of government, America's real-estate industry welcomed public funds that would line its pockets. Some organizations, like NAREB, remained opposed to any federal policy toward housing, but many in the industry began to understand that a federal commitment to urban renewal would provide vast profits for the industry that would be called upon to rebuild America's cities. Dropping their historical opposition to federal programs, conservative developers agreed to support a housing act if it contained a large-scale commitment to urban renewal, the larger, the better. Those industry representatives who moved to the "left" by agreeing to support federal legislation were met in the center by progressive reformers who moved to the "right" by accepting urban renewal and by shifting their emphasis from structural change in the housing market to the promotion of growth. The Wagner-Ellender-Taft bill united the conservative notion of urban renewal to the liberal concept of public housing and passed them both in an ecstasy of harmony. Urban growth, it was hoped, would ensure that both goals would be reached.

There was only one problem. Housing, like matter, can either be created or destroyed. The purpose of urban renewal was to tear houses down while the purpose of public housing was to build them up. Progressive reformers who joined the growth coalition concluded that a bipartisan approach to housing reform would work to the advantage of the poor by ensuring that enough public funds would be left over from economic growth to build decent housing. It was a dubious conclusion. It requires only an introductory course in political science to know that the private sector controls the administrative process more effectively than it does the legislative process. Once the twin goals of building houses and destroying them were turned over to the bureaucracy, it did not take long for the latter goal to dominate the former.

The 1949 act mandated the construction of 810,000 housing units, a minimal goal given the shortage in the United States. Yet, by the end of the Truman administration, only 60,000 had been built, and these were "projects" that were made deliberately unattractive so as not to compete with the private sector. Moreover, by 1964, only 325,203 had been constructed. Indeed, as one authority has noted, "More families lived in substandard housing in 1965 than in 1949."[10] In other words, in order to obtain an insufficient number of underfunded, badly built, and often uninhabitable housing units, progressive reformers gave up a commitment to guarantee a home for every poor person, joined in a bipartisan alliance with Mr. Republican, agreed to sponsor an urban renewal program that would devastate minority communities, and alienated themselves from a reform tradition that sought to use pressure from below to force change at the top. Subsuming political choice to urban growth allowed legislation to pass, but it did not materially change the conditions that prompted the legislation, except, perhaps, to worsen them.

Yet the story does not end here, for liberals in the growth coalition paid one more price to have a housing law—they put themselves squarely on the side of racial segregation. During the debates on the Housing Act of 1949, the conservative bloc in the Senate sponsored an amendment calling for the elimination of segregation in public housing. (This was intended as a demagogic move to embarrass the bipartisan coalition favoring the bill.) Such an amendment gave liberals an excellent opportunity, not only to go on record favoring an extension of civil rights, but also to expose the hypocrisy of the conservative bloc: had liberals supported the amendment, the right would have been forced to vote for it or to retreat. (Sex discrimination in America was later outlawed because conservatives inserted it in a civil rights bill in order to defeat the legislation, only to see it pass, again over liberal objections.) Faced with a choice between justice and growth, reformers opted to lead the fight for segregation. Paul Douglas, for example, gnashed his teeth and said, "I am ready to appeal to history and to time that it is in the best interests of the Negro race that we carry through the housing program as planned, rather than put in the bill an amendment which will inevitably defeat all hopes for rehousing 4,000,000 persons."[11] It is unclear where Douglas received his figures, for, as I will show momentarily, the housing act left more people homeless than it succeeded in rehousing. But the point remains that growth priorities dictated to the reformers that they abandon liberal goals. (Thus was a cycle begun. In 1956, prominent Democrats like Adlai Stevenson and Senator Richard Neuberger of Oregon would oppose the Powell Amendment to abolish school segregation on the grounds that it would endanger federal aid to education, and, in 1966, Senator Muskie of Maine dropped an antisegregation clause from Model Cities legislation in order to broaden support.)

It makes little sense to characterize the Housing Act of 1949 as "a milestone in the broad sweep of twentieth-century reform,"[12] as one historian has done. It was not a piece of reform legislation at all. It did very little for the homes of poor people except to tear them down; indeed, the poor would have been better off if the law had never passed. (The construction industry would have been worse off, as would real-estate developers, insurance companies, banks, and local Democratic party officials.) The Housing Act of 1949 was one of the greatest public works boondoggles in American history. It financed the destruction of America's cities, while sustaining a rebuilding machine that united politicians, bankers, and developers into a powerful coalition that took over the Democratic party. Its passage was not a victory for equality, less a triumph for the poor. The Housing Act of 1949, when compared to the New Deal, marked the *end* of twentieth-century reform, not its beginning. It did, however, signify the emergence of growth as an alternative.

Americans were not only poorly housed in the late 1940s, their medical care was far less than adequate. Worried about the extensive amount of poor health in the United States, Franklin Roosevelt recommended a comprehensive health insurance program in 1935. Wartime conditions then stimulated an interest in health care as an issue. Americans were shocked to learn that up to 40 percent of the 22 million men of draft age in the mid-1940s could not pass the military's physical examination.[13] (A Presidential Commission on the Health Care Needs of the Nation, organized by Harry Truman in 1951, would document extensive inequalities in both the geographic and social class availability of health care.[14]) Workers, unprotected by their government from the financial uncertainties of illness, began to pressure management for concessions the minute the war ended. In short, by 1946, the lack of a comprehensive system of health care combined with increased demand from below to make the issue of public support for health care an extremely popular one.

Harry Truman, at the urging of liberal advisers like Leon Keyserling and Clark Clifford, proposed legislation in November 1945 that would have created a national health insurance system in the United States. Modeled on the Wagner-Murray-Dingell bill, which had been stalled in Congress since 1943, the plan would have financed a general program of health insurance by imposing a 4 percent tax on the first $3,600 of income made by each American. Exceptionally needy people would be financed out of general revenue, but the plan as a whole was based on the self-financing nature of the social security system. Truman's bill was quite cautious. It did not address itself to the structure of health care delivery. It did not advocate reforms in the health sector. All it did was to provide a federal subsidy for health care consumers to buy an unchanged product. At best, it was a minimal first step toward decent health care for all.

The fight over this legislation was so bizarre that Truman, for one, could never understand it. Rather than support a bill that would enrich doctors at the public expense, the American Medical Association (AMA), mimicking the real-estate industry, denounced the measure vehemently: "This is the kind of regimentation that led to totalitarianism in Germany and the defeat of that nation."[15] Senator Taft, who would be won over to the housing bill, called Truman's plan the most socialistic measure ever to appear before Congress. Opposition was so fierce that Truman never expected the bill to pass; he merely wanted to scare the doctors who opposed it. Given the inevitable defeat of the bill—though repeated attempts to pass a health care bill had been introduced, not a single measure had made it to the hearings stage until 1946— the question was what would be forthcoming as an alternative. The AMA and other conservative groups could not ignore the fact that reforms were needed, given the popularity of reform and the manifest inadequacy of the existing system. They set out to devise a "reform" that was more compatible with their privileges.

As early as 1942, the American Hospital Association (AHA) had begun to worry about the inevitable postwar demand for health insurance. Creating a commission on hospital care with funding from the Kellogg Foundation, the AHA asked Thomas Gates (later Eisenhower's secretary of defense) and Edward Ryerson (chairman of the board of Inland Steel) to come up with proposals to reform the health care system that would not threaten vested interests. After due deliberation, the commission recommended a massive federal spending program directed toward hospital construction. Such a program would eliminate the shortage in hospital beds; subsidize part of the costs of businessmen's expenses (unhealthy workers produce less); give the impression that health care reform was taking place; stimulate the economy through federal expenditure; and preserve untouched, if slightly expanded, the profit system in medicine. The commission's proposals became the basis for the conservative alternative to national health insurance: the Hill-Burton Act of 1946, which promised extensive federal money for a program of hospital construction.

Hill-Burton was a dream come true for the AHA, the AMA, and other opponents of reform in the health sector. *Hospital Management*, for example, noted in 1946 that

> . . . the Hill-Burton [b]ill is a commendable effort to do a necessary thing whereas the whole Wagner-Murray-Dingell drive is a dangerously motivated attempt to do a wholly unnecessary thing. Every member of both houses of Congress should be given all possible aid in keeping clear the essential differences between these two measures and the groups who respectively support them.[16]

Taft, who had strongly opposed Truman's bill, was a fighter for Hill-Burton. The AMA just as militantly supported one as it denounced the other. Hill-Burton, like the Housing Act of 1949, was another example of reform without reform, substituting growth notions for structural change in the markets that deliver services. The Housing Act of 1949 was inspired by progressive reformers and compromised to win industry support, while Hill-Burton originated within industry and was broadened to include liberal support. Both, regardless of origin, were expressions of a centrist crusade for growth and not of a policy that made a choice between competing conceptions of politics.

Hill-Burton, like the Housing Act of 1949, was an expensive proposition. It called for a $3 million survey of hospital needs and then $75 million for hospital construction over a five-year period. So popular as a public works measure did the act become that between 1946 and 1975, it has been estimated, over $4 billion was spent to build hospitals.[17] Construction, however, is not health care. The growth dynamic inherent in Hill-Burton meant that by the 1970s a surplus of hospital beds existed in the United States; one estimate put the number of excess beds at 100,000, costing some $2 billion per year and some $8 billion overall in waste.[18] Moreover, because of the administrative character of the act, the whole method by which health care in America was delivered went through a change. To Hill-Burton can be attributed, in whole or in part, the following: the rise of the hospital as the primary deliverer of health care; substantial unnecessary surgery; inflated medical costs; the supremacy of Blue Cross in the health insurance industry; the decline of the family doctor; the withering away of preventive medicine; and the growth of bureaucratic medical complexes standing imperialistically in the heart of inner-city neighborhoods. Led by a conservative network that denounced intervention in the health sector as inflationary and wasteful, Hill-Burton helped create a system of health care delivery so expensive, inefficient, and irrational that, in the 1980s, not even the federal government wants to pay for it.

Between them, the Housing Act of 1949 and Hill-Burton set in motion the forces that would cause America's domestic impasse a generation later. It was difficult to deny in the late 1940s that there were a significant number of Americans who lived in poor housing and received inadequate medical care. Action by the federal government to promote equality and social justice was demanded. Yet, when it was discovered that equality and justice impose costs on those who profit from inequality and injustice, political reform gave way to economic growth. Making a choice between the conservative desire to leave profits untouched and the liberal inclination to achieve equality would have been wrenching, destabilizing, ugly, and emotional. Making a commitment to economic expansion through public works, by contrast, offered to unite the manufacturers who supplied the materials, the bankers who put up the funds, the construction trades that furnished the men, the bureaucrats and politicians who dispensed the rewards, the intellectuals who proclaimed the resulting harmony, *and* the poor who would have access to the housing and the hospitals. It seemed too good to be true. Business and organized labor would have a common interest. The South could be as much a part of it as the North, if appropriate installations were built in Dixie. Republicans as well as Democrats could be attracted to it, Westerners as well as Easterners, suburbanites and slumdwellers, rural America and downtown, the military and the universities—everybody. Americans would be linked by a program that built and, because it built, stimulated the economy to build some more. A pro-growth coalition, uniting conservatives interested in profits with liberals committed to equality, could seemingly dominate American politics forever.[19]

The pro-growth coalition was a brilliant answer to the political stalemate in America. So long as public works drove the economy forward, not only would the privileged obtain more privileges, but there would be benefits for the poor as well. Yet the very success of the growth coalition would turn out to be the reason for its eventual failure. The growth coalition was created as an alternative to making political choices. As the economy succeeded, the ability of government to make policy effectively failed. So long as the boom continued, the paralysis of government did not seem to matter. But after the growth stopped, the price that had been paid to achieve it became clear. America had neither a policy toward correcting injustice nor a constituency that could bring one into being. Having been preoccupied with growth, progressive reformers deprived themselves of the one force that can create a more equal society: the support of the mass of people to force through changes upon a recalcitrant elite.

# III

AS POLITICALLY TAME as the growth coalition had become, it was still a bit too radical for General Eisenhower. Elected president in 1952, Eisenhower appointed as director of the Housing and Home Finance Agency (HHFA) a congressman who had led the fight against the Housing Act of 1949. He encouraged the Federal Housing Administration (FHA) to continue blatantly segregationist policies. His Council of Economic Advisers deliberately emphasized slum clearance and urban renewal at the expense of public housing.[20] Yet, unable to find any substitute means of housing the poor—Eisenhower discovered what all politicians learn, that the private housing industry had no interest in meeting the housing shortage for the poor—the president never completely abolished the 1949 act. The growth coalition was slowed under Eisenhower, but it was not stopped.

Public works projects did exist during the 1950s, most notably the National Defense Highway Act. Deprived of other outlets, urban growth coalitions made the most of it, building Interstate highways through the cities and thereby providing jobs and political muscle. But the decade was uncomfortable for the pro-growth liberals. They had hoped to prove that profits and a crusade for social justice could exist together. Eisenhower was anxious to support the former, reluctant to acknowledge the latter. The truly unique feature of the growth coalition—its blending of conservatism and reform—was eclipsed, and it would take a new president to prove that an expanding economy could provide social justice without tampering with profit and privilege.

Eisenhower's reluctance to spend money on the cities gave liberal advocates of urban growth eight years to see the flaws in their program, but most of them did not. Instead, the architects of the growth coalition damned the administration for not spending more money to cement their power. Key advocates of urban growth—such as Mayors Richard Lee of New Haven and J. Richardson Dilworth of Philadelphia, city planner *par excellence* Edward Logue, developer James Scheuer, and others—formed a committee within the Democratic Advisory Council to argue for the new urban policy that they hoped would be begun by the Democrat to be elected in 1960. Their report was incorporated, almost word for word, into the 1960 Democratic platform and then became the basis of John F. Kennedy's housing program. "Just as the Marshall Plan restored the cities of Western Europe from the devastation of war," the committee noted, "so our program will restore urban America from the ravages of spreading slums and disorderly growth."[21]

When Kennedy became president, he quickly adopted the Marshall Plan metaphor: "Most of us know what needs to be done, and I think we know that most of what needs to be done requires one ingredient—and that is money."[22] It was forthcoming. In all eight years of the Eisenhower period, $1.6 billion was authorized in Title I grants; Kennedy reached that figure in two years.[23] Federal spending, moreover, stimulated private investment. Preliminary loans for urban renewal amounted to $44 million in 1954, which expanded to $239 million in 1958 and then $706 million in 1960. But in the next decade, it multiplied an additional fivefold, rising to $2.8 billion in 1968 and $3.8 billion in 1970.[24] The total money that flowed to the cities during the 1960s has been estimated by John Mollenkopf as follows: "Since 1949, the federal government has committed over $8.2 billion in direct outlays and more than $22.5 billion in bonded debt. By 1968, private investors had sunk an estimated additional $34.3 billion into 524 renewal projects around the country. In addition, some $70 billion had been expended on interstate highways, a substantial portion of which went to high-cost urban areas."[25] Rarely, if ever, have so many cities received so much money in so short a time.

Little of this flow of funds reached the poor. If anything, Kennedy's policies were harder on the urban poor than Truman's. At the insistence of progressive reformers, the Housing Act of 1949 contained a "predominantly residential" requirement, mandating that funds spent under the act be concentrated on housing rather than office buildings or redevelopment plazas. That requirement had been ignored in practice. Kennedy's response was not to enforce the law but to change it; a key feature of the Housing Act of 1961 was to broaden the exemption from the residential requirement. (Lyndon Johnson would broaden the exemptions still further.) Nor did Kennedy fight for racial justice in housing with any enthusiasm. Though he criticized Eisenhower for not abolishing by executive order discrimination in the sale of federally assisted housing, Kennedy delayed his own order for two whole years, and when he did sign it, he exempted both existing facilities and homes financed by the Federal Home Loan Bank Board. (This delay was extraordinary, given the pressure put on by blacks and the fact that the usual argument that Kennedy advanced for this conservatism— that Congress would not go along—was inapplicable to an executive order.) Although Kennedy appointed a black as director of the Housing and Home Finance Agency and introduced legislation for a cabinet-level urban affairs department, these were symbols, not policies. He simply refused to upset the bipartisan and centrist nature of growth politics by introducing into a harmonious consensus such political matters as racial justice or equality. Kennedy's main concern was how to spend the money in urban areas in a way that would keep the growth coalition unified.

Buoyed by the flow of Title I grants, nearly every city in the United States created a corporate-dominated planning body to allocate the funds.[26] Downtown business interests realized the bonanza that awaited them and allied themselves with reform mayors who understood their point of view. (Old-line machine politicians, corrupt as they were, often were too closely connected to neighborhoods about to be destroyed and to working-class constituencies to be effective partners in the growth network.) Men like Robert Wagner, Jr., in New York and Joseph Alioto in San Francisco (a late starter) joined New Haven's Lee and Philadelphia's Dilworth as effective leaders of the growth coalitions at the local level. Uniting diverse constituents into a nonideological quest for greater funding, the growth coalition showed the same apolitical utopianism at the local level that counter-Keynesians were demonstrating at the national level. Managers were hired, like Edward Logue in Boston and Robert Moses in New York, men interested in power, not in ideas, in money, not in votes. Moses, indeed, became the living legend of the growth coalition, the physical embodiment of the new force unleashed in America's cities. Rejecting an earlier career as a municipal reformer and "do-gooder," Moses's life history was the biography of growth politics writ large: greater access to power and money matched by increasing distance from a concern with social justice and equality. Like that of the economic tinkerers of the new economics (chapter 3) or of the national security managers of the cold war (chapter 5), Moses's vision was more technological than political, dominated by a concern with means, to the exclusion of the ends the means were supposed to serve.[27]

(During the 1960s, the similarities between urban planners and cold war managers would become more than metaphorical. The RAND corporation would offer its advice equally to the air force and New York City, while Pentagon economists like Alain Enthoven would become the social policy technicians of the 1970s. Once politics is sublimated, then management is management. As General Bernard Schreiver noted in 1968: ". . . When major programs are created in the future to rehabilitate our cities we will need a means for rapid and centralized decision making. The arrangement may not be identical with the one worked out in the Department of Defense. But I think it would have to be similar in principle.")[28]

While federal money was pouring into the cities, city residents were pouring into the suburbs. To a significant degree the postwar suburban boom was a product of Title II of the Housing Act of 1949. Its mortgage provisions far outstripped all public housing in terms of federal housing subsidies, and the bulk of Title II money went to the suburbs. FHA preference for segregation, the national highway program, and federal tax policies all contributed to the suburban boom.[29] Politically, suburbanization had the effect of guaranteeing the bipartisan character of the growth coalition. Republicans, who had once opposed federal boondoggles as wasteful, learned the virtues of guaranteed profits and, in the form of Nelson Rockefeller, joined the growth bandwagon with a vengeance. The Housing Act of 1949 linked pro-growth Democrats with construction-oriented suburban Republicans to form a centrist consensus that seemed unshakable. The battle between the ins and the outs at the state and local level, like the pattern in Washington, was not fought over policies but over alternative methods of spending money.

Growth, which Lyndon Johnson would describe as "the most powerful weapon in our hands,"[30] was magic. It made possible an approach to social policy that was different in form and content from both conservative ideas about the free market and social democratic theories about equality and social justice. Among the accomplishments of the growth coalition were the exploration of space; the expansion of public education; suburban shopping malls; Interstate highways; downtown office plazas; the military–industrial complex; Houston, Texas; and the state of California. As it plowed along on its nonideological course, sweeping away political choices the way the bulldozers were sweeping away blight, the coalition that was transforming America was too busy spending money to take note of the flaws that had begun to appear by the mid-1960s. As time went on, those flaws would turn into faults, and then the faults would become quakes. There were, in retrospect, four inherent problems with the pro-growth coalition: fiscal irresponsibility; ideological eclecticism; planning difficulties; and the creation of artificially induced inequalities.

There was a certain irony in the fiscal irresponsibility of the pro-growth coalition, for from the start conservatives worried about the costs of a housing program for the poor. Yet the urban renewal schemes dreamed up by downtown business interests, banks, real-estate speculators, and planners turned out to be far more fiscally irresponsible than any program oriented to promote equality. One certainly cannot know whether an alternative program of granting funds only to the poor to improve their lives would have averted a fiscal crisis, but one can be certain that the public works consequences of the Housing Act of 1949 helped create one. Between them, conservatives like Martin Anderson and James Q. Wilson and radicals like Robert Goodman have documented the incredible waste brought about by Title I spending.[31] Between 1950 and 1960, for example, more homes were destroyed under urban renewal programs than were built. Moreover, it was poor people who lost their homes and middle-income and wealthy people who gained them. The funding schemes developed by the pro-growth coalition were so arcane that no one can know for sure how much was ever spent. True costs were hidden, financial manipulation was endemic, and the burden on the taxpayer never clarified. Detailed case studies of specific projects—like Chester Hartman's long-running critique of San Francisco's Yerba Buena[32]—reveal that, with protection from the government, private interests lined their pockets with impunity. A campaign organized to promote social justice had become a growth industry in the 1960s.

There were social and political costs that were added to the fiscal ones. Before the Housing Act of 1949, housing and real estate was a competitive industry, one of the few areas of enterprise in the United States that had not become monopolized. That changed with the infusion of federal funds. Developers like William Levitt could not have built and sold their mass-produced homes without governmental assistance. Solidified with public funds, the growth coalition spawned quasi-public "authorities," like New York City's Triborough Bridge and Tunnel Authority, that made major political decisions with all the publicity and public participation of the Kremlin.[33] By the late 1970s, even the real-estate broker—the last gasp of localism and grass-roots civic responsibility—was being organized into two or three national networks, advertising on television and making huge profits off of a national housing shortage. The American public, which faced large-scale and politically untouchable monopolies when it bought cars, filled them with gas, and changed tires, now also faced them when it drove its cars home.

Whether in the marketplace, the political arena, or the culture, the pro-growth coalition was irresponsible because it displaced competition and diversity with monolithic uniformity. The architecture of the projects matched the business and political practices of those who built them—intolerant of dissent and relentless in their quest for efficiency and sameness. Political pluralism, local diversity, neighborhood distinctiveness, and economic competition were all subordinated to the quest for growth. And yet the growth machine, once started in motion, did not know how to stop. Despite massive dislocations and the expense of urban renewal, the growth network in Pittsburgh geared up for a Renaissance II project in 1980 over the determined opposition of neighborhood groups. Henry Ford II spent astonishing sums to recreate downtown Detroit even as the city faced the highest unemployment rate in the United States. And, most extraordinary of all, during New York's fiscal crisis, when hospitals, schools, and libraries were being shut down for lack of funds, the federal government approved money to transform the West Side Highway into an interstate. Politicians and business interests, without growth projects, simply did not know what to do.

A second set of problems for the pro-growth coalition concerned its ideological eclecticism. Legislation like the Housing Act of 1949 and Hill-Burton passed Congress with large majorities because they deliberately avoided taking a political position. Yet it remained true, despite the compromises fashioned, that there was a

difference between the conservative notion that profits should take
first priority and the liberal concern with social justice, equality,
and income redistribution. Both the right and the left, on this
matter, had long traditions of political philosophy behind them to
which they could appeal in order to create constituencies that
would fight for their programs. Notions of business freedom have
led to revolution in the past, and visions of equality put a world in
ferment in the present. Yet growth, unlike either conservatism or
radicalism, had no such vision, no ability to arouse passion or
political concern. Basing itself neither on the right's commitment to
the market nor on the left's concern with justice, the growth coalition was incapable of developing the kind of articulate and consistent philosophical justification that could sustain it once economic
expansion, which was the only basis for its unity, began to atrophy.

The most intelligent criticism of the ideological mishmash of
the pro-growth coalition has been offered by Theodore Lowi.[34] He
argues that every approach to public policy is based upon a conception of the public good, whether articulated or not. For most of
the history of the United States, classical liberalism served as the
public philosophy. The rise of the growth network displaced the
free market, but at the same time it did not substitute socialist
theories, which were the most ideologically consistent alternatives
to laissez faire. Instead there developed what Lowi calls "interest
group liberalism," a position that argues, in essence, that private
interests should be given public money in order to secure their
power. Insofar as the pro-growth coalition justified itself at all—its
reliance on electorally unaccountable authorities obviated a major
need to develop an ideology in the first place—it did so by claiming that growth would give everyone more. Employing neither the
conservative doctrine that "whatever is, is right" nor the radical
idea that "whatever is right, should be," the growth coalition offered a third formulation: "whatever works, has to be that way."
Nothing works like the workable, and so long as growth happened,
the lack of a consistent system of justification made little difference. But in a slow-growth economy, the notions of the growth
coalition could be attacked from two sides. Conservatives denounced federal policies on the grounds that the poor were ungrateful for what little they had been given, while an emerging left
and black-power movement confronted the growth coalition with
community organizations and militancy. Unsatisfactory to radicals,
the growth coalition also aroused the ire of conservative whites,

who organized thinly disguised racial campaigns—Hicks in Boston, Procaccino in New York, Imperiale in Newark—that blamed reformers as vehemently as blacks. In the face of all these attacks, all the growth coalition had was money; it tried to buy off its opposition. When the money ran out, there was nothing left. Not having ideas had consequences.

Third, the growth coalition suffered from an inability to plan, which was ironic since a core element in the coalition was the newly created urban planning network. Title I of the housing act had been hailed by city planners as a Magna Charta. "The adoption of the Housing Act of 1949 is the most significant recent event in the development of city planning in the recent history of the United States," wrote William L. C. Wheaton, who later served on the Democratic Advisory Committee's task force on urban affairs.[35] "The planners have been challenged," added G. Holmes Perkins, then the editor of the *Journal of the American Institute of Planners*.[36] This legislation brought city planners from the university and the local community into the seats of power but, at the same time, it also deprived them of the ability to plan, just as the political triumph of counter-Keynesianism was based on economic impotence. Planning theory had been developed by critics of laissez faire who had argued that the free market, by itself, was incapable of meeting such social goals as a safe environment, adequate public power, coordinated policy, or rational transportation. Experiments like the Tennessee Valley Authority and the National Resources Planning Board had been based upon the assumption that the private sector had simply failed, requiring a corrective dose of public action. Yet the Housing Act of 1949 repudiated this trend. By calling for the greatest possible reliance on the private sector, and by turning public policy over to local authorities dominated by industry, the act made planning impossible. Although few realized it at the time, growth and planning were antithetical; so long as a major commitment was made to the former, the latter would not take place.

Not surprisingly, then, policy under the housing act consistently achieved the opposite results from those advocated by the planners. Designed to remedy a housing shortage, for example, national housing policy dehoused more people than it housed. In New Haven, cited by many as a model of growth propelled by Title I funds,[37] ten times more low-rent housing units were destroyed than were bulit; overall, by 1960, 140,000 units of low-rent housing had been torn down, replaced by only 40,000 units, 95 percent of which were for middle- and upper-income people.[38] Moreover, a law that was designed to constitute an urban policy weakened cities at the expense of the suburbs; the 1949 housing act bears the major responsibility, of any federal legislation, for the decline of the cities as viable and safe places to live. Last, the inability to plan was reflected in the fragmentation of administrative responsibility toward housing. There had, in the past, been three distinct federal housing agencies, each serving its own constituency. The Federal Housing Administration (FHA) promoted suburban expansion; the Urban Renewal Administration (URA) oversaw slum clearance and redevelopment; and the Public Housing Administration (PHA) built homes for the poor. Each tended to work at cross-purposes to the other: the FHA wanted to kill urban renewal; the URA was determined to undermine public housing; and both the FHA and the URA attacked public housing and racial integration. Rather than helping to resolve these disputes, the Housing Act of 1949 brought all three agencies together in one place, creating the Housing and Home Finance Agency. As a result, bureaucratic warfare became the outlet for the social choices that were not being made by the legislation. Instead of the public sector's bringing order and planning out of chaos, the ragtag pattern of the private sector was incorporated into the state. For all the rhetoric about planning, the housing act's refusal to confront the industry produced a lack of coordination and a preference for waste and duplication, whatever statements to the contrary were made.

The most serious flaw in the growth coalition—and the one most responsible for stopping it—was the impact it had on the group in whose name it was originally created: the poor. One of the unusual attractions of growth politics was that it conferred privileges upon the privileged while seeming to do so out of a concern with poverty. Too good to be true, such a utopian fantasy could not perpetuate itself forever. In reality, cities that had once been racially integrated were becoming segregated as a consequence of federal policy.[39] The Hill-Burton Act, which had successfully created hospitals in poor rural areas, had negative impacts on inner-city ghettos, where medical empires displaced housing and exacerbated racial tensions.[40] Federal sponsorship of urban highway programs tore healthy neighborhoods apart, and, even when mass transit came, it often did so, as San Francisco discovered, in a way that would cost poor people more in taxes than they would receive in benefits.[41] Rather than uniting all, including the poor, the growth coalition was separating the poor from everyone else. The social problems it produced included a kind of induced poverty, not poverty caused by a badly performing economy, but a poverty that was a direct result of governmental action.

When, starting in 1964, poor people took to the streets to register their rage at, among other things, the effects of urban renewal, highway construction, and the creation of a medical–industrial complex, they set in motion the forces that would stop the growth coalition. As Frances Fox Piven and Richard Cloward have argued, opportunities for the poor to express their discontent are historically limited; most poor people at most times accept their lot, for they see no other choice.[42] Had a program of viable reform been possible in the late 1940s, the riots of the 1960s might never have happened. But since the growth coalition could come to power in the former period only by subsuming questions of social justice, the anger of the latter period had a certain Greek-like inevitability about it. Excluded from a coalition operating in its name, the poor could articulate their perspective only outside established institutions. The rage of the 1960s may have been self-destructive, but it made its political point: for not much longer would it be possible to argue that the lot of the poor would be improved by making the well-off better off.

## IV

BOTH LYNDON JOHNSON AND RICHARD NIXON, each in his own way, tried to respond to the coming collapse of the growth coalition. Johnson, unlike either Truman or Kennedy, responded to the cry of anguish from below and sought direct governmental programs to improve the lot of the poor, but, when he found out how high the costs would be for the growth coalition that had become the core of the Democratic party, he backed off. Nixon, and especially Gerald Ford, responded to the problem by pretending that it did not exist, but found that expectations of growth were still strong enough among the voters to bring the Democrats back to power in 1976. In other words, both administrations recognized that the growth coalition no longer made economic sense, but neither could develop a political alternative to it.

Stung by the uprising in American cities, and determined to leave his mark upon history as a domestic reformer, Johnson created the Great Society, which promised the poor some participation in the decisions that affected their lives.

The notion of "maximum feasible participation of the poor" was proposed as part of the Economic Opportunity Act of 1964, which established community action programs as part of a "war" on poverty. Within six months after the passage of the law, big-city mayors, speaking for the growth coalition, made a successful plea to Johnson through Vice-President Hubert Humphrey to redirect the program away from their power base. In September 1965, a little over a year after the program started, Johnson ordered the Bureau of the Budget to slash funds for the poverty program and demanded an administrative shake-up to bring the Office of Economic Opportunity in line with traditional urban politics. The Democratic party had become far more closely tied to considerations of growth than it was to considerations of social justice and equality.

The war on poverty foreshadowed Johnson's attempts to deal with the fallout from the Housing Act of 1949. As urban specialists watched the havoc spawned by unchecked commitments to expansion financed by public works, they developed two basic critiques of postwar urban policy.[43] One school of thought, associated mainly with the Brookings Institution, argued that these programs were ineffective because no agency existed for coordinating them. A second point, emerging from social critics at every point in the political spectrum, stressed that urban renewal was making the poor poorer. Responding to both criticisms at once, Johnson appointed a task force in the fall of 1965 to recommend legislation that would correct the abuses of the 1949 act. Chaired by Robert Wood of MIT and containing leading specialists from Brookings, from the growth coalition itself, and from the civil rights movement, the task force proposed that a few "demonstration" cities be singled out for a coordinated attack on bad housing. With some modifications, Johnson adopted the recommendation, and on January 26, 1966, he introduced "Model Cities" legislation in Congress. ("Demonstration" had another meaning that Johnson did not especially like.) Model Cities, as proposed, went right to the core of the problem. Implicitly it placed the blame for the failure of Title I programs on the lack of policy coordination and the capture of social policy by downtown financial interests, both of which had been concessions made by liberal growth advocates to win conservative support. Any attempt to change these policies raised a major question: was the political stalemate that brought such compromises into being in the first place still strong enough to prevent reforms that would alter them?

Despite the size of the Democratic majorities in Congress, the political stalemate of 1938 had not disappeared. As soon as it received the Model Cities proposal from Johnson, Congress busily went to work changing it in order to ensure that the power of the growth coalition would not be hampered. One tactic was to dilute the program in the guise of expanding it. Whereas some people like Walter Reuther wanted to see one demonstration project and others favored two or three, Johnson, looking over his shoulder at Congress, extended it to sixty, while Congress, looking over its shoulder at reelection, broadened it even further. Dispensing with an experiment designed to see whether a concentrated attack on poverty in one or two places could eliminate it, Congress passed instead a public works measure that gave funds to every medium-sized city in America. Second, Johnson assured Congress that Model Cities would in no way interfere with the engine of urban renewal, even if the program had to in order to succeed. "We are not robbing Peter to pay Paul in this program," Housing Secretary Robert Weaver testified,[44] even though Paul was impoverished because Peter had been stealing from him for years. Third, Congress amended the legislation in order to make it more acceptable to the South, dropping a requirement to "counteract the segregation of housing by race or income."[45] By the time that Model Cities was on its way to passage, it had become a law designed to expand the growth coalition, not to curb its abuses.

Model Cities won the support of the National Association of Home Builders, the National Association of Housing and Redevelopment Officials, David Rockefeller, and Henry Ford II. It passed Congress. It also failed to halt the growth coalition. Not only were no effective programs against the destructive consequences of urban renewal undertaken, but the cities were given so much money under Model Cities that a number of them were never able to develop ways of spending it. By 1968, the National Commission on Urban Problems, ironically chaired by the same Paul Douglas whose compromises made Title I possible, pointed out the obvious: ". . . over the last decade, government action through urban renewal, highway programs, demolitions on public housing sites, code enforcement and other programs has destroyed more housing for the poor than government at all levels has built for them."[46]

A similar statement on the issue of medical care had similar results. Hospital construction had boomed under the Hill-Burton Act, but health care was getting worse. In spite of fairly obvious flaws in the health care system, and in the face of strong public support for reform, no progress had been made on a national health insurance bill since the defeat of Truman's plan except for the Kerr-Mills Act of 1960. This act, supported by the AMA, gave money to the states to help them improve medical coverage if they chose to do so. Hoping to revive the New Deal coalition, Johnson wanted a national health insurance bill, and he directed his secretary of health, education, and welfare, Wilbur Cohen, to come up with one. (Cohen had been one of Truman's advisers on health care.) Recalling the devastating defeat of the Truman years, and uncertain of the conservatism of Congress, Cohen decided to restrict the goals of medical coverage to the narrowest possible basis in the hopes of winning broader support. Such "consensus mongering,"[47] as Theodore Marmor called it, doomed any effective reform of the delivery of medical services.

The tactic developed by the AMA and other opponents of structural reform in the industry was to criticize Cohen's bill for not going far *enough*. With Republican urging, the AMA introduced legislation to broaden the coverage and then, in return for its "liberalism," won agreement on a point to have this expanded system be provided by private insurers. Faced with a choice between Cohen's bill and the Republican alternative (and in addition an AMA version closer to the latter), the House Ways and Means Committee, in the spirit of the growth coalition, reported out what was called a "three-layer cake," combining elements of each approach. Now assured of passage, Medicare and Medicaid became features of the American political landscape.[48] But neither was directed to correct the abuses in the medical system. As anyone with a sense of history might have concluded, ideological eclecticism makes for broad political support and economic disaster at the same time.

In the first year after the passage of Medicaid, the rate of increase in doctor's fees doubled, while hospital costs increased by an unprecedented 21.9 percent.[49] This jump in the cost of medical services initiated an inflationary spiral that made health care one of the leading culprits of inflation by the 1970s. (In proposing a bill to control hospital costs in 1979, a bill deliberately toned down to win conservative support and yet unable to be passed by Congress, Jimmy Carter pointed out that, in one decade under Medicare and Medicaid, health costs had increased by 340 percent.)[50] Another effect of "consensus mongering" was an outbreak of nursing home construction that continued the spurt begun by Hill-Burton and would become, for a while, a major source of graft necessary to keep the growth coalition unified. Finally, Medicare, following the example of the Housing Act of 1949, turned federal money over to the states, and as a result funds were spent uncontrollably, state governments refused to offend health providers, and no federal review authority was thoroughly exercised. Johnson's legislation was a federal subsidy for graft, inflation, and waste, with something left over for health.

So great was the economic expansion of the 1960s that there was something left over. The Great Society as a whole illustrated the point made by Brookings economist Henry Aaron, who noted that the war on poverty "was a by-product of programs intended primarily for the middle class."[51] Once the growth coalition took its cut, in other words, prosperity ensured that enough of the surplus would be left to make genuine progress in the fight against injustice and inequality. Medicare and Medicaid made health care available to two groups that had generally been denied it: welfare recipients and the aged.[52] Similarly, community action programs accomplished one of their objectives: they successfully mobilized poor people to make demands on city governments for social services.[53] The number of public housing units constructed under Model Cities increased, reaching its crest in 1970.[54] Manpower training and education programs had a measurable effect in improving people's lives.[55] Progress toward equality and social justice could be made, but the Great Society achieved it in a perverse way. Fantastic growth made possible the best of both worlds: a political system that rewarded the poor and rewarded those who lived off the poor at the same time. Always implicit in that paradise, though, was its negation: the possibility that in a declining economy, both the poor and the growth coalition would suffer.

Richard Nixon felt little allegiance to the cities, even less to their residents. Running for president in 1968, he pounced on the Great Society: "For the past five years we have been deluged by government programs for the unemployed, programs for the cities, programs for the poor, and we have reaped from these programs an ugly harvest of frustration, violence, and failure across the land."[56] Nixon's conservatism was reenforced by a host of evaluation studies concluding that the Great Society had failed to bring about significant reform. The Great Society did indeed fail to achieve equality; but not commented on by these studies, and certainly ignored by Nixon, was the fact that the Great Society did not achieve equality because it did not try to. The most deleterious legacy of the growth coalition was the opposition it spawned. Having promised benefits for the middle class and a residue for the poor, the architects of growth politics ensured a conservative response that could blame the poor for the waste of subsidizing the middle class. When the economy worked, the poor were able to benefit from growth after the middle class received its share, but when the economy failed—and under Nixon it began to fail badly —the pattern was reversed: an attack on the poor would spill over onto the growth coalition itself.

Mobilizing public resentment against an approach to social policy that was wasteful, inflationary, and ineffective, Richard Nixon eliminated the gap between the promise and the performance of domestic policy by eliminating the promise. To his credit, Nixon understood, as liberal growth advocates never did, that growth was no substitute for reform. But rather than reverse the priorities and seek to achieve the latter at the expense of the former, Nixon chose to avoid both. Earlier in this chapter, I argued that an effective social policy requires five elements: a national commitment; the creation of an effective agency; strong enforcement powers; adequate funding; and a capacity to plan. Nixon's approach to the problem of equality and social justice was to uncover whatever progress had been made in each area and to overturn it.

National commitments had been made under Kennedy and Johnson to a number of goals, most notably the elimination of poverty. Nixon's response was to try and eliminate the bureaucratic agency that embodied the commitment, the Office of Economic Opportunity. He appointed a conservative named Howard Phillips to head the agency with the specific mandate to terminate its existence. Some presidents try to abolish poverty, others to abolish the abolition of poverty. Neither task is easy, but there was less opposition to eliminating the agency than to eliminating the problem. By the end of the Nixon–Ford presidency, there was no longer a federal commitment to improve the lives of the poor.

Through his much-heralded plans for a New Federalism that would be based on revenue sharing between the federal government and the states, Nixon also managed to undermine federal efforts on behalf of social justice. In a country still under the intoxicating fumes of Jeffersonianism, transferring power to the states and local communities has democratic appeal, even if it becomes the chief means of conservative elites to preserve their power. As badly as poor people may fare in Washington, there is more sympathy for their plight there than there is in the state capitals. Picking up one of Walter Heller's more ambiguous notions, Nixon adopted revenue sharing as the major "reform" of his administration. Switching from categorical grants (i.e., money allocated for specific objectives like garbage collection or libraries) to block grants (i.e., lump sums to an agency of government to spend as it pleases), the New Federalism ensured that unpopular programs would starve. In addition, revenue sharing undermined the power of those administrators who did try to create effective programs; Floyd Hyde, for example, Nixon's head of Model Cities, was unable to get a commitment from the White House for urban programs so long as Nixon was intent upon decentralizing public spending.[57]

A particularly ingenious method characterized Nixon's approach to the funding commitments made by Congress to Great Society programs: he would just refuse to spend the money. Immediately after his decision to bomb Southeast Asia in December 1972, Nixon announced that he was not going to spend any money on low-rent public housing, rent supplements, homeownership assistance, and rental housing for a period of eighteen months. Citing studies showing that these programs were wasteful—studies that in fact were undertaken after the impoundment was announced— Nixon never questioned whether the money spent on the bombing was equally as wasteful. (Senator William Proxmire noted that the effect of both policies was "to increase the housing shortage both in Asia and in the United States. That is reorganizing priorities with a vengeance.")[58] Nixon combined impoundment with overall budgetary outlays for social programs that were minimal in scope. The 1975 and 1976 budgets included major cutbacks in programs like food stamps, maternal and child health care, and nutrition—an approach carried forward by Gerald Ford. Nixon and Ford solved the problem of inequality by declaring that it no longer existed.

Given the lack of commitment, funding, and federal enforcement, there could be no effective policy planning to meet social objectives under Nixon and Ford. The one major attempt by the Nixon administration to bring about some order and direction in social policy was in the area of welfare, and there his commitment was ambiguous at best.[59] For a president who was preoccupied with government reorganization—going further than any other president in recent times to centralize power—Nixon was surprisingly uninterested in policy planning. And even in those areas where Nixon did try to bring about a coordination of policy (see chapter 3), his personal paranoia, preoccupation with Watergate, and appointment of Gerald Ford all guaranteed that effective coordination would be, in Richard Nathan's phrase, "the plot that failed."[60]

Nixon's attempt to destroy the preconditions of effective social policy could not have occurred without the growth coalition's preparing the way. By the 1970s, the pursuit of economic growth through public works had created a puzzling domestic situation. Reform had become highly unpopular in America, even though reforms had barely been tried. In order to fashion a compromise that could maneuver around the political stalemate in the United States, policies were followed that combined the worst of two worlds. On the one hand, conservatives could point out that domestic programs were expensive, inflationary, and wasteful. On the other hand, such programs were also tame, impotent, and counterproductive. It was truly an amazing creation: a governmental apparatus that was too expensive to please the right and too impotent to please the left. Yet the reason for it seems clear: one can develop a program that makes a genuine attempt at social reconstruction, which would be expensive but which might show results, or one can spend no money at all, which does not show results but also does not cost money. By trying to do both things at once, the growth coalition gave birth to a monstrosity.

# V

## Paying an Imperial Price

G ROWTH ABROAD was pursued as relentlessly by postwar America as growth at home. Emerging out of World War II with fantastic economic and military advantages relative to the rest of the world, Americans felt themselves truly blessed by history. After some hesitation, the United States speedily went about creating a *Pax Americana*, reorganizing the world, not only to maintain American power, but also to provide an imperial dividend in the form of domestic economic benefits. The expansion of American economic and military power abroad became the organizing principle of both foreign policy and strategies toward international economic issues. Bolstered by its privileged position, America found itself fatally attracted to empire, for affairs went very smoothly over there when contrasted with the domestic stalemate over here. Relying on overseas expansion as an alternative to needed domestic reconstruction, America, slowly at first, rapidly later, sacrificed more and more of its domestic strength in order to keep alive its overseas influence. By the early 1980s, the call of empire had become so seductive that no political party could resist it, no matter how destructive its pursuit. Americans, who had received such a munificent imperial dividend, had little choice but to pay an exorbitant imperial price once the world changed more rapidly than did American politics.

### I

THE SINGLE MOST IMPORTANT FALLOUT from America's military and economic strength in the late 1940s was that it prevented America from developing a foreign *policy*. A workable approach to the affairs of other countries requires two ingredients. For one country to arrive at a workable approach to the affairs of other countries, it must first be able to make choices, to distinguish between what is important and what is not. Without that ability, a country may find itself staking its prestige on an adventure that will have little to do with its national interest. The making of choices in foreign policy is generally called diplomacy, and the successful diplomat is one who knows what to give away in order to retain what is essential. But even the best diplomat will be hampered unless a second condition is satisfied. Without some sense of the values for which the diplomat's own society stands, there will be little chance of building long-term domestic support for foreign actions. And without such support, even the most acutely made diplomatic choices will be for naught.

As it emerged from World War II, America faced a political stalemate over foreign policy as deep and divisive as the one that existed over domestic policy. Isolationism—the only genuinely American contribution to the art of diplomacy—had been the traditional approach of the United States toward the rest of the world. Discredited because of its tolerance, and sometimes affection, for Hitler, isolationism was not as inappropriate to the modern world as it would later be made out to be. As embodied in the world view of a man like Robert Taft, isolationism made a claim that the national interest of the United States should be the preservation of competitive capitalism. To the degree that foreign actions might be necessary to protect that way of life, they should be supported. But if any foreign activity required the destruction of a system of low taxes, protectionism, small government, and localism—such as a peacetime draft or the creation of a permanent military establishment—it should be resisted. The isolationists, in short, were guilty of premature anti-imperialism, opposing, from the right, the trend toward the emergence of the United States as a global power.[1]

Isolationism would always retain a secure foothold in the American imagination. Buoyed by the reservoir of popular support that existed for isolationism among the general population, the Republican right emerged from World War II prepared to dismantle the global apparatus that had been set up to fight that war. Politically popular as it was, however, isolationism was marred by its irrelevance to the economic transformations that World War II had capped. A Wall Street-based financial and industrial elite, linked to emerging global corporations, was not about to yield power to a group of characters out of a Sinclair Lewis novel. America, this elite claimed, needed to preserve and extend its influence abroad, not to "retreat" to within its own borders. Foreign policies are made by an unstable combination of elite preferences and popular sentiments; isolationism, with much of the latter, had little of the former.

The most critical opponents of isolationism were global humanitarians who saw themselves at the left end of the political spectrum. Stunned first by the Great Depression and then by fascism, a number of intellectuals, and some policymakers, argued that America must take the lead in reconstructing the world along idealistic lines. There would be a world government of some sort, a state capable of bringing about the rule of law. Foreign aid would bring the New Deal to the world, while international cooperation between the victors of World War II would be strengthened to ensure the peace. Eleanor Roosevelt often articulated sentiments like these, ones that would be most strongly advocated by Henry Wallace. Global humanitarianism, like isolationism, was not as naive and unworkable as was later claimed. Its hallmarks were a statement of the national interest—the preservation of peace—and some thoughts about the choices that would have to be made to reach it: the United Nations; foreign aid; and programs of international reconstruction. But if the isolationists were made redundant by the economic realities of World War II, the internationalists suffered from not being in accord with the political changes wrought by war.

Winning the war necessitated friendly relations between the Roosevelt administration and the corporate and military leaders who controlled the key to victory. Businessmen, suddenly as popular as they once were detested, were instinctively distrustful of anything that smacked of a "giveaway." An anticommunist consensus fashioned at the end of the war discredited a key plank in the humanitarian program: cooperation with the Soviet Union. (Indeed, the global humanitarians could never successfully avoid the communist problem, as Henry Wallace would discover in 1948 when he tried to propose a left alternative to a program of global American hegemony.) But the most important stumbling block to a genuinely internationalist foreign policy was the emergence of the military as a dominant force in American life. This was brand-new. Traditionally suspicious of militarism, which it associated with the decadence of European feudalism, America was unprepared for the incorporation of militarist considerations into civilian decision making. Guardians of the nation state, the military's mission was to prevent international cooperation, not to facilitate it.

So long as first Roosevelt and then Truman were dependent on the military, they had no choice but to weaken and then silence the international idealists in their administrations.

Deprived of the popular appeal of isolationism and the idealism of global humanitarianism, America developed an approach to foreign policy that combined elements of both but resembled neither. Working around the domestic political stalemate, a centrist consensus was fashioned that stirred economic expansion, military intervention, and international idealism into an extraordinary imperial mix. The creation of a *Pax Americana* seemed to solve the problem of the domestic political stalemate, but in actuality it simply postponed it. For the growth of American economic and military power in the world was premised upon *not* making diplomatic choices and *not* articulating a clear statement of the international interest. So long as there was little resistance to growth abroad, and so long as growth at home facilitated overseas expansion, this failure was inconsequential. But when the limits appeared, America was left without a capacity to distinguish the important from the trivial and with little popular support for an effective foreign policy. One of the strongest roots of America's impasse in the 1980s was the one that was planted as policymakers tried to develop an approach to the world in the bitter and divisive atmosphere of the late 1940s.

## II

CAPITALISTS, Joseph Schumpeter has argued, are inherently pacifistic, more attuned to English liberalism than to Prussian militarism.[2] Some of America's leading businessmen seemed, at one time, to give credence to Schumpeter's hypothesis. A number of important policymakers in the Roosevelt and Truman administrations—Secretary of State Cordell Hull, his economic assistant Will Clayton, Secretary of the Treasury Henry Morgenthau—looked upon the mass mobilization of World War II as the aberration, not the rule. They all believed, to one degree or another, that the ultimate goal of postwar foreign policy should be the removal of barriers to world trade. So far as they were concerned, the role of the state was to keep out of international transactions, thereby allowing commerce to bring about peace. Armies were suspect because they were run by governments and required high taxes to support them. Such men were not militarists, but nor were they radicals; their program, in fact, was a genuinely conservative alternative to what would develop. They did, however, reject the notion that the Soviet Union was the major threat to American security, and they looked with disdain upon those who argued for a fundamental transformation of the American system in order to meet the "challenge" posed by communism.

Free-trade notions dominated the making of foreign policy in the first two years of the Truman administration. Dean Acheson, at first, was much influenced by them, and even James F. Byrnes, in his first year as Truman's secretary of state, did not seem overly concerned about external military threats to the security of the United States.[3] To these men at that time, creating a peaceful environment in the world required diplomatic methods, carried out by a hereditary elite with little overt appeal to "common sentiment." The Department of State, with its ties to aristocratic American institutions, was the proper vehicle for such activities. Elites in other countries, including even the Soviet Union, could be induced to follow America's leadership, because the tremendous wealth of the United States in the postwar period ensured its influence. Had these trends continued, American foreign policy would have established links with its pre-World War II past: somewhat isolationist, very elitist, substantially conservative, and significantly antimilitarist.

Free trade, like Aristotle's noble-born hero, had an internal flaw: while it made certain economic sense, it was not capable of resolving the political stalemate in the United States. Too conservative for activist New Dealers, free trade was insufficiently anticommunist and militarist for the strengthened right wing. In order to pass through Congress, free-trade legislation would have military considerations drafted upon it, producing a whole new approach to foreign policy that was politically broad if internally inconsistent.

An illustrative example of what happened in the charged political atmosphere of the late 1940s is provided by the case of aid to Europe.[4] There can be no trade if there are no traders, and the European economies in the postwar period were not in a position to trade for anything, including the products of American manufacturers. Substantial aid to Europe could overcome this problem, and a number of policymakers—including an ambitious assistant to Under Secretary of State Will Clayton named Paul Nitze—urged upon Truman something called multilateralism: a Wilsonian pro-

gram encouraging the United States to trade with as many partners
as possible. Nitze's position was strongly seconded by one of
Truman's closest personal advisers, Clark Clifford, who had argued
in 1946 that the Soviet Union was not a major enemy of the United
States and that economic aid to Europe was far more sensible than
American rearmament. (Clifford, like Nitze, would soon change
his emphasis.) Multilateralists united around the European Recovery Program, soon to be called the Marshall Plan, which would provide generous loans and grants to European countries in order to
stimulate their economic reconstruction. It was a bold and imagi-
native program, but Truman delayed its implementation on the
grounds that Congress and the American people were too isolationist to accept what seemed to be an international giveaway.

Truman was probably right; political opposition to free trade
was fierce in the late 1940s. A treaty negotiated in Havana to lower
American tariffs and to create an international trading order was so
strongly opposed by a protectionist Congress that Truman would
not allow it to come to a vote. Moreover, a proposed loan to the
British, viewed by the administration as a pre-Broadway tryout for
the Marshall Plan, ran into severe congressional opposition. The
country that seemed to constitute the strongest opposition to the
free-trade agenda of the United States was the United States.
There seemed to be no question that the Marshall Plan would never
be approved by Congress. Yet approved it was, for between 1946
and 1948 America discovered the Soviet threat and, with it, the
answer to the political stalemate that blocked Marshall Plan aid to
Europe.

Certainly the Soviet Union, with its interventions in Eastern
Europe and Iran, contributed to a worsening of international relations in the postwar period. But, as I argue at much greater length
elsewhere, the cold war cannot be understood without some appreciation of the role of domestic politics in the United States.[5]
Once anticommunism was grafted onto the multilateralist program, the political logjam in the United States was broken. Free
trade, an inherently elitist notion, transformed itself into an ideology with mass appeal when it adopted anticommunism as its rationale. Every one of the limitations of the free-trade position
could be overcome by an emphasis on the threat that the Soviet
Union posed to the United States: Europe could be turned into a
trading partner capable of buying American surplus production;
labor and capital could become united in their opposition to com-

munism; the resistance of Congress to globalism could be overwhelmed; and the American public's instinctive attraction to isolationism could be dented. Acheson, Clifford, and others learned this quickly and dropped their single-minded emphasis on multilateralism. Byrnes, knowing better all the time, realized that the operating language of the day was the Soviet threat and that he must mouth the appropriate clichés or find himself back in South Carolina. Negative perceptions of Soviet conduct could do what nobody in the United States was capable of doing, which was to unify a contentious society around a set of foreign policy goals that could win broad support.

We have it on the authority of the men involved—Acheson and Nitze, for example—that they deliberately chose to exaggerate the Russian threat for internal domestic purposes.[6] Nitze, in particular, played a major role in winning political support for the new position. Although a multilateralist believer in free trade in 1946, Nitze was arguing by 1948 that the Soviet threat had become an omnipresent reality, one that only immediate rearmament could counter. Instead of viewing the Russians as a global power with whom one negotiated through diplomacy, Nitze argued that the antagonist was a messianic, expansionary force that needed to be dealt with militarily. His most dramatic opportunity to push this perception came when the Soviet Union exploded an atomic device in August 1949. Truman's response was to commission a highly secret report from the National Security Council on Soviet intentions and capabilities. Nitze became the chief draftsman of NSC-68, the resulting document. This report, declassified and released to the American public in 1975, indicated how far elite opinion had changed from the relatively pacifistic ideals of the free traders.

The key conclusion of NSC-68 was that the U.S. military budget would have to be vastly increased in order to meet the threat posed by Soviet expansionism. This was a controversial conclusion, for military spending in those days was unconventional, if not somewhat radical. The secretary of defense, Louis Johnson (a former commander of the American Legion), was opposed to larger appropriations for his own department and was aghast at the direction taken by NSC-68. The whole idea of a drastic rise in military spending was so untoward that NSC-68 did not press for a specific commitment, although Nitze made it known that he would like to see the military budget rise from $13 billion to $35 billion or even to $50 billion within a couple of years. His desire, however,

seemed hopelessly naive, for it was considered axiomatic by conservatives and isolationists that in a capitalist economy government spending, for whatever reason, would undermine prosperity.
Given strong opposition from a conservative secretary of defense,
Nitze searched for allies.

He found an important one in an unlikely place. As I indicated
in chapter 3, a number of Truman's domestic advisers were
pledged to economic expansion through government stimulation,
but were meeting opposition from the president. Much talk of
using the military budget as a stimulant was heard within the
Council of Economic Advisers, for example, but the chairman,
Edwin Nourse, registered his opposition, and the idea was tem-
porarily shelved. But Nourse, like Louis Johnson, had his own Paul
Nitze to confront. The informal leader of the CEA at the time of
NSC-68 was Leon Keyserling, and he spoke of economic expansion
with the same passion that moved Nitze on the question of rearmament. Keyserling became chairman of the council on Nourse's
retirement, and lent his aide, Gerhard Colm, to Nitze to work on
the economic sections of NSC-68.[7] As a result, the chief planning
document for an expansionist U.S. foreign policy was based on an
expansionist domestic economy. Macroeconomic stimulation, NSC-
68 claimed,

> would permit, and might itself be aided by, a build-up of the
> economic and military strength of the free world; furthermore,
> if a dynamic expansion of the economy were achieved, the
> necessary build-up could be accomplished without a decrease
> in the national standard of living because the required resources
> could be obtained by siphoning off a part of the annual incre-
> ment in the gross national product. These are facts of funda-
> mental importance in considering the course of action open to
> the United States.[8]

NSC-68 was never formally adopted by Truman, but its existence indicated what would need to be done to work around the
political stalemate in the United States. In retrospect, the outstanding feature of NSC-68 was the alliance between Nitze and Keyserling; indeed, this alliance constituted a breakthrough in American
politics, for it symbolized the emergence of a growth consensus
that would increasingly exercise an iron grip on the making of
American foreign policy. On this issue, as was the case with hous-

ing policy, liberals took the lead in fashioning a centrist coalition that could unify the elite. Keyserling and Nitze were advocating a program that could appeal to economic activists and New Dealers, calling, as it did, for an expansion of the economy. At the same time, their program nullified isolationist opposition, for it emphasized national security and thereby put the right into the uncomfortable position of seeming to be soft on national defense. In addition, NSC-68 incorporated the free-trade position, offering a vision of a perilous world that made aid to Europe a matter, not only of economics, but of survival.[9] And finally, NSC-68 envisioned a healthy role for the military, thereby bringing within its scope one of the most powerful interest groups in Washington and winning support for the new position in the South and West, where military facilities were located. Although it would take some time before the world view outlined in NSC-68 would become adopted by the United States, foreshadowed in that document was a whole new approach to the problem of American foreign policy.

The program outlined in NSC-68 became the overseas equivalent of the domestic economic expansionism of the pro-growth liberals. Cold war containment was not just a policy of stopping Russian "aggression." America would have to play a more active role in world affairs, necessarily extending its influence into other countries in order to prevent the Soviets from getting there first. This meant the creation of an American empire, something opposed to the national self-image, but one that need not stir profound worries for it would more than pay for itself. Imperial expansion would stimulate economic prosperity abroad, thereby rebounding to American advantage. It would create a protective apparatus for American investment in other countries. It would, through its explicit endorsement of militarism, provide jobs, profits, and growth. A *Pax Americana*, like a domestic building boom, could resolve all contradictions, once conservatives could be convinced to overcome their opposition and support it.

Aggressive overseas expansion through the creation of a national security state, like both counter-Keynesianism and the pro-growth coalition, was a brand-new force in American political life. America's approach to the rest of the world would no longer be hampered by the isolationist strain that had prevented Roosevelt from playing a more active role in world affairs; eventually, right-wing resistance to higher military spending would simply disappear. Nor would the U.S. stance follow the gentlemanly instincts of

the free traders, men who had a proper understanding of the role
of American business overseas but were insufficiently appreciative
of the role that the military needed to play to support such ventures. And even though the interventionists adopted the name
"internationalists" to distinguish themselves from isolationists, they
bore little resemblance to the global humanitarians who had originally called for international cooperation and world government.
NSC-68 steered a course that rejected both the historical right and
the existing left. Nitze's shift from multilateralism to militarism
and Keyserling's move from reform to rearmament drew the con-
tours of a centrist, nonideological approach to foreign policy.
There would be no attempt to change the world, only an attempt
to police it. Political conceptions of how to organize the world—
either the conservative preference to make it safe for capitalism or
the liberal concern to make it safe for democracy—would be
downplayed in favor of emphasis on managing events through the
use of military force. The emphasis, as in domestic policy, was on
the accumulation of power, not on the ends that power was expected to serve. As men like Reinhold Niehbuhr repeatedly
stressed, political visions were hopeless obstacles to the necessary
realpolitik.

The principles of NSC-68 would not be adopted until the
Kennedy administration, and when they were, a solution to the
political stalemate over foreign policy would be at hand. Yet, as
time went by, the costs of achieving unity would turn out to be
high. To anticipate, NSC-68 was premised upon shaky contingen-
cies. Its emphasis on national security enhanced the power of the
military. Unleashed as a permanent force in politics for the first
time in American history, the military would come to exercise veto
power over the policies of civilian administrations. Democrats in
particular would find it necessary to court the support of the military for their foreign policy in a way quite similar to their need to
win business confidence for domestic policy. Hostage to the military, Democratic presidents would become more aggressive in
their overseas policies, expanding the empire as rapidly as they
could. At some point down the road, the limits to such expansion,
such as the desire of other countries to shape their own destiny,
would reveal how precarious the strategy had become.

Moreover, NSC-68 assumed domestic expansion at home, for
unity would prove to be expensive. To increase military spending
while at the same time providing economic security for the voting

blocs of the Democratic party necessitated perpetual economic growth. Liberals like Keyserling were convinced that military spending would sufficiently stimulate the economy, and for a time he was correct. But in the long run, military spending would also produce inflation, undermine the balance of payments, and act less and less as an effective stimulant. Under those conditions, the unity achieved would prove to be transitory, and many of the same conflicts that existed in the late 1940s would emerge in the early 1980s.

These problems, though, would not reveal themselves until liberals like Keyserling and Nitze had their chance to reshape American foreign policy. That chance did not come automatically. Adlai Stevenson did his best to bring the new coalition to power in 1952. Fortified by men like Nitze—and other spokesmen for an aggressive foreign policy like Thomas Finletter and George Ball— Stevenson gave speeches that, to the initiated, sounded like transcriptions of NSC-68. ("Strength is the road to peace," Stevenson pointed out during the campaign. "Weakness is the road to war."[10] The candidate made it clear which party stood for which.) But the public was not as impressed as the elite. Advocates of an expansionist foreign policy needed an atmosphere of crisis, and crisis was not on the minds of most people. Nitze and the cold war liberals would have to wait eight years to have their chance.

# III

THE STRUGGLE for Europe was easy compared to the struggle for Washington. Men like Nitze had been able to win support for the Marshall Plan, but they never managed to convince Truman of the necessity for a dramatic increase in the military budget. Moreover, the American public seemed stubbornly attached to values that the foreign policy activists claimed to be irrelevant to the world emergency. The popularity manifested for General Douglas MacArthur, as he slowly motored down Wall Street after being fired from his post in Korea by Harry Truman, seemed to indicate that sentiment in favor of a quasi-isolationist, Asia-first, low-defense-budget, big-bomb mentality was still warmly received by the American people. In the form of Robert Taft, that mentality threatened to capture the presidential nomination of the Republican party in 1952.

Taft's defeat by Eisenhower was a relief to the foreign policy expansionists, although many of them were unsure where they stood with the general. (A number had supported him for the *Democratic* nomination in 1948.) They soon found out. Not worshipful of militarism, Eisenhower sought to reconcile isolationism with anticommunism, relying on nuclear weapons to do it. Thus, the public stance of the Eisenhower administration became John Foster Dulles's notion of massive retaliation—threaten us, he said to the Russians, and we will blow you to bits. Massive retaliation was both belligerent and isolationist, the former because it was rationalized in terms of severe anticommunism, the latter because it implied neither military intervention in other countries, nor heavy military spending (nuclear weapons are cheaper than standing armies), nor a permanent war economy. In short, massive retaliation was a sort of nonforeign foreign policy. It was cheap. It did not require troops. It appealed to conservatives. And it favored the air force at the expense of the other two services, and the air force—based in the West and politically to the right—was the most Republican sector of the armed forces. Although it looked like a foreign policy, and was often called one by the press, massive retaliation was actually a domestic strategy—the best available means of holding together a Republican party split by internal dissent.

Under Eisenhower, decisions taken in the area of defense policy seemed to repudiate the future foreshadowed in NSC-68. The administration labeled its approach the "New Look," by which it meant an emphasis on the retaliatory potential of U.S. nuclear weapons to deter the Soviets from acting against American interests. But the New Look, as Samuel Huntington has argued, was formulated with Republican party considerations in mind.[11] Above all else, the New Look promised that defense would be cheap. An overriding goal of the Eisenhower administration was to hold down the costs of empire. As late as 1957, Eisenhower tried to impose a 10 percent cut on the Department of Defense. His plans were carried out by Secretary of Defense Charles Wilson, who introduced a long-range budget-cutting plan at the National Security Council meeting of July 25, 1957. Under this plan, Pentagon expenses from 1959 to 1961 would be held at $38 billion. Big cuts would be made in manpower, with the army being the most severely curtailed. In the 1959 military budget, the services were given ceilings in terms of expenditures rather than obligations for the first time.[12] Although Eisenhower had been both a general and a loyal army man, neither militarism nor the older services were faring well during his administration.

Off in academic exile, men like Paul Nitze watched these events with scorn and dismay. A forum was needed to keep alive the spirit of NSC-68, and, when the Security Resources Panel of the Science Advisory Council was asked to make a report to the NSC in September 1957, an opportunity presented itself. The final report, named after its chairman, Rowland Gaither, rewrote NSC-68 and brought it up to date. Paul Nitze served as a project member of the Gaither Report, as did other foreign policy activists like John Mc-Cloy and Robert Lovett. Projecting the military spending of both the Soviet Union and the United States, the report concluded that America would soon lose the cold war. The appropriate response was held to be a rapid increase in military spending, from 8.5 percent of the gross national product to 15 percent. New military programs, the report noted, implied an increase in the Pentagon budget of up to $11.9 billion over five years "and further un-estimated expenditures thereafter." To the conservative argument that higher expenditures on war preparations would flirt with economic disaster, the Gaither Report responded with expansionist economics: ". . . large additional expenditures of this sort are still within the economic capabilities of the United States." Counter-Keynesian economic techniques were specifically endorsed:

> Aside from its psychological impact, increased defense spending would have some influence on capital investment. If a moderate recession is impending, tax receipts would decline, but the increase in Federal expenditure would help to sustain pro-duction and employment. Under conditions of full employment, the program would have some inflationary effects, requiring a continuation of monetary and credit restrictions.[13]

Like NSC-68, the Gaither Report was an attempt to fashion an alliance in the center. Preparedness was sufficiently nonideological to win broad political support, at the same time offering policies that would stimulate economic growth. Military spending gave its advocates the security of respectability and the self-righteous-ness of dissent at the same time. Nitze and his allies were, on the one hand, clearly at odds with the status quo; in the 1950s, they were reformers, urging new and untested policies upon a hide-bound elite. But, on the other hand, their reformism was not really of an upsetting sort, for they were calling for changes that would enhance the power of some of the most conservative sectors of American society, particularly among business and the military. Calling for a vast increase in military spending in the 1950s was as controversial as calling for greater sums for urban renewal.

Maxwell Taylor's attempt to reorient the national security posture of the Eisenhower administration was typical of the simultaneously reformist and complacent notions of the foreign policy activists. Taylor, chief of staff of the army, proposed a budget and a program directly at odds with the narrow vision of conservatives like Admiral William Radford and Defense Secretary Wilson. According to his analysis, the United States and the Soviet Union, each possessing nuclear weapons, confronted each other like two giants so draped in armor that neither was capable of moving. The United States required a strategy that would give it some flexibility. (This would become a key word in the Kennedy lexicon.) Some example of the flexibility sought was provided by Taylor in a memo he circulated within the Pentagon in October 1956, advocating a new military program that

> . . . must be suitable for flexible application to unforeseen situations. It cannot be geared to any single weapons system, strategic concept, or combination of allies. It must be capable of supporting our national policy in all situations. It should attract essential allies and not repel other allies. In short, the military posture of the United States should include all reasonable measures to prevent general and local war and at the same time contain the potentiality of waging any war, large or small, in such a manner as to achieve our national objectives and to bring about a better world upon the successful conclusion of hostilities.[14]

Taylor's argument was truly remarkable. Urging an end of ideology for defense policy, he suggested that anything and everything should be used—so long as it worked. His was a new tone in strategic thought, implying the absence of any recognizable limits to military power. Taylor was saying that the United States could fight any kind of war, in any way, and at the same time bring about a better world. Such utopianism ran counter to an almost instinctive skepticism about military power that generals, before they won access to ongoing political power, used to have. Taylor and other activists needed to overcome what Henry Kissinger, then a liberal, called "the traditionalism of our military thinking"[15] in order to achieve their program. But if there were few models for their kind of thinking within the Pentagon, there was one conspicuous one outside of it. A strategy of fighting war and also bringing about a better world sounded like a strategy of destroying housing while improving the lot of the poor. Taylor's program, in other words, was the strategy of urban growth brought to foreign policy: spending in one area, as in the other, could provide the unity necessary to prepare the way for new options.

In truth, Taylor had a point: there were similarities between Eisenhower's hostility to urban public works projects and his support for the New Look. In both areas, Eisenhower was suspicious of using growth to reconcile political differences. Distrustful of big government and high taxes, Republicans in both domestic and foreign policy sought solutions that were fiscally orthodox. Eisenhower seemed happier mouthing homilies than cultivating an image of problem-solving toughness. Just as laissez faire had about it the aura of the musty, the New Look was a bit complacent, unmoved by perceptions of an immediate crisis. (The cold war was constantly analogized by liberals to the Great Depression; both were seen as sudden emergencies requiring immediate and extensive action by government.) For all these reasons, those who sought to extend the American empire abroad developed criticisms of the Eisenhower administration that resonated with those who wanted to expand the economy at home. We need verve and action, they claimed, new notions, the best ideas from the universities and think tanks. We need to wage an educational battle to win the support of the American people who, if left untutored, will slip back into a faith in both budget-balancing and isolationism. At the same time, and this would be true in both foreign and domestic policy, our solutions should not be too controversial, they should not ruffle popular prejudices too much, and they should be tailored to win support among those who hold positions of authority.

Just as the domestic reformers of the growth coalition sought equality and social justice without tampering with profit, the military reformers fought for a reliance on conventional weapons while leaving the nuclear arsenal untouched. The crucial argument made by the growth network was that one did not need to reject capitalism—indeed, one could strengthen it—in order to help the poor. Likewise, the foreign policy activists argued that the welfare state need not be dismantled—in fact, it could be extended—in order to increase military spending. As growth in the empire facilitated expansion at home, expansion at home would result in growth in the empire. The secret of success for foreign policy, then, was the exact same as it was for domestic policy. A new strategy could be adopted only "assuming continued and uninterrupted high employment and growth" as the Gaither Report expressed it.[16] This would be an empire without sacrifice, a show of military force abroad that would not only pay for itself but produce a dividend besides. The hope—and it was, in retrospect, only a hope—was characteristically articulated by Henry Kissinger. "While there is undoubtedly an upper limit beyond which the injury to the economy would outweigh the gain in military strength," he wrote, "it is also the case that this theoretical ceiling has been consistently underestimated."[17]

By the end of the 1950s, a program had been set in place that would seek to revitalize America's military force in order to make it more capable of being applied around the world. Basing themselves on the notion that the Soviet threat was growing by the hour, activists like Nitze and Taylor were calling for preparedness on all fronts: more aggressiveness to confront the Russians over Europe and more conventional weapons to win the hearts and minds of the Third World. America was preparing for action, although no one seemed to know what form the action would take.

# IV

LIKE THOROUGHBREDS held back from the start of a race for reasons they do not understand, the foreign policy expansionists burst into action when they assumed power in 1961. Kennedy's election gave them their opportunity to test the theories they were developing in academia. Men like Nitze and Taylor were ready for the world; the only question was whether or not the world was ready for them.

The first order of business was to make American military power, in the word adopted by Defense Secretary McNamara, "usable,"[18] a notion that apparently had escaped Eisenhower. The trouble with the Defense Department, according to the Kennedy men, was that it did not formulate policy. As two Kennedy defense officials put it, under Eisenhower "the defense budget was far from the vital policy instrument it should have been: rather than a mechanism for integrating strategy, forces, and costs, it was essentially a bookkeeping device for dividing funds between services and accounts and a blunt instrument for keeping a lid on defense spending."[19] The secretary of defense, they argued, too often acted as a broker, mediating disputes between service branches and trying to preserve harmony. Instead, the United States needed a secretary who was "active," who would be an initiator of new ideas rather than a mediator between old ones. This preference for action would imply higher costs. Although the Kennedy men talked a great deal about "cost effectiveness," their desire to use the national security machinery in new ways implied that at some point military spending would go up. As the new president noted, "The greater our variety of weapons, the more political choices we can make in any given situation."[20]

If the military might of the United States was actually to be used, the crucial questions would be when and where. Traditionally, answers to questions like these were provided by the State Department, which was, after all, in charge of foreign policy. But the Kennedy men thought of State as too conservative and complacent for their tastes. It was not diplomacy that they craved, but action, and, in truth, the State Department was not well-organized to offer the latter. Presidential advisers like McGeorge Bundy and Maxwell Taylor would make the key decisions about foreign expansion, not tradition-bound bureaucrats. And make it they did. It seems clear from the vantage point of the 1980s that America found a crisis, not that a crisis found America. Foreign policy expansionists were determined to flex America's military might somewhere, to demonstrate to all concerned that the United States was now in its imperial glory, acting, like Britain in the nineteenth century, to police the world in its image. There were no serious threats to American security in the early 1960s, and so the Kennedy administration invented them. Like a corporation president picking a new plant site, it roamed the world searching for a place to apply military force, ultimately resting on a small, Southeast Asian country. The fact that the country they chose was Laos, and not Vietnam, only indicates that it was the demonstration of power, and not the situation in which it was to be demonstrated, that concerned these men. In the first two months of his presidency, Kennedy spent more time concerned with Laos than with any other issue. "We cannot and will not accept any visible humiliation over Laos,"[21] he told Walter Lippmann at the time (thereby apparently concluding that invisible humiliation was okay). Ultimately, Laos did not prove to be the correct site, and the planning that went into its choice was then shifted next door, to Vietnam.

The Vietnam intervention, a number of its planners would later conclude, was the wrong war in the wrong place at the wrong time.[22] But from domestic considerations, it was the perfect one, which may help explain why it happened. Because it was in Asia, Vietnam would rectify the U.S. mistakes in Korea; that effort failed, many believed, because the United States had relied so much on the big bomb that it had not provided itself with sufficiently flexible conventional forces. Moreover, the timing was right. A war at the start of the Kennedy administration would prove that the activists really were activists, that they would be more willing than the Eisenhower Republicans to use force. To be sure, there was some muttering, particularly from the generals, about a land war in Asia, but the civilian activists did not contemplate that it would ever come to that. Any country serious about imperial pretentions had to be prepared to take the steps necessary to demonstrate its will.

Later, after the costs of Vietnam were finally calculated, all kinds of people would wonder why the United States became involved in the first place. From the viewpoint of national security, one might indeed wonder, for Vietnam bore little relationship to any threat to the American way of life. In retrospect, one must conclude that Vietnam came about because of the dynamics let loose in the United States when anticommunism was drafted onto free-trade liberalism to produce a consensus about U.S. expansion overseas. By the early 1960s, activists in the Kennedy administration, having preached preparedness, found themselves in an awkward position. Whenever an event occurred anywhere in the world that could be interpreted by conservatives as an extension of Soviet power, liberal presidents had to respond. Just as Kennedy found himself domestically sponsoring programs that would increase business profits, and meeting opposition from business in so doing, he was also in the position of pursuing military adventures abroad, all the while facing opposition from the military for so doing. Growth policies, in short, produced the same puzzling pattern in foreign policy that they did in domestic policy: liberal presidents were forced to carry out conservative programs over conservative objections. This pattern of politics made Vietnam, or something like it, well-nigh inevitable. As Kennedy, and then Johnson, repeatedly said, he would not expose himself to the right by appearing to be soft on defense.

Thus, Vietnam, like the sponsorship of economic growth, was a major gamble for the imperial coalition. If an overseas adventure succeeded, then the United States would become unified. And if it succeeded without costing very much, a demonstration of American power would underline the privileged position of the United States in the world's balance of power. In short, expansion abroad, like growth at home, would work brilliantly if it worked at all. But —and this neither Kennedy nor Johnson ever seemed to understand—if it failed, there would be a debacle. By the mid-1960s, evidence seemed to be accumulating that the gamble was a failure. Three limits to overseas expansion were emerging. First, the objects of American policy simply did not roll over and play dead when the United States shot at them, a contingency that was apparently never considered by the architects of the war in Vietnam. Second, the assumption that the economy would be able to absorb rising defense costs through growth, though at first confirmed, was not holding true by 1967. And third, liberal expansionists, convinced that the American public would support their ventures if sufficient incantations of national security were offered, were finding themselves increasingly discredited.

Certainly the Vietnamese bear the major responsibility for the failure of the *Pax Americana*. As early as February 1965, McGeorge Bundy was on his way to Vietnam to see if he could avoid what might become, in his own words, a "disastrous defeat." While he was there, U.S. planes carried out Operation Flaming Dart, which involved the systematic bombing of Vietnamese territory. "The die was cast," Chester Cooper, a Bundy man and a CIA operative, wrote at the time.[23] Bundy then penned what may have been the most prophetic sentence contained in the *Pentagon Papers*: "The situation in Vietnam is deteriorating and without new U.S. actions defeat appears inevitable. . . ."[24] Bundy's 1965 trip to Vietnam raised the question implicit, but avoided, in Maxwell Taylor's formation of the strategy of flexible response: were there, indeed, limits to America's power? The Johnson administration was determined to prove that there were not. Operation Rolling Thunder, which commenced the major commitment of U.S. troops to Vietnam, was the administration's response. Limited war had been replaced by limitless war. Imperial dreams, Johnson and his advisers learned, were costly: one did not, after all, win a war without losing lives.

The failure of the Vietnamese to act out the role they were assigned also raised the financial costs of the war. New operations meant new weapons and more troops, both of which cost money. Whether or not the budget would be drained by providing them depended on how fast the economy could expand, and as a result Vietnam drove the domestic liberals to spur the economy. As Richard Cooper, an economist who will figure in chapter 8, put it at the time, "The rate of economic growth at home will influence considerably the success of the United States in achieving its objectives of foreign policy: a high rate of growth will provide additional freedoms, and a low one added restraints, in the pursuit of our international aims."[25] Many liberals were convinced that the economy would prove reliable. As late as 1966, Walter Heller, recently of the Council of Economic Advisers, delivered his previously mentioned lecture arguing that the United States could expand its governmental commitments without having to worry about inflation.[26] Heller joined Bundy to link domestic growth considerations with overseas expansion in the same way that Keyserling had once joined Nitze. Any resemblance between bombed-out villages in Vietnam and devastated areas in the Bronx was more than coincidental: both were the products of actions taken by liberals that were tailored to win conservative support.

The hopes of the liberals were misplaced. As I argued in chapter 3, macroeconomic stimulation through expenditures on the demand-side can stimulate the economy, but it is a blunt instrument at best; and the expansion of the economy brought about by wartime expenditures was setting off an inflationary upsurge, particularly given Johnson's attempts to hide the true costs of an unpopular war. The strongest inflation since the Korean War forced Johnson to propose a 6 percent surcharge on personal and corporate taxes, effective July 1, 1967, for the purpose of financing the war. Congress, especially the then powerful chairman of the House Ways and Means Committee, Wilbur Mills, objected. Mills was willing to finance the war, but only if Great Society programs were cut. While this fight was taking place, the U.S. balance-of-payments deficit increased precipitously in the last quarter of 1967. By early 1968, U.S. economic troubles had caused tremendous speculation on the international gold exchange, severely draining U.S. reserves. On June 22, 1968, President Johnson's long-delayed tax bill was finally passed by Congress, but it leaned closer to Mills than to the president. Johnson, who in 1966 had refused to cut Great Society programs in order to fight the war, now no longer had a choice.[27]

Popular support for imperial goals disintegrated as the cost of achieving them became higher. Both NSC-68 and the Gaither Report had worried about whether the American people would make the necessary sacrifices to support an empire, but they remained confident that with proper education in the nature of the threat from abroad, Americans would live up to their "responsibilities." Here again they were wrong. Johnson's popularity declined in inverse proportion to the escalation of the war, from a high of 80 percent after he took office to below 40 percent in late 1967. Over 65 percent of the American population supported the war in late 1965, but that had fallen to 40 percent two years later.[28] Whether opposition to the war was based on sentiments favoring immediate withdrawal or a massive effort to win was irrelevant, for both options were critical of the idea of an extended American stay overseas. Ironically, America's effort in Vietnam, instead of producing unity, revitalized a formerly moribund global humanitarianism (the antiwar movement) *and* a reborn isolationism (the bomb-'em-back-to-the-Stone-Age notions of Curtis Le May). Between the radical peace movement and the conservative insistence on immediate victory, Johnson's centrist efforts to expand overseas lay in tatters.

One reason the peace movement had such a significant impact on the America of the 1960s, and a neo-isolationism was able to flourish, was that overseas expansionists were never able to develop an articulate rationale that could win popular support. The centrist compromise that unified the elite in the face of its political stalemate was premised on making no clear-cut ideological choices between competing conceptions of foreign policy. Therefore, when the crunch came, there were no appropriate justifications for what Johnson was doing, no credible appeals that could sway public opinion. Vietnam was rationalized on grounds that were either negative, like anticommunism, or simply untrue, like national security. Johnson, in other words, could not justify his efforts because his efforts were unjustifiable. The very factor that gave overseas expansion its appeal in the first place—its political ambiguity—was the reason it was unable to win for itself the kind of popular passion that makes foreign policies effective in the world arena.

The final blow to the strategy theory of the imperialists was the TET offensive of March 1968 and the domestic reaction to it. Some overseas expansionists, like Walt Rostow, believed, and continue to believe, that TET was a defeat for the Vietnamese, but most of Johnson's men saw in that offensive an end of their hopes for a unified imperial strategy. Limited war, one that demonstrated American will abroad with no domestic costs and a few domestic benefits, was simply a failure. Maxwell Taylor, out of power, had suggested that America could fight any war and bring about a better world as well. Maxwell Taylor, in power, lost a war and bitterly divided the world against the United States and the United States against itself. Stunned and at a loss for understanding, Lyndon Johnson asked one of the original formulators of the imperial compromise, Clark Clifford, to take over the Department of Defense and to find out what should be done. "Give me the lesser of evils," were the president's words to Clifford, and they suggested how hemmed in by contradictions the pursuit of empire had become.[29] Clifford, convinced that if the Joint Chiefs' recommendation for an additional 206,000 men were granted, the effect on Wall Street would be "appalling,"[30] underwent a political reconversion and argued for disengagement. America was back to where it was in 1946, disunited, facing a domestic stalemate over foreign policy, and seemingly incapable of producing a coherent policy toward the rest of the world.

So shaken was the national security establishment by this impasse that it committed an unprecedented act: it met. Imperial dreams for these men had become a way of life, a set of assumptions and goals so common that they never needed to be articulated and ratified. By coming to the State Department on March 25, 1968, the overseas expansionists were demonstrating that what once went unexamined would have to be scrutinized. Clifford summoned to this historic meeting Dean Acheson, George Ball, McGeorge Bundy, Douglas Dillon, Cyrus Vance, Arthur Dean, John McCloy, Omar Bradley, Matthew Ridgeway, Maxwell Taylor, Robert Murphy, Henry Cabot Lodge, Abe Fortas, Arthur Goldberg, Dean Rusk, W. Averell Harriman, Walt Rostow, Richard Helms, Earl Wheeler, Paul Nitze, Nicholas Katzenbach, and William Bundy. The meeting was acrimonious. While some defended the whole strategic thrust that had culminated in Vietnam, the majority called for a reexamination.[31] One can only imagine Lyndon Johnson's reaction as the entire Eastern establishment revealed its disarray. Recognizing the depths of the stalemate that he would have to face, Johnson withdrew from his reelection campaign, paving the way for the possibility of a post-imperial strategy for the United States.

The men who came to the White House had good reason to be upset, for the United States no longer had a foreign policy. Since 1945, a major change had come over the external behavior of the United States. Diplomacy, as I argued in the preceding section, is the art of negotiating for what you want by giving away what you do not want. Successful foreign policies are based upon choice, yet utopian strategies like the one advocated by Maxwell Taylor negated choice. Taylor wanted everything: U.S. economic domination of the world; containment of the Soviet Union; nonrevolutionary sentiment in the Third World; and the love and respect of all other people at the same time. By trying to obtain everything, the Maxwell Taylors obtained nothing. Any group of people that could commit as much money and arms to a country as strategically and economically unimportant to the United States as Vietnam, was living in a fantasy world (as, indeed, these men sometimes recognized). They were not controlling the world, the world was controlling them. For all their emphasis on activity, they were quite passive, developing defensive and futile reactions to events beyond their purview. A reliance on military force to ensure influence abroad, in other words, turned out to be incompatible with an effective foreign policy. By opting for the one, the United States inadvertently foreclosed the other. Vietnam was a particularly difficult way for the growth coalition to learn what most elites have to learn: that there are always limits to the use of military power and that a meaningful foreign policy has to be based on the recognition of those limits.

By this standard, Hubert Humphrey was part of the problem. Running for president in 1968, he faithfully stuck to the Vietnam script even though few were listening. Humphrey was a living monument to the American impasse, a man who clearly recognized that what he was saying was untrue and yet who was not in a position to say anything else. It would not be the Democrats who would have the first opportunity to end America's reliance on military expansion overseas.

## V

THE IRONIES of Richard Nixon's presidency were countless. Fascinated by foreign affairs, Nixon never developed a coherent theory of national security policy, responding on an ad hoc basis to one crisis after another.[32] A belligerent conservative, he approved of policies that had last been seriously considered by Henry Wallace in 1948. A Quaker, he waged terrible and costly war. From an isolationist past, he operated in an interventionist present. One of the underlying reasons for Nixon's seeming inconsistencies was that the whole imperial vision that had brought about Vietnam was discredited, but there did not exist substantial political support for any alternative. The right-wing faith in isolationism had been sublimated into an advocacy of military budgets and overseas intervention, depriving Nixon of movement in that direction. Meanwhile, global humanitarianism, discredited by America's anticommunist mania, was confined to small segments of the left and to intellectuals. And so Nixon existed as a man in limbo, one who understood that a new approach to the exercise of American power abroad was essential, but one who was constrained by the domestic political stalemate from developing a coherent policy. The ambiguities that resulted can be seen in three areas where Nixon tried to modify the strategic assumptions of the postwar growth compromise: the termination of the Vietnam War; the pursuit of détente; and the search for a new nuclear strategy.

Nixon's path for extricating the United States from its involvement in Vietnam constituted a repudiation of Maxwell Taylor's strategic utopianism. The purpose of efforts like Vietnam, according to men like Taylor, was not simply to win: with its power, the United States should be able to win anything. The purpose was to accomplish American objectives through the use of flexible conventional forces, for only in this way could the United States prove to the world the capability of its ongoing imperial ambitions. Whatever his other blunders, Nixon understood that limited wars kill Americans. Attempting to reduce the level of U.S. troops by relying on an unusually intensive bombing campaign, Nixon shifted American strategy away from the army to the air force. What he produced was not, technically speaking, massive retaliation, for no nuclear weapons were involved, but it did resemble Dulles's emphasis on bigger bangs for the buck than it did Kennedy's open-ended commitment to troops. In thus repudiating the growth coalition's strategy, Nixon solved two of its three problems. By lowering the casualty figures, he overcame some of the domestic opposition to the war. And with less money spent on manpower, the economic crunch eased. But Nixon could never solve the problem of Vietnamese resistance, and the United States ultimately was unable to achieve *any* of its proclaimed objectives in Vietnam. If the purpose of the war had been to make a point, by the time Nixon ended it, no one could be sure what the point was. There would be no more attempts by expansionist liberals to involve the United States in overseas military ventures until Zbigniew Brzezinski, during the Carter administration, would demand that the United States overcome its Vietnam hang-up, a strategy then adopted by the Reagan administration in El Salvador.

The pursuit of détente also undermined the assumptions of the overseas expansionists who had first made their mark in the Truman administration and then came to power under Kennedy. "In the late 1940s," Henry Kissinger testified at a Senate Foreign Relations Committee hearing in September 1974, "this nation engaged in a great debate about the role it would play in the postwar world. We forged a bipartisan consensus on which our policies were built for more than two decades. By the end of the 1960s the international environment which molded that consensus would be transformed."[33] Specifically, Kissinger concluded that the Soviet Union had achieved a situation of "military bipolarity" with the United States. Given this new "environment," a stable international order, and therefore peace, could be fashioned only if the two major powers began to cooperate in limited areas to prevent the world from fragmenting. Détente, then, was an acknowledgment that the obsessive anticommunism and instinctive cold war inklings of the liberal activists were no longer appropriate to the world as it had become.

Henry Kissinger, hoping for a job in the Reagan administration, would later criticize the Carter administration for being "soft" on the Russians, but it was he who had prepared the way. While the means used by Kissinger to promote détente were often disreputable, the ends themselves allowed the United States more room to exercise diplomacy than had been the case under Kennedy and Johnson. First, détente's emphasis on cooperation with the Russians reduced the American need to rely on military solutions and resulted in lower military budgets. Second, it produced an opening

with China that expanded the diplomatic possibilities. Finally,
détente suggested a negotiated arms agreement as an alternative to
endless military expansion. Kissinger understood that the American
public was losing its automatic support for perpetual cold war
policies: "The American people," he said, "can be asked to bear the
cost and political instability of [an arms] race which is doomed to
stalemate only if it is clear that every effort has been made to
prevent it."[34] Over tremendous opposition from both the Pentagon
and cold warriors in the civilian sector, Kissinger used all his considerable skills to win agreement for the SALT I treaty, which,
despite its flaws, was based on assumptions quite different from
those expressed by Paul Nitze in 1949.[35] For thirty years, the bottom line of American foreign policy had been the image of Soviet
expansion; Kissinger was posing the question of whether America's
foreign policy could finally exist without it. (Both the Carter and
Reagan administrations would discover that it could not.)

The third leg in Nixon's tripartite rejection of cold war liberal
strategic assumptions was his attempt to fashion a new doctrine for
the use of nuclear weapons. Here Kissinger may have been too
tainted by his own liberal past, for he lost the battle to other Nixon
advisers, particularly James Schlesinger, the secretary of defense.
Vietnam, in Schlesinger's view, was a disaster, for, by not winning
the war, the United States had come dangerously close to destroying its credibility as an imperial power. America's defeat, especially
when combined with Russian advances in strategic weapons,
meant that if the United States was to convince the world that it
was serious, it had no choice but to spend massive amounts on a
whole new generation of nuclear weapons. Even as Kissinger
accepted military bipolarity with the Russians, in short, Schlesinger
was set to undermine it, thereby giving Nixon's foreign policy so
much of its contradictory character. Since the McNamara days,
American strategic planning had been based on a theory of deterrence—American missiles should be developed and aimed in
such a way as to discourage the Russians from launching a first
strike. From the 1950s onward, liberal expansionists believed that
nuclear weapons were of limited offensive use and argued that
they should be preserved mostly for defensive purposes; conventional arms were more compatible with the needs of empire.
Schlesinger repudiated this emphasis, suggesting instead that
America rely far more heavily on its strategic forces, and that those

forces be aimed directly at Russian missiles, implying thereby a first-strike capacity for America.

While détente was a shift to the left, Schlesinger's counter-force doctrine was a swing to the right. But the conservative option was no longer what it had been under Eisenhower and Dulles. Their reason for relying on nuclear weapons was to keep costs down, but Schlesinger was proposing, not only that the military budget go up, but that America's willingness to deprive itself of other amenities in order to expand it was a test of its moral character. Thus had isolationism been transformed. Those areas of the country that once supported Republican notions of minimal defense costs, in part due to the placement of military facilities in their midst, had become advocates of ever higher Pentagon funding. The political power of the military–industrial complex, closely linked to government spending while supporting conservative causes, prevented Nixon from ending America's reliance on military force as a substitute for diplomacy. With both conservatives and liberals calling for defense spending, debate centered on who should receive the money—liberals preferred the army, conservatives the air force—and not on whether the money should be spent. The oddest legacy of the liberal tolerance of militarism was that it gave birth to a form of belligerency more extreme than its own. At one time America had had an isolationist tradition that opposed the creation of the national security state; now the heirs of that tradition found themselves extending it. America's impasse intensified because no domestic political force existed capable of ending the country's reflexive tolerance of the military option.

The Nixon administration, then, went off in two different directions at once. On the one hand, just as Nixon was more Keynesian than the counter-Keynesians of the Democratic party, he was more willing to adopt humanitarian goals like détente and arms control than were the cold war interventionists. But by unleashing James Schlesinger, supporting the B-1 bomber, intervening in the domestic affairs of Chile, and generally talking tough when it suited his purposes, Nixon undermined whatever contribution he might have made toward a saner foreign policy. For the first time in a generation, America under Nixon had begun to exercise choice, to practice the art of diplomacy. Nixon had a sense of appropriate limits —the Nixon doctrine, for example, which called on Asian countries to organize their own defense, made far more sense than Kennedy's open-ended commitment of resources to corrupt dictators in the region. Moreover, there were attempts during the Nixon years to formulate a set of goals for American foreign policy around which popular support could be fashioned. Kissinger, in his statements on détente and in his advocacy of SALT I, developed conceptions of the national interest that were more thoughtful and positive than the utopian speculations of Maxwell Taylor or the knee-jerk anticommunism of Paul Nitze. But it all went for naught. Anticommunism and dependence on the military had become so much a part of the theory and practice of America's outlook on the world that there was no political and economic base for an alternative, either to the left or to the right. By 1980, Nixon had published a book claiming that the Russians were winning World War III, and Kissinger had become one of the most intransigent belligerents in Washington.

The generation that had brought about the *Pax Americana* was not especially thrilled by Nixon's attempt to find an alternative to it, no matter how half-hearted. The foreign policy expansionists of the 1960s regrouped, trying to develop a critique of Nixon's foreign policy, but they were hampered by the same problem that faced the incumbent. In the real world, America no longer had the hegemony that it possessed in the 1940s when the cold war began: the Russians had caught up to the United States in nuclear weapons; other countries were surpassing the economic performance of America; China was emerging as a global power; and the Third World was more nationalistic and independent. Yet, in Washington, a coalition based on military expansion was as politically and economically powerful as ever—in many ways stronger than it was in the late 1940s. As the journals, think tanks, conferences, and option papers considered a new foreign policy for the United States, one problem dominated: was it possible to go beyond a reliance on military force when, given the political stalemate at home, a reliance on military force was the only way to gain domestic unity for an active foreign policy? Nixon's critics divided into two schools of thought on this question and, ironically, what divided them was the same set of issues that in 1946 separated multilateralist free traders from cold war militants.

One trend of dissident national security thought during the Nixon years emphasized that the failure of overseas expansionism lay not in the theory but in the practice. There was nothing wrong with a *Pax Americana*, according to the advocates of this position; the problem was that Vietnam was the wrong place to test its principles. Therefore, the United States should return to an emphasis on global expansion, but with less of the "do-everything" gusto of Maxwell Taylor. As Paul Nitze, for example, viewed the matter, two contrasting answers had emerged when Defense Secretary Clark Clifford asked his staff for a way out of Vietnam in 1967. (Nitze had been Clifford's under secretary.) "In one view," he went on, outlining his own, "U.S. foreign and domestic programs would continue, indeed might become more serious as a result of Vietnam, and could well call for ever more emphasis and greater prudence than had been devoted to them in the past."[36] Nitze was suggesting that the United States had not been resolute enough in its quest for empire and would have to do better next time.

"In the contrasting view," Nitze continued,

> the problems of the past had arisen largely from our own errors springing from overemphasis on foreign policy, and particularly its defense aspects. Those taking the latter view believed that the USSR presented our only military threat and that that threat could be deterred with forces less than those that had already been authorized. Therefore—so the argument ran—significant cuts could and should be made in a wide variety of defense programs requested by the executive branch. It was hoped that the Soviet Union would agree to make certain parallel cuts, or at least reciprocate by restraining some of its own programs.[37]

With these words, Nitze was trying to summarize the point of view of his own assistant in the Defense Department in 1967, Paul Warnke. (Nitze's feelings for this position were emotional; he viewed Warnke's ideas as "screwball, arbitrary, and fictitious. . . .")[38] What Nitze had to recognize was that a significant group of cold war expansionists had recanted; chastened by their failure in Vietnam, they were willing to consider an alternative to a reliance on military force as the chief tool of American foreign policy.

The yawning gap between Nitze and Warnke, both of whom had worked together at one point, was symbolic of the disarray that had come over the national security managers as the limits to a reliance on cold war militarism were revealed. On the one hand, there was a vocal coterie of former Democratic policymakers who formed the Committee on the Present Danger and the Coalition for

a Democratic Majority. These men—Nitze, Dean Rusk, Walt Rostow, and others—believed, with Eugene Rostow, that "the program
of Soviet imperialism is based on a military build-up without parallel in modern history. . . . In many significant categories of military
power, the Soviet Union now has more military strength than the
United States."[39] Rostow called for "true détente," by which he
meant a sharp increase in the cold war. His position was a reitera-
tion of NSC-68 and the Gaither Report—a third incantation of the
Soviet threat and the need for the United States to beef itself up
militarily in order to meet it.

This time there was strong opposition to a resumption of
automatic anticommunism. Men like Warnke, Cyrus Vance, Leslie
Gelb, and Anthony Lake all began to articulate, during the Nixon
years, a position that called for a greater reliance on diplomacy
as an alternative to military force. Gelb, for example, claimed that
Vietnam should have taught policymakers a number of lessons,
among them that military power is meaningless where the political
conditions do not permit it and that the "domino theory" was absurd.[40] Vance and Warnke endorsed a report of the United States
Committee for the United Nations that called for reduced military
spending.[41] Lake had resigned from Kissinger's State Department
with a blistering attack on imperial pretentions in southern Africa.[42] As they groped toward an alternative, these men's views
began to resemble the multilateralist free-trade position of 1946,
before it had been linked to militarism. They were the heirs of
Cordell Hull and Will Clayton, men trying to formulate a global
strategy that would enable America's economic might, unfettered
by an atavistic tolerance of military force, to dominate the world.

The critics of military expansion had a program that made a
certain amount of economic sense. Lower levels of defense spending would reduce inflation, strengthen the dollar, leave more
money in the budget to counter sluggish growth, and enable the
United States to regain a positive sense of self. But as sensible as
their strategy might be economically, it faced the same political
stalemate that existed in 1946, only intensified. No such program
could hope to win political support unless it mobilized a popular
majority for peace in order to overcome the entrenched power of
the military–industrial complex.[43] Yet men like Vance and
Warnke, gentleman free traders, were simply too aristocratic and
tied to elite institutions to conduct a popular campaign for anything. Much more than the unreconstructed expansionists, they

possessed a program that might enable the United States to exercise political choice; but much less than those expansionists, they lacked the ability to fashion a domestic basis that would enable them to do it.

The reverse was true of the imperial activists like Nitze and Rostow. These men were urging a return to the cold war; but they were doing so at a time, unlike the 1940s, when the dollar was falling, when other countries (less dependent on inefficient military production) were increasing their share of the world's trade, and when domestic inflation was rampant. Under the economic realities of the late 1970s and early 1980s, the foreign policy of the 1940s would play havoc. Yet, although a return to militarism would flirt with economic disaster, politically it was still the only popular response. Congress would respond positively to increased Pentagon spending; foreign adventure would distract attention from domestic disabilities; and the old pattern of bipartisan support for overseas expansion could be reestablished. As was the case with domestic policy, there was no viable political alternative to expansionism.

These two groups—chastened empire builders and unreconstructed expansionists—would clash when the Carter administration assumed office in 1977. Each side was flawed, one by its political naiveté, the other by its economic irrelevance. How the unreconstructed expansionists won is a story that must await chapter 8. For the moment it is enough to emphasize that, by the late 1970s, America's political stalemate was even more severe than it was in the late 1940s. In terms of foreign policy, America had an elite in despair, one faction knowing what to do but not how to do it and the other knowing how but not knowing what. So long as each side managed to prevent the other from winning, America's foreign policy was tied in knots, incapable of acting, but also unable not to act.

# VI

# Nationalistic Internationalism

WITH THE DISCOVERY of a *Pax Americana*, the United States solved, for a time, the problem of how to organize the world's power, but still unresolved was how to structure its wealth. Creating a set of global economic rules was as compelling an issue to postwar policymakers as developing a set of political ones. Because the most fundamental decisions about the international economy are made by nation states, Congress and the executive branch would be called upon to determine the direction that America would take toward the economic systems of other countries.

International economics is an arcane subject, replete with impenetrable jargon and passionate devotees of diverse schools. As much as one might be tempted to sympathize with those who resist these matters, one must not succumb. For the decisions that were made by the United States on subjects like currency and trade—more properly, the decisions that were not made—would come to reenforce America's impasse, as anyone who has watched the value of the dollar plummet can testify. As the 1980s begin, America finds itself at the mercy of worldwide events: the Germans and the Japanese make goods more efficiently than the United States; countries once dependent on America have higher employment rates and lower inflation rates; jobs flow overseas faster than oil flows in; to win the confidence of international bankers, the United States must put its own economy into recession; in the absence of an effective international currency, the Europeans have created their own monetary system; international economic disorder promotes analogies to 1914; and the entire world economy seems enmeshed in a recession, heralding a new era of protectionism and slow growth. Not all these effects can be attributed to a single cause, but the peculiar way in which expectations of growth shaped America's participation in the international economy over the course of the postwar period played a major role in bringing this impasse about.

# I

SPEAKING ABSTRACTLY for the moment—specific details follow shortly—there are two general ways in which any national economy can relate to the rest of the world: autarky and integration. While the advocates of each position often mimick the scholastics in their denigration of the other, each approach has its merits, each its defects. In addition, the advantages and problems of each depend upon whether one is considering issues involving trade or issues involving currency and finance, for they are different in their implications. While every political system will combine elements of autarky and aspects of integration, the choices of whether to lean one way or the other in trade and currency matters are among the more fundamental political decisions that a system has to make.

Debates over the degree of free trade constitute one of the longest-running soap operas in the drama of economic controversy. Autarkic notions, which trace their modern roots back to Friedrich List and the Prussian campaign to catch up with the British, seek through governmental actions to carve out an area in which the domestic economy can have some room to shape itself. By following a protectionist course, government attempts to establish a haven that will influence the overall level of domestic investment, the amount of money in circulation, and the rate of employment. Protectionism, in other words, has the sure advantage of bringing human intervention to bear on forces often held to be outside control. But there are costs. Free-trade advocates claim that autarky brings about slow growth; and in general, though not for the reasons they sometimes state, they are right. It is not so much that with free trade capital and labor can move about to the most efficient utilizers. It is more that autarky implies restrictions on the freedom to invest abroad or to participate freely in international transactions, leading international business to threaten a "capital strike" if their desires are not fulfilled. Regimes that carry through on their economic nationalism can lose the confidence of international business and suffer less growth, though more for political than economic reasons.

Currency questions are quite different. Monetary internationalists generally favor the creation of a reserve currency that will add liquidity to the world economy and enable it to grow. International expansion enables poorer countries to obtain access to wealth; and, like domestic income redistribution, it acts with a multipler effect to stimulate demand. Thus, John Maynard Keynes, who was something of a protectionist on trade matters, was a confirmed internationalist on monetary affairs. Since his objective was full employment, he supported national planning, which required restrictions on free trade, but he also supported international liquidity, for that would increase the overall performance of the world economy and therefore increase domestic employment as well. The great advantage of international liquidity, then, is that it enables some planning to take place in the world economy, shifting resources from surplus areas to scarcity areas, for example. The disadvantage of internationalism is that national elites must relinquish some of their sovereignty, which not only courts extraordinary political opposition but also leaves the nation state less able to engage in domestic planning.

It should be clear from even these introductory remarks that while debate on autarky versus integration rages over the presumed economic advantages of each, the decisions about them are taken politically. Countries that dominate the world economy gravitate toward free trade on automatic pilot, while those in a less privileged position instinctively try to close their economies. Even within any particular country, the position taken by a specific firm often has more to do with its power than with its production process. The most powerful firms, such as monopolistic industries insulated somewhat from competition (domestic and overseas), will promote free trade, while less powerful sectors are drawn toward autarky. The Chrysler Corporation, for example, generously free-trade in outlook when few Americans drove Datsuns, shifted to protectionism when more of them did. Finally, arguments against free trade will be heard from labor when policies that once expanded the economy seem to throw people out of work, from small businessmen losing out to concentrated industries, and from farmers protected by high price supports. Those who search for consistency on free-trade questions will be as frustrated as those who look for legal logic in arguments to the Supreme Court; in both cases, it all depends on who is being harmed. Much of the confusion surrounding international economic policy is based on the fact that political questions are discussed as if they were economic strategies.

As a political decision, the choice of whether to be open or closed to the world economy after World War II was one of the most important decisions the United States faced. All signs pointed to integration with the world economy. Free traders were in the ascendancy in the State Department under Cordell Hull, and monetary internationalists were strong in Henry Morgenthau's Treasury Department. Yet, because this decision was so crucial, in neither trade nor currency matters, I will argue, was it made. Free trade, at least in its pure form, was incompatible with the strategic interests of the United States, especially in Western Europe, and was too elitist for a political culture still attracted to conservative isolationism. Monetary internationalism, which made substantial economic sense, faced relentless opposition from Congress and from a united banking establishment. The domestic political stalemate, in other words, was just as powerful in this sphere as it was in so many others. Needing to develop an approach to other countries, but unable to do so, the United States simply linked its most intense domestic nationalism to institutions and policies that seemed international in appearance, giving itself the benefits of both autarky and integration at the same time. This combination, politically remarkable, was so replete with internal contradictions that it could not, except under one highly unusual condition, work. Unfortunately for America, that one condition—unrivaled economic power—existed. Confident that the world economy and the American economy were the same, policymakers developed a solution to trade and currency issues that was completely unique, a blending that I will call nationalistic internationalism. Exempted from the dilemmas that face most societies at most times, America went about the business of strengthening its national economy and the world economy at the same time.

The flaw in an otherwise perfect picture was fairly easy to spot from the beginning. What is good for the nation state is not necessarily good for the world, and vice versa. Protecting the former, the United States incorporated the national interest into its international activity, but the hegemony over the world economy that made such an eclectic approach possible was undermined as the approach itself began to work. As that took place, the United States either had to suppress growth abroad in order to maintain its advantage, or to channel growth into American-based multinational companies. Both were tried, yet there was no way that the fantastic American advantage over the rest of the world could be maintained forever. As other countries closed the gap between themselves and the United States, the one condition that enabled nationalistic internationalism to overcome its internal problems disappeared, and the compromise no longer made any economic sense. Yet, even though policymakers at home knew it no longer made sense, they were prevented by the domestic political stalemate from finding a new approach. Thus, the same program that worked to American advantage at the start of the postwar period worsened America's economic performance at the end. As the United States continued to pursue a nationalistic course when the international economy was no longer synonymous with its domestic economy, it left other countries no choice but to seek their own course against America in the 1980s.

## II

AMERICA HAS GENERALLY BEEN SUSPICIOUS of the rest of the world, but in the years before World War II its nationalism was particularly virulent. After rejecting the League of Nations treaty, the United States insisted that German war debts be repaid and that repatriations be collected. (Both actions, aside from their dubious political wisdom, placed financial strains on war-weakened economies and thereby held down global economic growth.) American bankers, making huge profits as they expanded into the world's vacuum, did not seem especially interested in allowing the dollar to assume the role once played by the pound sterling as a currency reserve. Finally, American trade policies contributed to the instability. Interested in selling its goods overseas, but also searching for ways to protect domestic markets, the United States oscillated, finally adopting the highly protectionist Smoot-Hawley Tariff Act of 1930. As was the case with the more traditional aspects of foreign policy, America's approach to international finance was shot through with isolationism.

Even before America's entry into World War II, the Great Depression convinced a number of Roosevelt's policymakers that such nationalism was inappropriate for the postwar order, should it ever arrive. In its initial zeal, the New Deal was somewhat protectionist; advocates of economic planning like Rexford Tugwell and Raymond Moley sought bilateral trading relationships and quantitative restrictions on imports that would enable Washington to retain some control over the domestic economy. More conservative free traders, especially Cordell Hull at the State Department, fought against this perspective, emerging victorious with the adoption of the Reciprocal Trade Agreements Act of 1934. As the New Deal slowly swung in an internationalist direction, it turned to global economic expansion as a solution to domestic unemployment. Planners in the Treasury Department took the lead in articulating the notion that if the New Deal concerns with economic expansion and income redistribution were applied to the world economy, such a global Keynesianism would rebound to the domestic advantage of American workers.

While Hull and his assistants developed plans for a free-trade order, Secretary of the Treasury Henry Morgenthau and his economic assistant Harry Dexter White concerned themselves with the shape of the postwar monetary system. Between 1939 and 1941, when White was busily writing papers on monetary reform, a similar effort was being undertaken in London, where an unpaid adviser to the British Treasury, John Maynard Keynes, was also considering the nature of the postwar world. As Keynes and White began to meet together, their thoughts, despite differences in tone and nuance, were unusually similar. Hoping, to reorganize the international system to prevent depression and war, both men put their faith in international liquidity. Their idea was that an expansion of the global economy would give each national economy more wealth, thereby providing a "floor" that could prevent a vicious cycle leading into depression. "The lesson that must be learned," wrote Harry Dexter White, "is that prosperous neighbors are the best neighbors; that a higher standard of living in one country begets higher standards in others; and that a high level of trade and business is most easily attained when generously and widely shared."[1] Toward this end, White proposed, as did Keynes, that an international mechanism be created that could provide liquidity to countries hit by adverse economic circumstances. Whether called a Stabilization Fund (White) or a Clearing House (Keynes), both ideas represented what a Treasury Department memo called "a New Deal in international economics."[2]

White's plan for a Stabilization Fund was an attempt to introduce government-based economic planning on an international scale. The Treasury Department experts, as Richard Gardner has commented, "considered government control of financial policy as the key to the objectives of high employment and economic welfare"; and for that reason, their aim "was not to restore a regime of private enterprise but to create a climate of world expansion consistent with the social and economic objectives of the New Deal."[3]

Not surprisingly, such an objective ran into intense opposition from the forces that gathered after 1938 to limit domestic reforms. "Franklin and I moved the money capital from London and Wall Street to Washington, and they hated us for it, and I'm proud of it," Morgenthau wrote in his diary. "The important issue was who governs, and the New Deal made the government govern American banking and monetary affairs."[4] Hoping to remind the secretary who, in fact, did rule, businessmen and bankers were determined to fight White's plan. Schemes to promote international liquidity, said the Guaranty Trust Company, are "dangerous"; they would "substitute fallible human judgment and discretion for the impersonal action of the markets in regulating balances of international payments and foreign exchange rates."[5] Having fought, and lost, a struggle with reformers during the early phase of the New Deal, conservatives were determined to make up the ground they had lost once the war came to an end. There would be no New Deal in international economics if they had any influence.

Keynes and White met together periodically to coordinate their plans for postwar financial institutions, agreeing finally on the need for an International Monetary Fund (IMF) to provide liquidity and for a World Bank to spur overseas investment. Keynes, representing a declining industrial power, sought a highly expansionist role for both of these institutions. To the British negotiator, any effective postwar monetary body should be "a genuine organ of international government."[6] To perform this idealistic role, the fund and the bank had to be given substantial resources, and, more important, their decisions had to be removed from the political control of any one nation state (by which point Keynes had in mind the United States). Although White understood that, economically speaking, Keynes's ideas made a good deal of sense, he also knew that, politically speaking, he could never put his signature on any agreement that diluted American sovereignty. By 1944, when both men arrived at Bretton Woods, New Hampshire, to negotiate their remaining differences, White, who was as ambitious as he was brilliant, decided to compromise, even eliminate if need be, the New Deal aspects of his plan in order to win domestic approval.

Both the fund and the bank were significantly altered at Bretton Woods to bring them more in line with the nationalism of Republicans, bankers, and isolationists. On every major issue that came up for discussion, White argued against his better judgment.

Choosing political acceptability over economic theory, White defeated Keynes's notion of providing the fund with $32 billion in liquidity, sponsoring instead a plan to give it $9 billion (which would be reduced by $1 billion when the Soviet Union dropped out). White went even further in rejecting Keynes's plea to have the fund's resources be unconditional. The United States insisted on the following conditions with respect to drawing rights: they must be limited to contributions; they must be taken in the currency in which they were to be repaid; they must be dependent on making internal economic adjustments; and they must be contingent on no outflows of capital. Rather than protecting vulnerable economies from a depression, which had been the original idea, the fund was becoming a device to ensure the dependence of poorer countries on the market. The IMF that came out of Bretton Woods, like domestic macroeconomic planning in the United States, was counter-Keynesian, designed to do the opposite of its original, reformist intention. Keynes himself agreed to these changes only with the greatest reluctance, knowing that America had the power in these matters and that the choice was between a fund on American terms or no fund at all.

The transformation of the World Bank was also drastic. In his original 1942 proposal to Morgenthau, White pictured the bank as a public lending institution actively engaged in sponsoring social reform. That notion had gone out the window as soon as bankers and the State Department had their input. Then the United States drew the bank's charter more tightly with every passing day of the Bretton Woods Conference. First, the U.S. delegation stripped the bank of its actual ability to lend money, giving it instead only the authority to guarantee loans made elsewhere. Then it tightened the criteria under which a loan guarantee could be made. (For the technically inclined, reformers wanted the ratio of loan guarantees to capitalization to be set at 300 percent of unpaid subscriptions, while conservatives argued for 75 percent; the final agreement was 100 percent.) Dean Acheson expressed the political imperative well. "The most important thing," he noted, was to "assure that the bank can function at all, and in order to function at all it must be sure to build up confidence—people must believe that it's guarantee is good, that it is conservatively run."[7] Winning business confidence was as much a Democratic party objective in international finance as it would become in domestic macroeconomic policy.

When the Bretton Woods Agreement was finally signed, a new

approach to the world economy had been created. New Dealers had been arguing for a system that would be international in scope, creating financial and commercial practices that would preserve peace and avoid depression by limiting the prerogatives of national business elites. The latter, conversely, were suspicious of globalism, arguing for a system in which domestic ruling classes would retain their privileges. What emerged from Bretton Woods was neither. A body of international institutions had been created, such as the IMF and the World Bank, but they did not have the power to contravene the national sovereignty of the United States. Possessing an international form but dominated by a national content, this approach can only be described as *nationalistic internationalism*, a compromise hybrid that took the principles of autarky and integration and placed them side by side. Under the plan that emerged from Bretton Woods, every country in the world save one would be subject to the imperatives of the international market. The one exception was the United States. America would be able to retain its nationalism, even while supporting globalism.

Yet the struggle over the form that nationalistic internationalism took had only just begun, for the Bretton Woods Agreement now faced a U.S. Congress that had been seized by an attack of demagoguery. Congressional Republicans seemed to agree with Henry L. Carr, president of the First National Bank of Philadelphia, who found White's ideas, no matter how compromised, "to be based upon the same idealistic but totally impractical collectivism that has characterized so much New Deal thinking of the last twelve years."[8] Robert Taft denounced the agreement as "pouring money down a rat hole" and made it known that "no international body should have any jurisdiction over the domestic policies of the United States."[9] Winthrop Aldrich of the Chase Manhattan Bank thought the agreement a dangerous innovation, while *The New York Times*, which in 1943 had called the gold standard "the most satisfactory international standard that has ever been devised,"[10] editorialized against it. That quirk in American political discourse that led conservatives to attack economic expansion or urban renewal as if they were socialist reforms motivated attacks on the nationalism of Bretton Woods as if it was world government. Harry Dexter White, seeing the virulence of the attack, asked Roosevelt to hold the line; we have given everything we could, he argued, and the time has come to defend internationalism on its own terms, to make a case for economic participation with the rest of the world. Roosevelt, who knew a stalemate when he saw one, gave as much ground as he dared to win conservative support. "The Congress," Gardner wrote, "would be given assurances that the fund would operate in accordance with the national interests of the United States."[11]

With passage of the agreement looking dubious, a critical political intervention took place. Up until 1945, the campaign for Bretton Woods had been led by New Deal reformers like White who moved sharply to the right to win conservative support. When there was no place left for such men to move, businessmen from the monopoly sector shifted to the "left" and came out strongly for Bretton Woods. Crucial testimony, for example, was provided by Beardsley Ruml, the treasurer of Macy's, former dean of the School of Business at the University of Chicago, and an activist in the Committee for Economic Development. The CED, which also played a key role among businessmen in winning support for counter-Keynesianism, jumped onto the pro-agreement bandwagon. Ruml was seen everywhere, talking to senators, badgering bankers, convincing industrialists.[12] Active support for the agreement from Ruml and other businessmen took the steam out of the right-wing lament. With advocates of Bretton Woods making strong claims about its contribution to world peace—"Less trouble, and less expensive, than building a bomb shelter would be a letter or wire to your senators and representatives urging ratification of Bretton Woods"[13]—the agreement handily passed the Senate. A strong coalition of the center, uniting New Deal reformers with monopoly-sector businessmen, made nationalistic internationalism possible.

Morgenthau and White were overjoyed to have Bretton Woods ratified, but their apparent victory was a dubious one. What had begun as a campaign to control bankers concluded by being controlled by them. Ratification was not the culmination of a New Deal in international economics, but a return to power of those discredited by the Great Depression, although this time in an international guise. The coalition that made the fund and the bank possible was based on two concessions: American national sovereignty would be preserved and no curbs would be placed on the private sector. In order to satisfy these conditions, the institutions created had to be stripped of the powers that they were supposed to embody. To be politically acceptable, Bretton Woods would have to be made economically ineffective. It would have neither the liquidity nor the international character that would enable it to avoid recessionary downturns.

Any remaining doubts about who "won" Bretton Woods were dispelled at the first meeting of the IMF in Savannah, Georgia. Keynes, who was still hoping for some enlightenment from the Americans, came to Savannah under the impression that, with the congressional controversy over, the fund could be reoriented to its original purpose. What he did not count on was the emergence of the Truman administration and the increasing American belligerence as the cold war began to heat up. Truman's economic advisers, Fred Vinson and John Snyder, seemed to take special pleasure in humiliating Keynes in Georgia. The British at one time had wanted the fund located outside the United States but, unable to win on that point, argued that it should be placed in New York, on symbolic parity with the United Nations. The United States refused even to consider the point, flatly declaring that the fund would be placed in Washington. ("This decision," Gardner wrote, "was an important victory for the idea of close national control of the Bretton Woods institutions. It was to have a profound effect on their future development.")[14] Other decisions—such as the high salaries paid to the executive directors and the veto power possessed by the American government over the U.S. representatives to these institutions—strengthened the point. Truman wanted the voters to know that the days of White and Morgenthau were gone for good. (White, who was called a communist by Elizabeth Bentley, had become a political embarrassment, and Morgenthau, who had hoped to prevent the reindustrialization of Germany, was out of favor with cold war expansionists like Paul Nitze.) The virulence of the nationalism expressed at Savannah shocked Keynes, who returned home to die in a couple of weeks, "his castles," as his biographer wrote, ". . . falling around him."[15]

The fate of the bank was similar. When its presidency became vacant, Truman considered it his mission to appease Wall Street (whose main contribution to the bank had been to oppose its creation). He appointed to the office John McCloy, who was emerging as a leading cold war expansionist. McCloy then, with a dramatic flourish, fired Harry Dexter White's disciple Emilio Collado from his staff position. (Collado was anything but a radical. He would become a major adviser to the Rockefeller interests; but, in the atmosphere of the late 1940s, simply believing in international business was somewhat suspect.) Under McCloy, as I will show in the next chapter, the World Bank worked to suppress growth in the Third World by imposing tight-money policies. Whatever lingering dreams of liquidity and internationalism remained by 1946 were destroyed. Institutions that had taken their name and form from liberal internationalism would become the vehicle for the triumph of conservative nationalism.

# III

NATIONALISTIC INTERNATIONALISM was a compromise so filled with contradictions that it never should have worked. Built into this hybrid from the moment of creation were tensions that would ultimately tear it apart: strategic and economic objectives worked at cross-purposes; the dollar was both a national currency and an international currency reserve; and a U.S. reliance on payments deficits to finance national objectives aroused international hostility. Yet, one factor would, for a time, mollify the impact of these tensions. So long as the United States was the dominant economy in the world, it could pursue national and international objectives at the same time. (Contained in that statement, of course, is its converse, that when the United States was no longer the dominant economy, the two objectives would begin to undermine each other.)

One of the strongest beliefs to emerge out of World War II was the idea that protectionist blocs cause war, while free trade preserves peace. As relentlessly argued by Cordell Hull, only the creation of a multilateral trading order in which no country or bloc of countries could prevent the free flow of goods would be able to avoid the mistakes of the past. Multilateralism, as I argued in the previous chapter, was the primal urge of the State Department, but its adoption was impossible in the postwar years because of its elitist nature and because it made America vulnerable to the rest of the world. Seeking some way to gain congressional approval for European economic cooperation, the Truman administration linked the Soviet threat with economic aid and won support for the Marshall Plan. But with national security, an overwhelmingly domestic objective, grafted on to international trade, a pattern was established that made multilateralism unrealizable.

Two of the most basic features of Hull's internationalism were reciprocity and nondiscrimination. The former meant that one country would pledge to reduce duties on goods in return for a promise from another country to do likewise, while the second principle established as policy a refusal to give preferential treatment to any specific country or groups of countries. (The British, for example, discriminated in favor of goods from the British Empire.) As the emphasis shifted from an international concern with free trade to national security considerations, the United States gave up on both objectives. By sponsoring the Marshall Plan, the United States substituted regionalism for multilateralism,[16] tying its commercial policy to the promotion of European recovery (and Japanese, when the United States, over European objections, negotiated *bi*lateral agreements with that country). Strategic considerations would ultimately become so important that the United States would encourage Western Europe to discriminate against *American* goods. The United States supported the creation of a European Economic Community (although insisting that American corporations in Europe be treated equally with European ones) out of a desire to replace global economic integration with regional power politics.

Once Marshall Plan aid subsided, the American desire to trade with Europe was financed by military aid in the form of rearmament. Five hundred seventy-six million dollars in direct military expenditure left the United States for Europe in 1949, but this increased to $2.6 billion in 1953 and then to $3.4 billion in 1958.[17] This overseas expenditure enabled the Europeans to buy American surplus production and therefore to keep domestic employment high; in this sense, European rearmament was a massive transfer of funds from the American government to American corporations, "laundered" by being passed through Western Europe. Rationalized as a security measure, aid for arms could pass a Congress that would oppose global trade in other forms, yet once again a strategic interest would come into conflict with an open world economy. Later on, U.S. arms for Europe would be found to have negative economic impacts, but because they had been provided as a "security" measure, the United States would have to provide them anyway, thereby contributing to its own economic difficulties. Militarizing aid was an inflexible, if politically feasible, way of providing it.

A second major problem that would emerge with nationalistic internationalism was the liquidity gap in the postwar world economy and the attempt to use the dollar to fill it. Under the influence of conservative nationalism, the United States had rejected at Bretton Woods Keynes's proposal to increase the amount of money available to the world. Given the fact that the world's supply of gold was limited, and that inflation would cut the real value of a relatively fixed supply, an automatic limit on liquidity came into existence. Yet the world was about to experience a growth boom and needed to find the funds for it somewhere. Since the United States had pledged to convert gold into dollars at a predetermined rate, the world's need for funds became tied to the accumulation of dollars. The American dollar took on a dual (and eventually contradictory) role in the world economy. First, it was the national currency of the United States, but, second, it was also the world's reserve currency, the major form in which international trade took place. Under this remarkable system, which was never planned but which was a direct result of the U.S. refusal at Bretton Woods to discuss the problem of scarce currencies, worldwide economic growth could occur only if the United States was willing to run large balance-of-payments deficits. For what may have been the first time in the history of world trade, the growth and stability of the international economy required that a major participant be in deficit.

An immediate consequence of American nationalism at Bretton Woods was that gold and dollars began to flow overseas. Although the U.S. deficit averaged around $1.6 billion between 1950 and 1956, it shot up to $3.8 billion in 1958 and 1959.[18] Long-term private capital left the country at increasingly higher rates, and government loans and grants contributed even more to the deficit. In addition, the United States lost its monopoly on gold. In 1950, the U.S. share of the world's monetary gold, reserve currencies, and IMF reserves was 49.8 percent and Britain's was 7.1 percent. Exactly twenty years later, the United States held 15.7 percent and Britain 3.1 percent. Most of the slack was taken up by Japan and continental Europe, their combined shares increasing from 7.3 percent in the earlier year to 37.7 percent in the latter.[19] These outflows were not perceived as all that serious during the 1950s— the Eisenhower administration seemed barely interested in the subject—but they would become increasingly problematic as time passed. Robert Solomon points out that visits by two American secretaries of the treasury to Europe symbolized what was taking place. In 1949, flushed with arrogance, John Snyder traveled to London to convince the Europeans to devalue their currencies.

Eleven years later, Robert Anderson more humbly visited Europe to ask for its help in reducing the American payments deficit.[20]

In and of themselves, payments deficits are not harmful. Just as a country can run domestic deficits in order to encourage economic stimulation, a balance-of-payments deficit under certain conditions can be a desirable objective of economic policy. The third major contradiction inherent in nationalistic internationalism was the particular way in which the United States treated its deficits. The outflow of dollars during the 1950s threatened to produce inflation and monetary instability, since there were more dollars in the world economy than countries or financial institutions wanted to hold. Yet the United States opted to defend the system because it could be turned to national advantage. Although there is some controversy about how to measure the phenomenon, the United States was able to rely on the dollar's role as an international currency reserve to finance part of its domestic expenditure. Since every country that held dollars was involuntarily paying for America's prosperity, this system enabled the United States to achieve its nationalistic objectives, even as it aroused international hostility. The first to indicate his displeasure was Charles de Gaulle, who devalued the franc against the dollar between 1956 and 1958 as a way of enabling France to obtain some of the benefits from growth that were flowing to the United States. The issue would return later when other countries made it clear that they did not appreciate the privilege of paying for the U.S. intervention in Vietnam.

These developments should have revealed the precarious nature of nationalistic internationalism. Every attempt by the United States to protect its domestic economy could at some point harm the international economy, yet that point seemed to lie somewhere beyond the horizon. "The central problem of international economic cooperation," writes Richard Cooper, a leading economist and policymaker, ". . . is how to keep the manifold benefits of extensive international intercourse free of crippling restrictions while at the same time preserving a maximum degree of freedom for each nation to pursue its legitimate economic objectives."[21] Cooper is saying that most countries at most times have to find the delicate balance between national and international needs. The most remarkable feature of nationalistic internationalism was that it enabled the United States to absolve itself from this quest. Under the practices established at Bretton Woods, the theoretical conflict between national and international imperatives simply disappeared. America was able to pursue domestic objectives like military strength, dollar growth, and the international financing of national projects, and at the same time, despite spoilsports like de Gaulle, to organize the world economy as well. For one brief period in human history, a society did not have to make a fundamental political choice between nationalism and internationalism.

The reason for the privileged position of the United States was easy to see: for a time, the U.S. economy and the world economy seemed to be the same thing. When Bretton Woods was negotiated, U.S. economic strength in the world was overwhelming. As I pointed out in chapter 2, nearly half the world's manufacturing in 1946 was produced in America, an astounding figure for that time or any other, while the United States controlled three-quarters of the world's gold supply. Such fantastic hegemony made it possible for American international economic policy to have the best of two contradictory worlds. It literally was true that what was good for America was good for the world, and vice versa. Under that kind of giddy unreality, a compromise like nationalistic internationalism made sense.

All America had to do to keep its compromise intact was to stop the world from changing. Since one of the outstanding features of capitalism is that it constantly transforms itself, nationalistic internationalism was premised upon an end to history, a utopian quest to do what every socialist revolution had failed to do, which was to freeze economic relations in place. The whole compromise, in a word, was based on a fantasy, simply impossible to maintain for long. Yet, even though policymakers knew that the solution was flawed, they could not develop an alternative to it, for the domestic political stalemate would prevent movement toward greater internationalism. In the way they obtained congressional support for Bretton Woods, the Roosevelt and Truman administrations had let an ornery cat out of the bag. By agreeing to the more extreme prejudices of nationalistic elites, rather than attempting to rely on the international spirit generated by the war effort, they set in motion a process by which any participation in the world economy had to be cast into conservative language in order to gain approval. Political realities in the United States prevented movement toward global integration, even as the global nature of trade and commerce prevented any movement back to autarky. The United States was stuck with a compromise that made less and less sense.

In every area of policy discussed in this book, the solution to awkward political compromises was found to be economic growth. Rapid expansion could cover up the internal defects, whether it was an economic policy that sought the opposite of Keynesian remedies or a domestic pursuit of social justice that was highly beneficial for those who made profits from poverty. This would become true in international economic policy as well, but with a unique twist. Nationalistic internationalism was premised upon American hegemony over all other countries. The pursuit of growth at home, then, could help the compromise, for the more rapidly America grew, the greater its potential advantage. But if the United States were to help expand the world economy, which it was committed to do for strategic reasons, then its relative share of the world's output would be likely to decline, for countries with less absolute wealth will grow at a more rapid ratio than those with more. In other words, to maintain nationalistic internationalism, the United States would be in a strange position, trying to expand its own economy while suppressing the growth of other economies. The growth coalition that sponsored public works, imperial adventures, and domestic expansion, unless it found a solution to its dilemma, threatened to become a growth coalition without growth, a group of people committed to expansion everywhere except in the world economy.

Over time, the growth coalition would find a workable solution to its dilemma. The expansion of American multinational corporations operating overseas gave the growth network what it needed, a way to expand in the world economy without detracting from American domination. But until multinational investment became more important in the 1960s, the growth coalition found itself in the uncomfortable position of suppressing growth in the world as a whole. For example, during the 1950s, a group of reformers urged that the IMF be expanded along the lines originally suggested by Keynes, but the United States argued for deflationary policies as a condition of receiving IMF funds. Another example was a plan put forward by the United Nations Economic and Social Committee to develop counter-cyclical policies aimed at full employment in foreign countries.[22] Both plans would have increased international liquidity, thereby relieving pressure on the dollar. Both would have enabled other countries to expand. Both, in a word, were the kind of policies that growth advocates should have favored. But, because either plan would have reduced American hegemony in the world economy, American policymakers opposed them. Although it seemed absurd for a growth coalition to prevent the world from growing, this was a direct result of the domestic political stalemate. It was not until an administration that was pledged to act came to power, but was prevented by political realities from taking any action, that the full import of these difficulties would be revealed.

## IV

WHEN JOHN F. KENNEDY became president, one of his first plans was to do something about the gold drain. Consulting Wall Street as he went about choosing a secretary of the treasury, Kennedy was told that the outflow of gold was the single most serious issue facing the country. He responded by appointing none other than Paul Nitze to report to him on the question. Nitze talked to his Wall Street friends and then told Kennedy what orthodox opinion had to say on the matter: "The early appointment of a Secretary of the Treasury who enjoys high respect and confidence in the international financial world would do more than anything else that your committee can think of to consolidate confidence in the international payments position."[23]

The choice was not an easy one for Kennedy to make. The gold drain was a direct result of the nationalistic proclivities that Wall Street had forced on international economic policy in the first place. (Had the United States accepted Keynes's idea of a Clearing House, remarks Richard Gardner, it "would have accumulated some $30 billion in unconditional liquidity—enough to finance virtually all the U.S. deficits in the 1950s and 1960s.") Wall Street, in other words, was demanding that something be done, but that the policy that was causing the problem not be touched, which is why Nitze's most important recommendation was a purely symbolic one, appointing a new treasury secretary. If Kennedy followed this advice, there would be only one way to stop the gold drain and that would be to deflate the economy at home. No wonder that nearly all of Kennedy's advisers, most of them passionate believers in growth, urged him to reject this course, for following Wall Street's advice would mean restricting the economy to achieve international objectives at the same time that the administration was expanding it to achieve domestic aims. In spite of the inherently absurd nature of what Kennedy was being urged to do, he did it anyway, for the new president felt that he would never be politically safe unless Wall Street accepted him. Nitze's suggestion was adopted and a Wall Street investment banker (and a prominent Republican) was appointed secretary of the treasury. (In an ironic parallel with the development of the *Pax Americana*, Kennedy cited the need to have a "bipartisan fiscal policy" as the reason for his appointment of Douglas Dillon, as if the making of economic policy could ever be beyond political controversy.) The choice of Dillon (over Tennessee's populistic Senator Albert Gore) was a signal to conservatives that although Kennedy's heart may have beaten with Morgenthau and White, his head leaned toward Acheson and McCloy.

Stymied in one direction, Kennedy thought of trying to control U.S. military expenditure abroad, another cause of the financial drain. "The surplus of our exports over imports," he noted, "while substantial, has not been large enough to cover our expenditures for United States military establishments abroad."[25] The easy way to solve that problem was to cut those establishments, which should have been easy, given the fact that European recovery had taken place and that the Soviet Union seemed willing to consider a European settlement. But just as Kennedy's domestic liberalism was an obstacle to deflation, his overseas expansionism prevented a diminution of the *Pax Americana*. Kennedy could not rely on a simple reason like economic sanity to remove American troops from Europe when the whole thrust of American policy hinged on a Soviet threat. If anything, Kennedy's advisers were Europe-firsters, determined to increase military spending on the continent after eight years of what they considered to be Eisenhowerian neglect. Economics seemed to demand cuts in American military spending overseas, but politics indicated otherwise. Kennedy tried to avoid the problem by asking the Europeans to assume more of the burden of their own defense, with farcical results. Understanding American politics better than Kennedy, the wily Europeans simply allowed notions like a Multilateral Force to die, knowing that in the end Kennedy could not allow himself to appear soft on military spending. In a sufficiently Jamesian denouement, Kennedy wound up increasing military spending in Europe, thereby worsening the gold drain that he was pledged to stop.

Understanding at some level that much of America's problems with the world economy was due to excessive nationalism, Kennedy did make an effort to shift in a more internationalist direction. Committed to trade liberalization, he introduced the Trade Expansion Act of 1962, strongly endorsed British membership in the Common Market, and began the Kennedy round of tariff negotiations under the General Agreement on Tariffs and Trade (GATT). Yet each of these starts was delayed. The political stalemate was still severe, and Congress did not pass Kennedy's tariff cuts until 1967, meanwhile amending the Trade Expansion Act to facilitate the growth of multinational corporations in Europe. At the same time, the French, still resentful of the postwar political compromises and fully as nationalistic as the United States, initially rejected British membership in the Common Market. Both domestic and international political realities, in a word, prevented Kennedy from taking the kind of decisive and immediate action that his rhetoric demanded.

Unable to alter the compromise over nationalistic internationalism, Kennedy could only tinker around the edges. The president entrusted the tinkering to an investment banker who had been an executive of the Federal Reserve Bank of New York, Robert Roosa. Roosa was, as tinkerers go, a maestro. He shuttled around the world managing crises, propping up the dollar, and using every ad hoc solution in the books to stop the gold drain. But what Roosa could not do was to shift the compromise one way or the other. "It does seem to me mistaken," he told the joint luncheon of the American Economic Association and the American Finance Association in December 1963, "to assert that international monetary reform is needed in order to eliminate the dollar as a reserve currency . . . or that much larger and more automatic availabilities of liquidity could have significantly modified the elements that have been found essential for the American balance-of-payments program in the conditions of these past few years."[26] Thus, Roosa strongly opposed a plan developed by the internationalists around Kennedy to use the IMF as a source of more flexible exchange rates, greater liquidity, and monetary expansion. That plan, like so many other proposed reforms, would have enabled the United States to sponsor greater growth abroad, but since it would detract from American hegemony (and court the opposition of Wall Street) Roosa combined forces with Dillon to block it. At the same time, Kennedy was presented with a plan from Hendrik S. Houthhakker and other Harvard economists to devalue the dollar by 15 percent, a conservative option. The administration was not permitted even to discuss the notion.[27]

By the time of Kennedy's death the situation had reached a complete impasse. Nationalistic internationalism was producing gold and payments deficits; yet, as problematic as they may have

seemed, both outflows presented the United States with enough of
an economic advantage to prevent any changes. In addition, any
basic reforms of the nationalistic compromise over internationalism
were impossible to bring about given the strength of conservative
opposition. The worst thing that could happen would be a sharp
increase in overseas spending, one that would so exacerbate the
payments problem that the compromise would be in danger of
crumbling. This was the step that Kennedy, and then Johnson,
took, the increase in overseas spending being called Vietnam. That
war took an international order that was showing signs of strain
and thoroughly disrupted it. Aside from the obvious domestic
impact from Vietnam, especially inflation, overseas intervention
also tore apart the compromise over international economic policy.
An estimate made by Michael Hudson concluded that "overseas
military spending represented the whole of America's balance-of-
payments deficit during the 1960s, deranging the Western economic system that the cold war had originally sought to cement."[28]

As the war exacerbated the trade and currency outflows, firmer
action to reorganize the nationalistic compromise over internationalism seemed called for. The most obvious solution was to
place controls on the export of capital, thereby reducing the
drain on gold in a more effective way than limiting what American
tourists could spend in Paris. But mandatory capital controls, like
wage-and-price policies at home, are an example of supply-side
intervention; Democratic administrations, unwilling to tackle one
type, were hardly willing to attempt the other. Fully counter-
Keynesian in their policies, the Kennedy and Johnson administrations sought tame measures that would not antagonize business.
Kennedy first proposed an interest equalization tax in 1963 and
then a voluntary program of export controls organized around
jawboning (highly visible attempts to talk businessmen out of
doing what they say they are going to do). Johnson's plan, tried
from 1965 to 1968, was to have the government consult with leading businessmen about how much investment abroad would be
beneficial to the U.S. economy as a whole.[29] (Eventually mandatory controls were proposed at the end of the Johnson administration and implemented under Nixon.) For most of the 1960s,
liberal administrations were prevented from placing controls on
the export of capital by their need to win business confidence.

In an analogous domestic situation, activisits, unable to intervene on the supply-side, chose economic growth as an alternative.

Such talk was heard during the 1960s for international economic policy as well. For example, a 1963 Brookings Institution study pointed out that the "U.S. balance of payments . . . improved during periods of rapid growth and deteriorated when growth was slow or absent. . . ."[30] Domestic expansion, these economists noted, should bring down the payments deficit in five years. The Brookings economists, like most Americans, did not count on the Vietnam War, the inflationary impact of which was leading a number of congressional leaders, especially Wilbur Mills, to demand slower rates of spending at home. With the traditional growth remedy inappropriate, Kennedy and Johnson, despite their self-proclaimed activism, were prevented from acting. Yet there was one solution to the payments problem that would not arouse firm opposition from Wall Street and could win Democratic presidents praise from business. While the difficulties being described here were taking place, so was a dramatic increase in the investments undertaken by American multinational corporations abroad. U.S. overseas direct investment, which was around $45 billion in 1960, increased to $71 billion in 1965 and then to $128 billion in 1972.[31] As multinational corporations expanded their operations, they financed their activities out of excess dollars held in Europe, thereby offsetting the effects of the balance-of-payments deficits.

As was the case with counter-Keynesianism, the expansion of the private sector, in this case the multinational corporation, became for liberal Democrats the solution to international problems in the same way that it had been used at home to finance social policy. "Faced with a deteriorating balance-of-payments situation," Robert Gilpin has written, "the United States government began to regard the multinational corporations and their growing overseas earnings as the means to finance America's hegemonic world position." Producing the foreign exchange to secure America's interests abroad, "The multinational corporation enabled the United States to resolve, at least in part, the conflict between American economic and security interests."[32] No wonder that Henry Fowler, Johnson's treasury secretary, could say that "the United States government has consistently sought, and will continue to seek, to expand and extend the role of the multinational corporation as an essential instrument of strong and healthy progress through the free world."[33]

Once they came to rely on the multinational corporation, Democratic presidents found a solution to the problems inherent in

nationalistic internationalism. A growth coalition unable to grow in
the world economy could lift off the shackles, so long as international growth was limited to American corporations operating
overseas. American policy increasingly inclined to support the
expansion of multinational enterprise, for example by providing tax
breaks for overseas investment, by demanding special status for
American subsidiaries in the Common Market, and, finally, by creating the Overseas Private Investment Corporation in 1969 to
subsidize losses caused by governments that had the temerity to
nationalize American operations in their countries. As liberal
administrations encouraged multinational investment, they found
the global equivalent of counter-Keynesianism. Whereas Keynes
had sought an international system in which nation units would
give up sovereignty to a form of world government, America had
created a system in which the international economy would give
up its privileges to support a national institution, the multinational
corporation. The same liberals who worked their way out of a
domestic impasse through the expansion of the private sector
found a way out of the international impasse through the same
method. No longer would a growth coalition have to suppress
growth; it could throw its energy into multinational corporate expansion and preserve American nationalism while simultaneously
participating in the international economy.

During the 1960s, there was an outburst of multinational investment so unprecedented that American politics still feels the
impact. The scope of this activity has been richly documented and
illustrated by writers like Richard Barnet and Ronald Müller, and I
need not repeat their figures and examples here.[34] Suffice it to say
that the expansion of overseas investment in the 1960s revitalized
the pro-growth network. Wall Street, which in the earlier part of
the decade had been suspicious of internationalism, now began to
see the virtues of overseas growth, so long as it was under the
control of Americans. Monopoly-sector business, more than ever,
gave its support to liberal administrations, particularly after the
Republican party became dominated by the Goldwater faction.
The growth coalition that was formed in the 1940s, in other words,
was given a new lease on life with the rise of the multinational corporation. Big business, finance, and a smattering of organized
labor—the ingredients that, mixed together, would produce Trilateralism a decade later—unified themselves around an international economic policy whose contradictions were overcome by

multinational investment. Nationalism, it turned out, was internationalism, and vice versa.

The new expedient was only a temporary one. No sooner had America come to rely on the multinational corporation than the flaw in this solution revealed itself. Overseas investment can be a blessing when the domestic economy is growing as well, for growth at home and growth abroad reenforce each other in symbiotic bliss. But if the domestic economy stagnates, as it began to do in the late 1960s, then multinational investment is not so wonderful. A somewhat schematic presentation may make the point clear. Before the drastic increase in multinational investment, policymakers were in the uncomfortable position of trying to expand growth at home while limiting liquidity in the rest of the world. When multinational corporations and the domestic economy grew together, as they did for most of the 1960s, then both national and international goals could be pursued together. But when the domestic economy declines, policymakers find a new stalemate: stimulating overseas expansion comes at the risk of intensifying stagnation at home. Any administration facing a declining domestic economy is in the reverse position of those on the upswing of the postwar growth curve. In an expanding economy, nationalistic needs shape international participation, but with the economy in decline international demands limit national options. The Nixon administration would be the first to have to deal with the new reality.

# V

IN THE SHORT TEN-YEAR PERIOD between 1965 and 1975, such fundamental changes took place in the world economy that generations from now the effects will still be felt. Major historical disruptions seem to occur in bunches. This was certainly the case as the world experienced the collapse of Bretton Woods; an international recession and ongoing slowdown; an unstable structure of basic commodity prices; the quadrupling of oil prices and an income transfer from oil-consuming to oil-producing states; a political awakening in the Third World; wheat sales from the United States to its ostensible ideological enemy; a setback to the world's food reserves; intractable inflation; excessively cold winters; currency speculation; famines; increased arms sales; international violence and terrorism; and the upsetting of entrenched political coalitions in one country after another. It was in this atmosphere that nationalistic internationalism began to unravel.

Underneath all the changes taking place was one that had extraordinary implications for American policy: the relative decline in the American share of the world's output. Although policymakers had done their best to stop the dynamics of capitalism, manufacturers and bankers will shift resources anywhere they can make profits, and the net result of interdependence was a narrowing of the gap between the rest of the world and the United States. The relative changes in the proportions of the world's gross national product in the time under discussion are given in the following chart:

Distribution of World GNP, Selected Years, 1950–74[35]

Percent

| Country or group | 1950 | 1955 | 1960 | 1965 | 1970 | 1974 |
|---|---|---|---|---|---|---|
| *Industrial Countries* | | | | | | |
| United States | 34.2 | 33.3 | 29.7 | 29.4 | 26.5 | 25.1 |
| Western Europe | 24.4 | 24.9 | 25.2 | 25.0 | 25.3 | 24.8 |
| West Germany | 5.2 | 6.5 | 7.1 | 7.1 | 6.9 | 6.5 |
| France | 4.8 | 4.7 | 4.7 | 4.9 | 5.0 | 5.1 |
| United Kingdom | 5.5 | 5.0 | 4.6 | 4.2 | 3.6 | 3.3 |
| Other | 8.9 | 8.7 | 8.8 | 8.8 | 9.8 | 9.9 |
| Japan | 2.8 | 3.5 | 4.3 | 5.5 | 7.3 | 7.7 |
| Other OECD countries | 3.8 | 3.8 | 3.7 | 3.8 | 3.8 | 3.8 |
| USSR | 11.4 | 12.1 | 13.0 | 13.1 | 13.1 | 12.8 |
| Eastern Europe | 4.7 | 4.8 | 5.1 | 4.8 | 4.6 | 4.9 |
| *Developing Countries* | | | | | | |
| Noncommunist | 12.3 | 12.5 | 12.5 | 13.0 | 13.1 | 14.6 |
| OPEC | n.a. | n.a. | n.a. | n.a. | n.a. | 2.8 |
| India | 2.7 | 2.6 | 2.5 | 2.3 | 2.2 | 2.1 |
| Brazil | 1.0 | 1.1 | 1.2 | 1.2 | 1.3 | 1.7 |
| Other | n.a. | n.a. | n.a. | n.a. | n.a. | 8.0 |
| China | 3.1 | 3.6 | 3.9 | 3.7 | 3.7 | 3.7 |
| Residual | 3.3 | 1.5 | 2.6 | 1.7 | 2.6 | 2.6 |

Source: Adapted from U.S. Department of State, *The Planetary Product in 1974*, Publication 8838 (November 1975), p. 14.

n.a. = Not available.

These figures indicate that with the exception of India the only countries or economic blocks whose relative position declined in the postwar years were Britain and the United States. America's share of the world's output dropped from one-third to one-quarter, a fairly drastic change for a twenty-year period.

As this decline in America's hegemony took place, disorder seemed to threaten the world economy. The two areas of the world that showed the most spectacular growth were Japan and that part of Europe that includes West Germany, the Benelux countries, northeastern France, and northern Italy (called "Lotharingia" after the name of Charlemagne's second son, who was once put in charge of the region). The emergence of these areas, in part due to U.S. support for their growth as a strategic move, undermined the entire postwar international settlement. Signs of cracking began to appear in trade policy: for example, disputes between the United States and Japan over textiles or between the United States and the Common Market over food. As the decline in East–West tensions closed the geopolitical umbrella under which joint economic ventures were taken, automatic cooperation between the United States and its allies could no longer be expected.[36]

"A declining overall world role for a country," C. Fred Bergsten has written, "produces a declining world financial role for its currency."[37] Monetary instability was a clear sign of the lack of hegemony. It was becoming impossible for the United States to continue to run balance-of-payments deficits as a means of providing liquidity to the world economy. As the United States became more reluctant to convert foreign dollar holdings into gold, dollars accumulated overseas took on their own momentum, constituting a source of vast currency speculation beyond the regulatory powers of any nation state. Gold reserves in the United States dropped so precariously in March 1968 that the most serious international financial crisis since 1929 seemed in the making. European and Japanese governments began to blame American deficits for inflation in their countries and increasingly sought cooperation among themselves as an alternative. Some of the pressure was alleviated with the creation of Special Drawing Rights as a source of liquidity in 1970, and by other ad hoc arrangements such as the German pledge not to convert gold into dollars in return for troop commitments in that country. But it was obvious to policymakers on both sides of the Atlantic (and Pacific) that the growth of Japan and Lotharingia meant at some point a basic change in the use of the dollar as an international reserve.

Richard Nixon's administration would be the first to try and develop an alternative to nationalistic internationalism in a situation of declining American hegemony. As he turned to the task, two difficulties presented themselves. First, multinational corporations were no longer the unmixed blessing that Kennedy and Johnson thought they were. Second, in part due to the first, the domestic consensus that existed on international economic policy was in a state of shock, so that making a move in one direction was sure to raise anger from another.

Multinational corporations pride themselves on making investments where they can obtain the maximum profits. So long as the domestic American economy and multinational corporations were growing together, overseas investment worked to the benefit of both. But with Europe and Japan becoming ever more profitable sources of investment, American overseas companies, aided by an expanding Eurodollar market that gave them access to liquidity, were less likely to repatriate profits back to the United States. Deprived of a dynamic new source of investment at home, America's economic troubles piled up. In 1971, the United States experienced a *trade* deficit for the first time in a century, indicating that it was losing some of its ability to compete with manufacturers in other countries. Since some of the manufacturers in other countries were U.S.-based corporations, the irony was clear. The interests of the American economy and the interests of American multinational corporations were no longer the same. If any incumbent administration were to do as Kennedy and Johnson had done, which was to facilitate the growth of American investment abroad, it would be paying for its own death warrant. The pro-growth strategy that had emerged in the 1960s to reconcile national needs with the international order, if continued, would produce a program of expanding the international economy at the expense of the United States. Richard Nixon would have to find some other method than relying on the growth of multinational corporations to solve America's problems in the world economy.

There was some constituency for a new approach. Organized labor, especially the AFL, was very unhappy about overseas investment, and businessmen from the competitive sector were upset at the gains being made by the multinationals. Uniting these forces, the Nixon administration turned in a protectionist direction, especially under the leadership of Treasury Secretary John Connally. But at the same time, multinational corporations had become so powerful and expansive in the 1960s that no president could ever ignore their influence and hope to survive. Whatever Nixon's protectionist sympathies, he was a Republican, close to big business, and his major national security adviser, Henry Kissinger, was a protégé of the Rockefeller family. As the domestic consensus over nationalistic internationalism fell apart, Nixon was in potential political trouble whichever way he turned. Too much protectionism, and the dreaded "establishment" would increase its criticism of him; too little, and he would upset the Republican heartland and lose his ties to conservative unions. Given these cross-pressures, the making of international economic policy under Nixon was contradictory and ad hoc, shifting back and forth from a program of national self-sufficiency and autarky to plans for global integration, as if one part of the administration did not know what the other was doing.

Nixon at first approached the problem by trying to do nothing. Borrowing a term from domestic policy, economists like Gottfried Haberler, Thomas D. Willet, and Lawrence B. Krause suggested that a passive strategy of "benign neglect" be adopted or, more precisely, not adopted.[38] The advocates of benign neglect proposed that the United States simply allow international currency markets to settle where they may and concentrate on other matters. Nixon was tempted. The idea of doing nothing seemed to suit one part of his personality (though it violated the other). Moreover, support could be had from conservatives like Milton Friedman who favor free-floating exchange rates, and such a strategy prevented a deflation of the economy that might hurt the president's reelection chances in 1972. (Under such conservative doctrines, the Republicans would announce free-floating policies once again in April 1981.) For all these reasons, benign neglect began to attract supporters. Much activity was devoted to the promotion of inactivity, and the absence of a policy was cited as evidence that a new policy had been found. A good way to deal with political problems was to deny their existence.

Benign neglect could only be carried so far, given the fact that the problems lay beyond American control. As the problems of the dollar sharply worsened, Nixon just as sharply reversed himself, and on August 15, 1971, he announced his New Economic Policy, which, like Lenin's, was a repudiation of what he had previously said. Nixon officially removed the United States from the Bretton Woods Agreement, formally ending the nationalistic internationalistic compromise. The United States would no longer convert dollars into gold; and America, looking out for number one, imposed a 10 percent surcharge on imports. In the eternal struggle between autarky and integration, Nixon was opting for the former. John Connally was unleashed to inform the world, and American-based multinationals, that the days of free trade were over. Henry Kissinger, intent on creating an opening with China, consistently exacerbated American trade differences with Japan. (Indeed, Kissinger was so preoccupied with strategic matters over economic ones that, of the 140 National Security Study Memoranda that he authorized in the first three years of the Nixon administration, only one dealt with a review of international monetary policy.)[39] The Republicans, the party so favored by big business, were courting opposition from the biggest businesses of all, the free-trade-oriented multinationals.

Had Nixon continued along this path, he might have been able to work his way out of America's impasse by shifting toward a more explicitly nationalistic solution. But dramatic events at home and abroad would muddy the waters. At home, of course, there was Watergate, and few multinational businessmen were sorry to see Nixon go. While Nixon was fighting to hold on to power, the earthquakes of 1973 hit the world. Between March and October of that year, the world experienced four major upheavals: a March currency crisis leading to the adoption of floating exchange rates; an April speech by Henry Kissinger that seemed to question the whole concept of an Atlantic partnership; a summer series of American export embargoes on agricultural commodities and scrap metal, the epitome of the new American protectionism; and, as if this were not enough for one year, the October Middle East war, the Arab oil boycott, and finally the quadrupling of oil prices.[40] These shattering events would have been difficult for any administration, but for Nixon, defending himself on the home front, they were especially severe. Not only had the ground been prepared for them by previous Democratic compromises over which he had had no control, but those same Democrats were prepared to attack him whatever he did. Nixon had the sense to understand that nationalistic internationalism would no longer work, but his attempt to find a nationalist solution was brief. Hobbled by these domestic and international events, Nixon could just hang on, a policy also adopted by Gerald Ford. If there was a solution to the collapse of American international economic policy, it would have to come from a new administration.

With Nixon and Ford unable to govern, America's economic problems intensified. A policy that had been designed to reconcile national needs with international order was now proving ineffective. On the one hand, the United States was suffering from all the problems of an open world economy. American workers were losing jobs overseas, productivity at home was declining, the United States was importing inflation from abroad, American consumers were at the mercy of overseas commodity producers, and currency instability was making the dollar as loved in Europe as the Black Death. The advantage of an open world economy should have been more rapid growth, yet, with increasing protectionism, the United States was also suffering from stagflation and lower rates of investment. Nationalistic internationalism, once the solution to contradictions, was itself a contradiction. Politically autarkic while economically integrated, America under Nixon was being punished by the very policies under which it had once been blessed.

Watching as Nixon helplessly shifted back and forth from one pole of the problem to the other, the multinationals and their allies, now confirmed internationalists, rethought Bretton Woods and realized that the United States had made a mistake. Forming the Trilateral Commission under the leadership of David Rockefeller, they mobilized the resentment that had built up against Nixon on the part of international businessmen and started preparing the way for a new growth coalition to come to power. The trouble with nationalistic internationalism, the Trilateralists concluded, was that it was much too nationalistic. "Today's Secretary of the Treasury," wrote Trilateralist Richard Gardner, "might well be tempted to summon the ghost of Henry Morgenthau and ask: 'Why didn't you accept Keynes' plan?' "[41] Forgetting that history rarely repeats itself, the commision met and suggested that the United States simply go back and adopt what it had rejected in 1944, even down to proposing the adoption of bancor, the name Keynes had given to his international currency.[42] Thirty years too late, investment bankers learned that you cannot combine autarky with integration in one package. Now that a choice had to be made, they would reverse Nixon's course and advocate internationalism over parochialism. But times had changed, and what might have been possible in the late 1940s would no longer work in the late 1970s. The Trilateral Commission, however, would not make this discovery until one of its members, Jimmy Carter, tried to revive an international course and found the domestic opposition too strong.

# VII

## Developing Development

IN THE 1970s, America discovered the world. The decade began with the United States unable to remove itself from a war that it could not win, proving, as the British had done with their Boer escapades, that its empire was less imposing than it seemed. Just as the limits of American military power asserted themselves, so did the limits of its economic power. When a group of oil-producing states announced a boycott, a shudder of anger and a premonition of impotence filtered into the heartland of the United States. A decade that began in ignominy ended in rage. Rioting Pakistanis burned down the American embassy in Islamabad, the American ambassador to Columbia was held hostage for two months, and Iranian students held for over a year the personnel that embodied America's interest in their country. It seemed as if a world divided into thousands of ethnic, linguistic, and regional differences had in common a distrust and suspicion of the United States.

It may seem hard to believe, but there was a time in the recent past when America's image in the Third World was quite favorable. Independence movements in former colonial possessions looked to the most successful war of independence of them all for guidance. (Both Ho Chi Minh and the Irish Republicans swore by the Declaration of Independence.) Too late to join the European scramble for colonies, the United States issued anticolonial pronouncements to the world, angering the Europeans, but stirring responsive chords from India to Africa. Americans, thinking themselves a generous people, had a tradition of organizing humanitarian missions, such as Herbert Hoover's relief work and the post-World War II reconstruction of Europe. Especially when compared to the older powers (including Russia), the United States came out of World War II in a marvelous position to benefit from friendly relations with the poorer countries of the globe.

Sympathy from the Third World was a tremendous asset for any country about to become a world power. At least four reasons to retain friendly relations with the newly emerging nations were fairly obvious. First, underneath the earth in nearly all of these countries, as the Paley Commission pointed out to President Truman, were vast amounts of resources to which the United States would clearly need to gain access some day. Second, some of the decisive battles of World War II were fought in places like North Africa and the South Pacific, making evident both the strategic significance of the Third World and the importance of friendly feelings on the part of the people who lived there. Third, the poor countries had high population densities, which businessmen automatically translate into large markets. As these countries became wealthier, they would be able to buy American goods and contribute to prosperity at home. Finally, a less quantifiable factor could not be ignored. The Third World was poor, while America was rich. Some program of humanitarian aid would simply be the right thing to do, and, because it was the right thing to do, it would win that ever-precious asset known as good will. One of the major policy items on the American political agenda as World War II ended was how to cultivate the positive feelings toward America that existed and to build upon them a creative approach to the majority that lived in the world.

The story of America's impasse is not complete until the chapter that tells of its failure to gain respect and sympathy where it would need both is recounted. In an era of limits, much talk is heard about the squandering of precious resources. Behind America's impasse lies the waste of the resource upon which oil, copper, and human labor depend: the world's good will.

Certainly the need to develop a policy toward the Third World was well enough understood. Liberals in both political parties made a compelling case, often based on the reasons just advanced, for why the United States should provide humanitarian assistance to the developing nations. A successful appeal was made to President Truman, who issued a ringing call for an aid strategy. Yet in spite of the intellectual recognition that surrounded the question of foreign aid, the United States was unable to offer the world help on terms that the world in good conscience could accept. The same political stalemate that blocked policy in so many areas blocked it in this one as well. Humanitarian aid could not come into existence until it was transformed into something acceptable to conservatives, the military, and businessmen; and when it was duly transformed, it no longer bore much resemblance to humanitarian aid.

The political problems facing a foreign aid program were many. For one thing, the mere notion of humanitarianism was suspect as America embarked on a course characterized by real-politik. In imperial America, more so than in most places, sympathy for the poor on moral grounds excludes one from the policymaking process; entry into the halls of power demands that one put aside humanitarian notions and enter the rough-and-tumble "realism" of the dominant discourse. Beyond that, liberals had to confront the fact that poverty, which may not be nice, can be very profitable, and a goodly number of American businessmen were making substantial profits from it. To bring about a new policy toward the emerging nations, moreover, tight-money policies favored by banks would have to be repudiated, military urges curbed, and isolationist sentiments suppressed. In short, humanitarian assistance required an extension of the New Deal overseas, yet the New Deal at home had already been stymied. How would a country unable to pass legislation improving the lot of its own poor fashion a program for a global attack on poverty? Conservatism at home was a sure check on liberalism abroad.

Unable to win support for a program of humanitarian aid, but needing to develop some kind of policy toward the emerging nations, America embarked on a course that resembled neither chintzy isolationism nor a global New Deal. Instead, America developed something called development. Aid would be given, not because it was right, but because it would make other countries more like America. Assistance would help the poor countries participate in the growth explosion, bringing them out of their poverty without tampering with the economic arrangements that caused their poverty in the first place. In order to fashion a domestic compromise over policy toward the Third World, the United States created an economic myth. It sponsored the notion that the world's majority was poor because of insufficient economic growth, not because a global structure of power deepened and extended that poverty. Ostensibly bringing growth to the Third World, America deepened the poorer countries' dependency on the very forces that made them poor in the first place. Development was a chimera, an absurd objective based upon a faulty analysis. Yet once it was discovered, so was a way out of the political stalemate. Growth abroad would link itself with growth at home to create a situation in which all would benefit.

When the postwar economic upsurge came to an end, America's development strategy was left in shambles. The same world that existed in the late 1940s—a huge gap between poverty in the South and wealth in the North—was discovered still to exist. But whereas the earlier period was characterized by some sympathy toward America, in the latter the United States stood isolated from humanity, trying to wriggle out of its impasse with little help from Lagos to León. Americans in the 1980s are angry that Third World countries treat them with so little respect. They must look to the fact that when the world asked for help, the United States offered it growth instead. A policy capable of producing domestic unity was premised on the exacerbation of international discord.

## II

FRESHLY INAUGURATED in 1949, Harry Truman characteristically expressed a particularly American form of idealism. After announcing the three major points of his foreign policy—for the record, they were support for the United Nations, European recovery, and military assistance—he paused dramatically and then announced a Point Four: "a bold new program for making the benefits of our scientific advances and industrial progress available for the improvement and growth of underdeveloped areas." Defending his call, Truman struck a note not unfamiliar to a population that had recently survived the Great Depression. "More than half of the population of the world are living in conditions approaching misery. Their food is inadequate. They are victims of disease. Their economic life is primitive and stagnant. . . . The old imperialism—exploitation for foreign profit—has no place in our plans. What we envision is a program of development based on the concepts of democratic fair-dealing."[1] His administration, he suggested, was not going to turn its back on the poor people of the world.

Seaching to discover a legislative outlet for its Point-Four rhetoric, the Truman administration consulted forty-three government agencies, created task forces, met with numerous congressmen, and eventually drafted what became the Act for International Development of 1950. The result of these discussions was that the bill introduced by Truman was recast in less heartrending language in order to win the approval of a conservative Congress. In the hearings on the bill, the administration emphasized two points. First, Truman and his advisers, concerned about domestic overproduction and possible unemployment, pointed out that development assistance would enable the underdeveloped countries to buy American products and thereby preserve jobs at home. Second, the administration stressed the security issues involved. As Dean Acheson testified, foreign aid, "as a security measure . . . is an essential arm of our foreign policy, for our military and economic security is vitally dependent on the economic security of other peoples."[2] Once expressed in a language appropriate to the political realities of the time, the act managed to pass.

But, though now law, foreign aid no longer bore much resemblance to the spirit of Truman's message when he announced his Point-Four program. Development aid might have been a wonderful idea in theory, but in practice almost every group that exercised some political power opposed it. Businessmen, especially those from the competitive sector of the economy, were still strong in Congress, and they announced their general opposition to foreign aid unless it were offered in the form of loans with strict (and profitable) repayment schedules. Congress, which was not disposed to offer money to a Western Europe presumed to be under the Russian gun, was even less likely to provide it to colored peoples who did not, in the congressional view of these matters, seem to want to work. Labor leaders had instinctive protectionist sympathies, looking upon humanitarian assistance as a plot to deprive Americans of their jobs. Given these attitudes, the Act for International Development had little immediate impact. The technical assistance programs begun under the law were absorbed into the military-oriented Mutual Security Program, and W. Averell Harriman, director of the program, announced that less than 10 percent of its funds would go to technical and economic assistance in the Third World. Business opposition, moreover, ensured that most of the money transferred overseas would be loans, and there were not many takers. Humanitarian assistance had gone from rhetorical declaration to oblivion in record time, about one year.

America not only refused to help the world's poor, it also seemed intent on punishing them. Such was the approach of the International Bank for Reconstruction and Development (or World Bank), created in 1944. The World Bank, as I pointed out in the previous chapter, was originally designed to provide loans to ensure both reconstruction and economic development. But with strong opposition in U.S. financial circles to any programs that violated strict principles of financial orthodoxy, Truman and Acheson redrafted the bank's charter to win conservative approval. This trend continued in the first years of the bank's existence. When John McCloy, for example, became president of the bank, he announced that he would not finance any "soft" loans, i.e., those which bypass in one way or another strict repayment criteria. Moreover, the bank insisted that loans be repaid in the currency in which they were borrowed, thereby making it impossible for many countries to make them. As if this were not enough, the bank then further imposed direct political criteria on the lending process. Under the policy known as "strategic non-lending," the World Bank insisted that recipient countries take no steps to curtail the scope of their private sectors. Like a cult leader who demands not just the absence of disloyalty but slavish devotion, the bank's priorities were spelled out by McCloy's successor Eugene Black:

> Governments must cease just tolerating private business. They must welcome its contribution and go out of their way to attract it. And there must be a fundamental reversal of the traditionally hostile attitude by Government and peoples alike toward the profit motive.[3]

One can understand sentiments and practices like these from the perspective of winning political support for the bank from the financial community, without whose cooperation the venture would fail. The bank's policies, as David Baldwin has pointed out, "became, in effect, the policies of the United States by tacit approval,"[4] and little American support could be expected unless steps were taken to overcome the domestic political stalemate in the United States. Yet, by making policies agreeable to powerful business interests at home, the bank lost any chance to be effective abroad. Any smart businessman knows that in order to win business in the future, one occasionally takes a loss in the present. Simple business acumen would have led the bank toward soft loans and even grants for long-term advantage. But, as was so often the case in the postwar period, political obstructionism was more compelling than economic wisdom. Conservative tight-money policies ensured that the World Bank would become a larger-than-life symbol of imperialism throughout most of the Third World.

Currency and trade policies in this period also worked against the interest of the world's poor, whatever else humanitarian rhetoric proclaimed. As I have already noted, the International Monetary Fund never became the device that Keynes had envisioned, helping vulnerable economies to protect themselves from the world market until they were over temporary troubles. Rather, IMF policies proceeded in lockstep with the World Bank. For example, under the principle known as "stand-by arrangements," the IMF would issue a line of credit to, say, a Latin American country in return for "reforms" that would bring the economies of that country more in line with the free-trade preferences of the United States.[5] (Free trade looks different on the two sides of an unequal arrangement; what the hegemonic power finds so pleasant is a crushing burden to the dominated power.) The fund actually did very little lending at all in its first years of operation, concentrating instead on trying to preserve sound money. Its first managing director, Camille Gutt of Belgium, won the praise of *The Wall Street Journal* for his fiscal "common sense," but also won the condemnation of Third World economists whose attempts to lead their countries out of stagnation were inevitably undermined by tight-money policies.[6]

Trade issues in many ways proved the most intractable of all. The United States, committed to free trade, was unreceptive to the Third World argument that for the poor, free trade meant production for export. As they created commodities for the world's markets, these countries would be prevented from diversifying their own economies and helping their own people. (Like the Irish of the nineteenth century who starved to death while growing crops for the world, African countries would send strawberries to New York while unable to feed their own population.) Ironically, Third World countries were asking for the trade policies once followed by the capitalist West, for most of the European economies protected themselves from the world market in order to cultivate infant industries. Third World protectionist demands were incorporated, to a very limited degree, into the Havana Charter of 1946, which created an International Trading Organization to oversee tariff disputes. The Havana Charter was a minimal first step toward an international trading order: it acknowledged temporary exceptions to free trade and placed representatives of the poorer countries on the various decision-making bodies created by the organization.

Dissatisfied by its limited character, Third World countries nonetheless approved the Havana Charter, but the American Congress did not. In a replay of the defeat of the League of

Nations Treaty after World War I (or a foreshadowing of the refusal to consider the SALT II treaty in 1979), Congress simply turned its back on the charter, hostile as it was to any program that was not cast in terms of immediate and direct self-interest. The world was left without a trade agreement, and as a result a parallel set of negotiations, ones never expected to substitute for the Havana Charter, became the basis of the international trading order. This alternative was called the General Agreement on Tariffs and Trade (GATT), and, unlike the Havana Charter, it was dominated by the richer countries and generally ignored the special circumstances of the poorer ones. With GATT setting the rules, free trade became the order of the day.

It was not so much that America was hostile to poor people, for at some level most Americans felt that poverty was a shame and agreed that something should be done about it. The problem was that the liberal concern with development was so heavily counterbalanced by the conservative domination of the policymaking process that only programs constructed to maximize profit in the narrowest possible way could be approved. When it was not making the life of the world's poor harder through needlessly blind financial practices, America was given to offering stern moral lessons about how to save and invest. Winning few friends and influencing fewer people, the United States might have never developed *any* plans for overseas development except for the fact that the underdeveloped countries began to intervene in the world's balance of power. Meeting in Bandung in 1955 and presenting unified demands for the first time, Third World countries proclaimed a certain neutrality between the United States and the Soviet Union that upset the expansionists in both camps. Once injected into the cold war, questions of development would take on a new momentum. It was no longer a question of whether foreign aid would be provided, but of how much and in what form.

# III

THE INCREASING STRATEGIC SIGNIFICANCE of Third World countries led a number of prominent organizations in the 1950s to begin to endorse programs for overseas development. Especially from the globally oriented elite centered around East Coast financial capital, a plea came forward for a new approach. In 1950, a report on foreign economic policy, written by Gordon Gray, had endorsed the transfer of some public capital to the Third World,[7] and the prestigious International Development Advisory Board, chaired by Nelson Rockefeller, agreed, even if cautiously.[8] Seven years later, the Committee for Economic Development issued a policy statement noting the importance of economic growth in the Third World and urging development assistance to supplement private investment.[9] To export-oriented, free-trade industrialists, the Third World was a major potential market and also a possible home for investment, so that building up its infrastructure made sense.

Eisenhower, although a Republican, was not particularly receptive to the notion of facilitating growth in the Third World, in part because his party was seriously divided on the issue. While a more "progressive" faction of the Republicans, called at the time the "Young Turks," were in favor of foreign aid, an intransigent group called the "4-H Club" (after four prominent conservative officials) fought against it. Unwilling to push too hard, Eisenhower searched for a compromise between the hard-loan advocates in the right of his party and the outright-grant advocates in the left, finally settling on a cautious program of "soft" loans tied to the Mutual Security Administration. It was a step, if only a tentative one.

As was the case in other areas of domestic and foreign policy, Eisenhower's conservatism gave rise to a rebirth of activism within the Democratic party. But what kind of activism was it to be? There was, during the 1950s, a feeling articulated by prominent liberals like Walter Reuther and Senator Brien McMahon of Connecticut that humanitarian aid would revitalize the New Deal idealism of the Democratic party. Basing themselves on the sentiments articulated by Truman in his Point-Four message, they urged a no-holds-barred program of direct assistance to the Third World. But, as was the case in 1946, such a humanitarian approach still had negligible political support and seemed hopelessly naive. As envisioned by Reuther and others (like Henry Wallace), development assistance was a measure that would redistribute wealth from the rich to the poor. It therefore relied upon public agencies and contained an implicit admission that the private market was failing. The justification for such aid was that it would provide long-term benefits to the United States, but neither businessmen nor politicians are paid to show a concern with the long run. Such a program, therefore, would be opposed, not only by the Republicans, but by Democrats who had committed themselves to growth policies as a substitute for liberal reforms. A society that was in the

process of adopting counter-Keynesianism, pro-growth urban policies, a *Pax Americana,* and nationalistic internationalism was hardly
likely to provide humanitarian assistance simply because it was the
right and proper thing to do.

There was no chance that the liberal programs advocated by
men like Reuther would be adopted. But there was also no chance
that nothing would be done. With the economic and strategic significance of the Third World becoming more important every day,
the need for an approach to these countries that could avoid the
liberal humanitarianism of the New Dealers on the one hand and
conservative isolationism on the other became everywhere apparent. What America required was an approach to global poverty
in line with the pro-growth, centrist, nonideological programs that
had been developed to deal with other policy matters. To create
such a program was beyond the capability of any politician. For
matters this difficult, academics are called in, and it turned out that
a number of the latter were becoming fascinated by the changes
taking place in the Third World and were in the process of re-
evaluating America's attitude toward those changes. Along the
Charles River in Cambridge, Massachusetts, for example, a number of economists began to meet regularly to explore the problem.
They had much in common. Most of them were already confirmed
counter-Keynesians, committed to reform, but not in a way that
would antagonize business. Many had worked together in the
Office of Strategic Services or the Strategic Bombing Survey during
World War II, where they learned about the world and about the
important role that correct attitudes play in shaping it. Nearly all
of them were attracted to a neighbor named John F. Kennedy who
was obviously running for president.[10] The task that these men—
Edward S. Mason, Walt Rostow, McGeorge Bundy, David Bell,
John Kenneth Galbraith, and Lincoln Gordon among others—took
upon themselves was finding a position in between the isolationism
of the right and the humanitarianism of the left. Their mission
would be to discover the pro-growth equivalent for the Third
World, the proper way to provide the poor countries with aid
without arousing the antagonism of corporate and military leaders.

Discover it they did. These men literally invented a policy that
offered a mechanism for aid in a way that conservatives could
accept. Aid, they argued, was a form of leverage, seed money to
encourage growth in the Third World while simultaneously expanding the economy at home. If growth was good enough for us,

it should be good enough for them. The United States should provide economic assistance so that countries on every continent could participate in the same growth miracle experienced by North America. There was nothing ideological or divisive about economic growth. Everyone believed in it, everyone would benefit from it. It required no radical experiments, aroused no unnecessary passions, and threatened no important vested interests (except landed ones, for feudalism abroad would be replaced by capitalism). Growth implied an economic transformation, not a political revolution; unlike a violent change in the existing order of power, it promised to revolutionize only "expectations." Giving their conception of growth a favorable name, the Cambridge theorists called it economic development. Foreign aid would promote development, earning the gratitude of the masses abroad while allowing the United States to believe that it was doing something good for the future of the world.

There was only one problem with the theory of economic development: it had very little to do with the reason why the poor countries were poor. In order to achieve political unity at home, the theory of development was compelled to ignore the role played by American business firms, the military, and the international financial community in reenforcing poverty. Third World poverty, the world would discover, was as much a political condition as an economic one, based on a lack of power in shaping one's destiny. By concentrating on economic growth, development theorists were avoiding the problem of political choice, which would make their theories irrelevant one day. But while development theories may not have had much to do with Third World economic realities, they had a great deal to do with First World political ones. Once foreign aid was placed into the context of a path toward economic development, assistance to the poor could be made acceptable to the rich. Implicit, and sometimes explicit, in the theory of economic development were a number of factors that softened the domestic stalemate over foreign aid.

First, the Charles River theorists argued that traditional societies were in the exact historical time period to benefit most from foreign aid. Walt Rostow's well-known contribution to the Cambridge seminar was his book *The Stages of Economic Growth.* For Rostow, aid was a form of primitive accumulation. Development, he argued, passed through a series of stages, including the famous "takeoff" stage after which a nation would step into maturity. But the most important stage was the one that came just before takeoff, when a nation faces the choice of what to do with the energies liberated during the anticolonial struggle: whether to direct them inward, outward, or into capitalist accumulation. It is precisely at this point, which, coincidentally, these societies were reaching in the late 1950s and early 1960s, when the intervention of foreign aid could help solidify the choice. Moreover, "It is in such a setting of political and social confusion, before the takeoff is achieved and consolidated politically and socially as well as economically, that the seizure of power by communist conspiracy is easiest. . . ."[11] Foreign aid just before takeoff was thus doubly blessed. First, it would prepare the way for capitalist accumulation, and, second, it would keep the Russians out. In this brilliant way, Rostow provided a crucial feature of the centrist compromise over economic growth. Using economic jargon and lots of graphs, but relying on simple concepts like the takeoff that even noneconomists could understand, Rostow showed how growth in the Third World was a major weapon in the struggle between capitalism and communism.

Humanitarians thought of aid as a goal, an end in itself. Poorer countries would be given money to help them out of poverty; it was up to them to spend the funds in ways of their own choosing. Distinguishing themselves from this notion, the Cambridge theorists made a second contribution to the debate by arguing that foreign aid was not a goal, but a means: in this case, a means toward integration into a global capitalist economy. The American policymaking process was ill-equipped to deal with what Max Weber once called an ethic of ultimate ends. By depriving the process of development of its revolutionary dynamic, by trying, in the words of Max Millikan, "to reduce the explosiveness of the modernization process,"[12] development theorists reassured the American Congress (and the American people) that the question was only one of technique. Debate would concern whether agricultural assistance should be chosen over balance-of-payments reform, avoiding thereby the more political question: development toward what?

Aside from defusing the visionary and idealistic aspects of foreign aid, an emphasis on development was compatible with domestic pluralism, a third major advantage. Within the United States, there would be numerous agencies that would want to administer foreign aid if the program became large enough. Aid, viewed as a means to some other end, could allow each agency and approach to have a say. The Center for International Studies at MIT, which became the home base of development theory, issued a report in 1957 that was read and debated within the National Security Council. Published by Max Millikan and Walt Rostow as *A Proposal: Key to an Effective Foreign Policy*, the report argued that private capital by itself was incapable of meeting the needs of development and called instead for maintaining "maximum flexibility between grants and loans."[13] Rather than placing its bets on any one approach to development, the report called for as many techniques as feasible for stimulating entry into the takeoff period. Such eclecticism helped build a consensus around foreign aid, promising the military one role, agriculture another, and commerce a third. Millikan and Rostow's pluralism was incorporated into the creation of the Development Loan Fund of 1957.

Fourth, the Cambridge people knew that a massive aid effort would be expensive, so they prepared arguments in advance to convince conservatives that costs could be kept down. For one thing, the notion of a takeoff point enabled them to argue that a finite point existed beyond which no more aid would be needed. Also, they suggested, comprehensive planning, using the latest techniques of social science, could be effectively used in the Third World. Evaluation studies and cost-benefit procedures would enable policymakers to eliminate waste. Furthermore, like the pro-growth housing activists described in chapter 4, the development theorists argued that a combination of public and private sources could do the job. While government would put up some of the money, there would also be opportunities for the private sector to build up Hué the same way it would build up Houston. (Brown and Root, a Texas construction combine, would indeed make fortunes in both cities.) The Cambridge group envisioned tax incentives to private corporations to invest in the Third World, low-interest loans, and other techniques of using the public sector to encourage the private sector to expand. On this point, in fact, they often moved further to the right than many business groups, insisting that the techniques they advocated would in no way interfere with sound business practices.

Finally, development was defined in such a way as to make it palatable to the American political culture. Development was just another term for growth, and growth was as American as a Chevrolet. The United States had once been a colony. It had reached its own takeoff point. Wealth, political democracy, and economic expansion all seem remarkably intertwined in North America. As Robert Packenham has shown, the social scientists concerned with development and the policymakers who emerged in the Kennedy administration (they tended to be the same) had a Lockean vision of the benefits of growth.[14] Foreign aid programs would establish democratic regimes abroad because democracy and economic expansion go together. When Kennedy proposed the Foreign Assistance Act in 1961, he asked Congress to help him demonstrate that "economic growth and political democracy go hand in hand."[15] Development, then, need not be controversial. Unlike the humanitarian left, which fooled around with naive visions, yet unlike the isolationist right, which refused to recognize the problem, growth could unite the center in the same way that public works projects, tax cuts, military ventures, and other features of the pro-growth coalition had already done.

Thus, economic development became one more technique in the hands of the pro-growth coalition, another method of developing policy to solve problems without upsetting the interests that were, at least in part, causing the problems. To many of the pro-growth theorists who formulated the approach toward development in the 1950s, making fundamental political choices was irrelevant because there were no fundamental choices to make. Having relied on growth to solve all the problems at home, why not rely on growth to solve them abroad? Here is how Millikan and Rostow viewed the home front:

> The United States is now within sight of solutions to the range of issues which have dominated political life since 1865. . . . The farm problem, the status of big business in a democratic society, the status and responsibilities of organized labor, the avoidance of extreme cyclical unemployment, social equity for the Negro, the provision of equal educational opportunity, the equitable distribution of income—none of these great issues is fully resolved; but a national consensus on them exists within which we are clearly moving forward as a nation. . . . If we continue to devote our attention in the same proportion to domestic issues as in the past, we run the danger of becoming a bore to ourselves and the world.[16]

I cite this passage not simply because it was wrong—fundamentally, dangerously, and myopically wrong—but because it was so much a quintessential part of the growth coalition's outlook on the world. The development theorists who were about to come to power with John Kennedy brought to the world the same apolitical utopianism and technocratic vision that characterized their approach to domestic life. It would not be their mission to create a better world, merely to enable the better world that already existed to realize itself more completely.

# IV

DEVELOPMENT, perhaps to avoid the boredom that Millikan and Rostow mentioned, became *the* issue of the 1960s, the one that mobilized foundations to call conferences and authors to write books. There were at least two reasons for this sudden concern. First, the poorer countries of the world began to speak more loudly. Various attempts had been made to put the issue of development at the center of world concern, such as the debates over a Special United Nations Fund for Economic Development (SUNFED) in 1953. Still in its conservative phase, the United States had opposed all such ventures in the United Nations, calling for further study or simply voting against them. Such opposition could not, however, continue forever. The admission of new states to the world organization created a numerical majority in favor of developmental assistance. Moreover, Third World countries were forming links with each other, eventually to emerge in the form of the United Nations Conference on Trade and Development (UNCTAD). Victorious socialist revolutions like the Cuban enabled nonsocialist regimes to call for aid on the grounds that the alternative was revolution. Third World countries themselves were creating an environment in which the question of development could no longer be ignored.

A second reason for the inevitability of a new approach to the Third World was cold war rivalry. Between the death of Stalin in 1953 and the Twentieth Party Congress of 1965, the Soviets conducted an about-face on the question of relations with the Third World. Repudiating their own domestic isolationists, the Russians contributed to the United Nations expanded program of technical assistance. They financed the Aswan Dam in Egypt and announced plans to help industrialize India, Syria, Indonesia, and Afghanistan. Some American response seemed called for. Douglas Dillon, who would become Kennedy's treasury secretary but who was in 1958 the deputy under secretary of state for economic affairs, expressed the need this way:

> It is of great importance that the American people, now well aware of the technical and scientific challenge posed by the Communist world, understand and rise to meet the equally great, and perhaps more subtly dangerous, offensive which the Sino-Soviet bloc has vigorously launched in the less developed areas. This offensive represents an attempt by the Sino-Soviet bloc to employ its growing economic and industrial capacities as a means for bringing the newly developing free nations within the Communist orbit.[17]

Because they viewed the world as a gigantic zero-sum game, in which any Russian advance was automatically an American defeat (and vice versa), the men who came to power with Kennedy could not help but give foreign aid significant importance once the Russians increased their own preoccupation with this issue.

The only question remaining was not whether large sums would be sent to the Third World but what form they would take. The split that had existed within the Democratic party on this question between humanitarians and the development theorists re-emerged once Kennedy assumed the presidency. Anxious to win the support of intellectuals and to carry forward the idealism of the New Deal, Kennedy brought to power men like Chester Bowles, John Kenneth Galbraith, and G. Mennen Williams, all of whom advocated foreign aid for substantially humanitarian reasons. Bowles, for example, spent a considerable amount of time trying to think through fresh approaches to the Third World. One of his most remarkable notions was a plan for a "neutral belt" in Southeast Asia designed to win Russian support as a counterweight to Chinese expansion.[18] Since it recognized the emerging split between the two great communist powers—something that Douglas Dillon, with his talk of a "Sino-Soviet bloc," was incapable of doing—Bowles's plan was far more realistic than the schemes advanced by the hard-line cold warriors like Maxwell Taylor. (Indeed, had Bowles's ideas been accepted by Kennedy, the United States might well have been spared its humiliation in Vietnam; in the 1980s, Vietnam *is* a Russian ally against China.) Brought into the new administration as undersecretary of state, Bowles pushed hard for a massive program of foreign aid to win the long-term political support of the Third World.

With the exception of Galbraith, the Cambridge development theorists detested Bowles and everything for which he stood. Determined to run him out of Washington, they undercut his influence, telling stories behind his back, holding him up as a buffoon, and demanding that he be fired.[19] For these men, steeped in counter-Keynesianism and overseas expansion, foreign aid was not a gift but an engine of economic growth. It must be provided as a weapon, suffused with realpolitik, stripped of its idealism, and sold to the American people as a hard-headed strategy for dealing with the tumultuous nature of the modern world. The world was in crisis, filled with forebodings of imminent doom. This was no time for woolly-headed idealism and humanitarian gestures but for firm resolve; after all, the "Sino-Soviet bloc" would get there first if we did not act quickly.

Faced with a political choice between two radically different conceptions of foreign aid, Kennedy acted in typical pro-growth fashion, avoiding the choice by adopting both. On the one hand, he proposed the Peace Corps, the Alliance for Progress, and other schemes that pleased the humanitarians. But he simultaneously oversaw an Agency for International Development that would become a weapon in the cold war, expanded the role of the military and the CIA, and chose the global struggle imagery as his theme for legitimating foreign aid to the American people. The new president did not seem to notice that he was adopting two policies, not one. The trick was to sponsor growth in the Third World and political harmony in the First, and a bipolar approach seemed to offer both. Idealistic young people and counterinsurgency specialists could go to Dacca together. Meanwhile, a congressman from Georgia could be as sympathetic to the program as an intellectual from Massachusetts. In other words, foreign aid made the most sense when it was stripped of politics, deprived of an explicit rationale for a specific purpose, and broadened to include as many different interests as could be fitted together within it. But by linking together the best of two worlds, Kennedy was setting into motion the forces that would deny one of them. Between the two conceptions of aid, peaceful coexistence was impossible. Only the unusual economic expansion of the early 1960s made them seem compatible. Gresham's law would work in policy as in currency; over time, the worst would drive out the best.

The Latin American experience offers a good example of the Greshamite inevitability of foreign aid. The area's proximity, some similarities to the United States in tradition (the republics there went through decolonialization long before the emerging nations of the post-World War II period), and the Cuban revolution all combined to give Latin America a particular importance in Kennedy's mind. With dramatic flair, Kennedy the candidate stood in front of the county courthouse in Tampa in October 1960 and announced his commitment to an "alliance for progress" ("development" was the original term chosen by his advisers, but it was rejected on the grounds that Kennedy would be unable to pronounce the Spanish word *desarrollo*; even at that, the president did not include the *el* before *progresso*). The alliance, the future president suggested, would provide long-term development funds, stabilize commodity prices for exports, stimulate land reform, expand technical assistance, bring about arms control for the hemisphere, enlarge student-exchange programs, and, icing on the cake, support democratic as opposed to dictatorial governments. Such an approach, Kennedy claimed, would produce "a great common effort to develop the resources of the entire hemisphere, strengthen the forces of democracy, and widen the vocational and educational opportunities of every person in all the Americas."[20] In short, the alliance would bring economic growth to Latin America and thereby allow the Southern Hemisphere to participate in that bounty of fine things already enjoyed by the Northern.

The alliance began auspiciously. In its first few years, it acted as if reforms were in fact necessary to prevent another Cuba. Projects were undertaken that aroused the opposition of the landowners; U.S. corporations were aghast at American support for social democratic, if strongly anticommunist, politicians; and the so-called winds of change began to blow. Yet the fact that development aid was deliberately stripped of its political character would become the reason that it would soon fail. The experience in Latin America was making clear to those who did not know it already that "growth" was a meaningless term. The problem all along in the Third World was not so much poverty as the structure of power that caused it; in other words, the *political* condition called dependency and not the *economic* condition called underdevelopment was in need of change. Yet America's strategy was the exact opposite, based on the idea that economic development deprived of any political content could bring about a better world. This was inherently utopian, when not deliberately sinister. It would not take long before economic aid confronted political power, and when that happened, as was the case with maximum feasible participation of the poor at home, then the vested political interests that made profits from poverty would attempt to block any economic programs that challenged their privileges.

In the case of urban programs at home, opposition came not only from business but from the pro-growth coalition that had come into existence out of an original concern with the poor. In Latin America, reforms were stopped, not only by American corporations (often working in direct partnership with the CIA), but also by the development establishment itself in the form of the World Bank and the IMF. Both of these essentially political institutions emphasized control over inflation, reduction of debt, and balance-of-payments adjustments, all of which worked to suppress growth in the Third World. The IMF and the World Bank, in other words, were insisting on conditions that made "development" impossible while the alliance was proclaiming the urgency of "development." Something had to give, and, by the time of the Johnson administration, something did.

Kennedy had created the Agency for International Development (AID) to house all Point-Four, Mutual Security, and economic aid programs; and before long, AID was attaching political criteria to the provision of economic assistance. Two officials of the program put it this way: "AID has increasingly recognized that economic aid can promote development not simply by supplementing the host country's limited capital and technical resources but also by exerting influence on host country policies and programs. As we have become more aware of AID's potential leverage role, we have experimented with techniques for exercising such leverage more effectively."[21] Throughout the 1960s, then, AID made its choice between two competing conceptions of development; in order to "exert influence" over another country's "policies and programs," the United States would "experiment" with such devices as program loans (lending money to a country in return for the promise to buy specific commodities from the United States) or other programs that extracted from the "host" a promise to follow tight-money policies in return for aid.[22]

Within Latin America, the Brazilian experience illustrated what the consequences of the U.S. choice came to be. This country had gone through various cycles of stagnation and growth by the time

that João Goulart became president in 1962. In a confusing political situation, facing demands from his own working class for
higher wages and demands from U.S. investors to keep a tight lid
on inflation, Goulart desperately sought some room to maneuver.
Economics Minister Celso Furtado and Finance Minister San
Tiago Dantas came to Washington and negotiated an agreement with the IMF for an austerity program. But Goulart was
unable to impose the program in the face of domestic unrest, and
instead he veered to the left, nationalizing some companies and
sponsoring land reform. Washington then intensified the political
character of its aid policies, sending assistance to anti-Goulart
governors, for example, while denying it to the president. The situation became increasingly untenable. If Goulart adopted reforms, even ones that just three years previously would not have
contravened the principles of the Alliance for Progress, he courted
opposition from the development establishment. If, on the other
hand, he sought to please Washington, he could not govern at
home. Democracy, in other words, was an obstacle to American aid
policies. The impasse was broken by abolishing democracy; the
military intervened, overthrew Goulart, and created a "development"-oriented regime that exists to the present day.[23] The Alliance
for Progress, a plan that linked democracy and development,
within three years saw the former destroyed to realize the latter.

The Brazilian coup revealed that politics and economics were
different when it came to the Third World. No country could
achieve political independence from the United States without
confronting all the forces, including the military, the CIA, and the
development establishment, that worked to perpetuate *depen-
dencia*. But on the other hand, economic development, as defined
by the United States, demanded political subservience to those
same agencies and institutions. In other words, the choice that
Kennedy would not make was made for him shortly after his
death. American foreign aid would be used to perpetuate American political control over the Third World, not to abolish poverty,
bring about a better society, or encourage the poorer countries to
copy the democratic practices of the richer ones. Out went the
humanitarians (Chester Bowles had been sent off to India some
time earlier); in came the cold warriors.

The Agency for International Development turned its attention
more directly to security questions. Between 1962 and 1965, for
example, military programs—training police and junior officers,

crowd and demonstration control, etc.—accounted for 20 percent of all AID funds, but this figure increased to 38 percent in 1966 (in part due to AID efforts in Vietnam).[24] AID funds to the Somali Republic, Yemen, and Afghanistan, in addition, were designated to be "counter-Communist" in intent, not developmental in nature. Lyndon Johnson, who viewed himself as sympathetic to the plight of the poor in North America, had little concern for the same people in South America. Johnson appointed as his chief official for the region Thomas Mann, who shared the Eisenhower approach of encouraging business expansion. In 1965, Johnson ordered the marines into the Dominican Republic in so blatant an intervention that it still stirs hostility throughout the continent. With the CIA, the American labor movement, and the mass media all competing with each other to intervene in the domestic affairs of Latin American countries, the United States was increasingly being viewed as much as an enemy close to home as it was far away from home.

As contrasting objectives overseas came into conflict, the compromises that enabled foreign aid to circumvent the domestic political stalemate began to collapse. The key toward winning conservative support for liberal aid notions was to broaden their character, to strip them of political meaning, and to unite a "mix" of broad-based techniques that worked at cross-purposes. The compromise had an air of absurdity about it from the start. The United States was perfectly within its rights to insist on tight money, and it was equally disposed, if it wanted, to offer humanitarian assistance. What it could not do, for any length of time, was to combine them. As soon as this became clear, there would be little domestic support forthcoming for foreign aid. It was ineffective, since it was directed against itself. It was expensive, since it pursued multiple objectives. Its recipients, like minorities displaced from their homes in American cities, were not gratified to receive it, realizing that their lives would have been better without it. Unable to achieve its objectives, foreign aid could win little public support, and isolationist criticisms of it began to be heard once again. The same eclecticism that gave foreign aid its popular support at the start of the decade was responsible for the deterioration in its support at its end.

Not only that, but America's approach to development created opposition within the countries that were supposed to receive it. When the attack came, it was launched against an economic theory. The Charles River theorists remained believers in the law of comparative advantage, originally formulated by David Ricardo. This law held that if every country specialized in what it did best, and then if all countries were free to trade their products, the poorer countries would ultimately be better off. Third World economists, particularly Latin American "structuralists" like Raúl Prebisch, offered a sharply contrasting view. By specializing in one or two commodities, they argued, poor countries produced substantially for export. This created a sector within the country that was firmly integrated into the capitalist world system, but it did so by impoverishing the rest of the country, ripping it out of its traditional balance without offering a substitute. What was required, in Prebisch's view, was a new global system of international trade that would take cognizance of the structure of the Less Developed Countries (LDCs).

Prebisch's ideas formed the backdrop for the first meeting of the United Nations Conference on Trade and Development held in Geneva in March 1964. Under pressure from the LDCs, who formed into an organization called the Group of 77, the United Nations became formally committed to a search for a new trading order that would be more compatible with Third World needs. Both UNCTAD I and a second meeting four years later in New Delhi indicated an emerging Third World cohesiveness, but also that the richer countries would not readily agree to any proposals that might result in global redistribution. For example, the LDCs proposed the creation of buffer stocks in commodities like tin and sugar. A buffer stock enables an international agency to accumulate sufficient amounts of a given commodity so that buying more or releasing some to the world market can counter climate conditions or production variations in order to stabilize prices. (The idea for such a sharp repudiation of the "free market" came from American farmers, who use buffer stocks to keep prices high when nature is ornery enough to be bountiful.) Wealthier countries were not receptive to the idea, unwilling to go beyond single commodity negotiations between only two trading partners. Even though a general system of preference for Third World exports was endorsed in principle, no concrete programs to protect the LDCs came out of the 1964 and 1968 meetings.

The Third World structuralist analysis also called into question the premises of the liberal trading order created by GATT. Between 1964 and 1967, GATT was also meeting, in a series of negotiations called the Kennedy Round, trying to flesh out the details of that order. The results were disappointing to the Third World. Few LDCs were represented in the Kennedy Round, and most of the negotiations involved commodities of only indirect importance to them. Consequently, protection from open world trade, which the poorer countries had sought as early as the Havana Charter of 1946, was put off for another time.

Events by 1968, then, had reached a stand-off. Two liberal presidents, Kennedy and Johnson, had overcome Eisenhower's reluctance and had poured money into the Third World to stimulate economic growth. The fate of peoples living in the southern half of the globe now became linked to the policymaking process in the United States. But, as was the case with the poor at home, Third World populations were more the objects than the subjects of policy. There was no effort to help them break their dependency on the forces that made them poor, only an offer to provide growth, yet one that was all the time contradicted by economic practices that intensified their supplication. Fashioned to reach contradictory goals, pro-growth policy extended to the Third World pleased few besides its own advocates. Ordinary Americans did not like it, because it seemed like a waste and its recipients did not sufficiently express their gratitude. The recipients did not like it because it worked to perpetuate the very conditions that they were trying to change. Like each of the other centrist growth mechanisms discussed in this book, development was flawed precisely because it had been broadened in order to overcome America's political stalemate. What made it politically possible in the United States made it economically disastrous abroad.

# V

THE EIGHT-YEAR REPUBLICAN INTERLUDE between 1969 and 1976 coincided with important changes taking place in the Third World. Increasingly suspicious of the United States, leaders of those countries seemed far less willing to be passive recipients of aid and continued their efforts to make themselves into an effective power bloc. The third UNCTAD meeting, for example, took place in Santiago, Chile, in April 1972, a country that had become symbolic of the new directions perceived by the Third World (and, at the same time, of the opposition to those directions that would exist in America). Addressing the conference, Chile's President Salvador Allende called for a recognition of the human conditions behind

aid policies: "At meetings like this, trade and development facts
and figures are often bandied to and fro without any real attempt
to consider how they affect the human being, how they affect his
basic rights, how they strike at the very right to life."[25] Yet the
UNCTAD meeting could accomplish little, for once again the rich
countries were unwilling to support trade preferences for the
LDCs; if anything, the American position had hardened, for domestic sentiment in the United States was moving in favor of
protecting local industries from cheaper Third World producers.
By the end of the session, it seemed as if UNCTAD had outlived
its usefulness as an effective voice for the poorer countries.

UNCTAD's problems pushed the dilemma into new arenas. By
the early 1970s, the Group of 77, representing the Third World,
had grown to over 100 countries and had won substantial support
for its positions, particularly in the U.N. General Assembly. Moreover, a nonaligned movement had organized that was more militant than the Group of 77, pushing the latter to take stronger
positions.[26] Producer organizations were being formed, such as
OPEC, which would soon become a major force on the world scene.
While the United States continued to glance menacingly at this
flurry of activity, other countries in the North began to respond.
Sweden's Development Agency, for example, targeted all of its
Latin American aid for Cuba and Chile on the grounds that their
commitment to equality made them worthy recipients.[27] Britain,
France, Holland, and Norway showed some sympathy to the
Group of 77 and urged other advanced capitalist countries to
negotiate on trade issues. The changing international atmosphere
was demanding new approaches, alliances, and policymakers.

One reason for the change was that Third World countries
were becoming poorer and richer at the same time. On the one
hand, food scarcities led to starvation conditions in the African
Sahel, which raised humanitarian concern around the world. The
famine simply called attention to what was widely known among
specialists. A World Bank study, for example, showed that if an
annual income of $75 were considered to be the poverty line, then
a majority of the population of Ecuador, Burma, Sri Lanka, India,
Pakistan, Chad, Dahomey, Tanzania, Niger, Madagascar, and
Sierra Leone lived in poverty.[28] So desperate were the conditions in what was being called the Fourth World (of especially
poor countries) that the question of humanitarian assistance simply refused to disappear. Canada's Lester Pearson, for one, headed

a commission that published *Partners in Development,* a major call for an increased program of developmental assistance for the South.[29] Sweden's Gunnar Myrdal addressed himself to the poor in the world the way he once helped make the question of poverty and racial discrimination an issue in domestic American politics.[30] At home, organizations like the Overseas Development Council kept the issue alive, publishing yearly summaries of progress in development and sponsoring a fairly radical critique of U.S. policy called *Beyond Dependency.*[31] Ironically, even the World Bank, which had done so much to reenforce poverty in the Third World, jumped into the crusade against it. All of the reports of all of these agencies told the same story: the poor were becoming poorer throughout the Third World.

Yet, while the poor were becoming poorer, some of the poor were becoming richer, and this fact as well made the question of North–South relations difficult to ignore. One and a half years after the inconclusive UNCTAD meeting in Chile, the oil-producing countries demonstrated their effective new economic power. In the wake of the successful oil boycott of 1973, producer organizations were formed in copper, bauxite, iron ore, bananas, and coffee. By 1974, Third World countries were able to unite around demands for a New International Economic Order (NIEO) and passed through the General Assembly of the United Nations a Charter on Economic Rights and Duties of States. The charter recognized the Third World's right to form producer organizations and called on the North to "respect that right by refraining from applying economic and political measures that would limit it."[32] Implicit in OPEC, the NIEO, and the charter was the very message that American policy had been unable to learn in the 1960s: the corrective to inequality in the world would necessarily rely on *political* organization, not *economic* "development."

The administration called upon by history to respond to these developments in the Third World was the Nixon administration. There was some faint cause for hope, since a president so willing to sponsor détente and an opening with China might have considered a repudiation of the centrist crusade for growth that was called development. Indeed, Henry Kissinger, who more than any other recent American policymaker understood that all problems were political, was in an ideal position to meet the Third World demands halfway. At first, the Nixon administration seemed to recognize its opportunity. Nixon and Kissinger indicated that they were responsive to the notion of "untying" aid, that is, of attaching fewer conditions to its use. In addition, after ignoring Third World demands for some time, Henry Kissinger did finally decide to hold a "dialogue" with the Group of 77. There was a period in which the United States considered a strategy of developing counterproposals to Third World demands as an alternative to outright rejection. This new spirit was reflected in a variety of developments: a U.S. scheme for policing multinational corporations through voluntary means; an agreement on tin and sponsorship of another on copper; support for a proposal at the 1974 Food Conference in Rome for the creation of an international reserve of food stocks; and a more open U.S. position at the Seventh Special Session of the U.N. General Assembly. With their instinctive sympathy for the *nouveau riche*, Nixon and Kissinger recognized the emergence of a capitalist elite in the Third World and seemed anxious to make a deal.

As it happened, Nixon was too much a product of his culture to see most of these initiatives through to their conclusion. The administration's political ties to the competitive, protectionist sector of the domestic economy, for example, were reflected in legislation that treated the whole Third World as an enemy. The decision to go off the gold standard in 1971 was accompanied by a 10 percent surcharge on imports that hurt the Third World badly. Nixon's major attempt to revise the international trading rules, the Trade Reform Act of 1974, did institutionalize preference schemes, but in a narrow-minded manner. Temporary, limited only to certain commodities, and biased in favor of American goods, the act was a disappointment to the Third World. Morever, it contained a strong refusal to grant preferences to any country that joined a producer organization, thereby eliminating OPEC in a single blow. When Nixon departed in favor of Gerald Ford, the intransigence intensified. William Simon, the Republican treasury secretary, stood guard over U.S. foreign aid policy and crushed any attempts to make it more enlightened. In his role as U.S. governor of the World Bank, Simon rejected even minimal reforms, insisted on market-determined interest rates, and tried to restrict the bank's special window for soft loans. Moreover, Simon was on a one-man mission against the NIEO: "To the degree that elements of the New International Economic Order conflict with the basic principles of free markets and free enterprise," he told Congress, "we must decisively reject them."[33] Simon was determined to bring back the "4-H Club" opposition to development assistance, to reaffirm his party's general parochialism about the world, and, to a remarkable extent, he succeeded.

Economically, the actions of the Nixon administration made little sense. The NIEO, as Michael Harrington has pointed out, had an ideology that was "impeccably capitalist."[34] Surely Arab sheiks and the Latin America juntas were not about to launch a campaign for socialism. Harrington, among many others, is puzzled about why, given the conservative character of the Third World's demands, Simon and Nixon were so hostile. The answer may have more to do with politics than economics. The Nixon administration was probably correct to perceive that behind the economic conservatism of the Third World was a political position that was suspiciously radical: the notion of a country controlling its own destiny. If the world's balance of political power were to change, and not just its distribution of wealth, then the American people would have to accept some scary new realities. Yet who, within the United States, was in a position to make those realities clear? Republican administrations leaned toward demagoguery, Democratic ones toward antiseptic notions of development. What neither party could confront was that a new approach to the Third World required a new approach at home. Sustained by a material prosperity that enabled it to ignore, and often ridicule, the Third World, the American public was not likely to acknowledge new realities. Old stereotypes were much easier to accept.

As demands from the Third World for social justice and equality grew stronger, the response in America was to withdraw into a sort of neo-isolationism. With détente making it difficult to whip up feverish attacks on the Russians, a fear of Arabs and Third World populations in general seemed to become a substitute. The American ambassador to the United Nations, Daniel Patrick Moynihan, ever sensitive to the changing winds, used all his considerable rhetorical powers to reenforce negative stereotypes of the Third World. Moynihan's speeches at the United Nations were received in stony silence in most of the world, but they touched a harmonious chord at home.[35] The ambassador was articulating a sentiment in line with an emerging conservatism toward the countries that just thirty years ago were colonies of the West. The rich, this point of view articulated, had done all they could. There was no more need to feel any guilt. The poor were on their own now, they would have to look out for themselves.[36] And so, Nixon, finally, gave up. Carrying forward his domestic policy toward poor people, the president married repression to ignorance and went about his more pressing business.

One effect of Nixon's retreat could be seen in the area that most embodied the contradictions of American policy toward the Third World: Latin America. Shortly after Nixon came to power, he sent his arch rival down south to make a report. While Nelson Rockefeller filled his resulting memorandum with calls to provide greater arms to the region, he also, quite surprisingly, endorsed some of the Latin American complaint against free trade.[37] Basing himself on Rockefeller's report (and to a lesser degree on a Latin American program worked out at Viña Del Mar in Chile in 1969), Nixon made a major speech in October 1969 that called for a fundamental review of U.S. aid policy. But a month before Nixon had become president, General Juan Velasco Alvarado proclaimed himself president of Peru and proceeded to expropriate an American-owned petroleum company. Faced with a direct challenge to corporate privileges—not only in Peru, but also in Uruguay, Bolivia, and especially Chile—Nixon dropped all attempts at reform in favor of direct reliance on multinational corporations and compliant military regimes.[38] Following Kissinger's dictum that no Latin American country should be allowed to exercise freedom to choose if it chose socialism, Nixon did everything in his power to undermine the Allende regime in Chile: economic boycotts, hard-credit policies, covert activities, and encouragement of the ultimate coup. After Allende's fall, it became difficult for the most conservative Latin American elites to trust the United States. Placing restraints on U.S. multinational corporations, even Brazil's generals discovered a path independent of slavish devotion to North American interests.

By 1976, America had failed the Third World twice. First, it had raised the hopes of the poorer countries for a greater share of the world's wealth, only to dash those hopes when it discovered that economic growth meant political change. This by itself was bound to lead to anger and dismay at American policies. But when domestic compromises over a growth strategy proved ineffectual and divisive, America then went and blamed the Third World for its own failures. In so doing, the United States combined interference with neglect. A policy that worked around the political impasse at home was, instead of achieving the best of two worlds, open to criticism from two sides. America was no longer isolationist; it meddled with unceasing regularity in the affairs of other countries. But nor was America humanitarian; its meddling consistently favored domestic elites that were unpopular and short-sighted.[39] Development, the Cambridge theorists promised in the 1950s, was a strategy that worked a middle course between conservative inclinations and humanitarian sympathies. In theory it offered both, but, in practice, the former inevitably drove out the latter. America, as Moynihan correctly suggested, was "in opposition," but it had brought its isolation upon itself. The country best in a position to gain by its international standing in 1946 had become the country most punished by its internal political stalemate by 1976.

# VIII

## Carter's Conundrum

During his futile effort to defeat Jimmy Carter's renomination in 1980, Senator Edward Kennedy, often to cheering crowds, condemned the incumbent for breaking with the traditions of the Democratic party. We need a president, Kennedy reiterated again and again, who will be faithful to previous Democratic policies, including those of a brother. Aside from the fact that Kennedy's strategy failed, it had one other flaw: it was wrong. Jimmy Carter's first term in no significant way violated the spirit of the Democratic party. In action and in rhetoric, Carter was the heir of the pro-growth centrist compromises that had seduced every Democratic president since Truman. It was not the policies that made Carter different but the context in which they were pursued. Whereas Truman, Kennedy, and Johnson followed pro-growth strategies in times of prosperity, Carter opted for them in times of austerity. The same programs that enabled the former to govern prevented Carter from doing so. Carter was the first Democrat to pursue growth politics in a no-growth economy, and his inability to establish a credible course (in both domestic and foreign policy) as well as his overwhelming defeat at the hands of Ronald Reagan were a direct result of that fact.

### I

In the years since World War II, neither political party took upon itself the task of restructuring American society to deal with the faults that had led to and sustained the Great Depression. Both parties deliberately sublimated the making of political choices into a quest for the proper conditions of economic growth. Conservatives, unwilling to acknowledge that the system had any flaws, waged their campaigns for office on the basis of symbols, while allowing private business to make profits. Liberals, more interested in building a program with majority appeal, were prevented by

America's political stalemate from controlling business and the military and instead channeled their energies into economic and imperial expansion, making them dependent on the very forces they needed to control. Thus was a pattern established. Democrats would come to power and, unable to carry out any reforms, would instill in the electorate a cynicism that would enliven Republican fortunes. Once the Republicans assumed the presidency, however, their own demagoguery would tire, preparing the way for the return of the Democrats and the start of a new cycle. So comfortable was this pattern, premised as it was on the assumption that one would come to power soon enough by doing nothing, that neither party had any incentive to correct the deficiencies in the economy that was making it all possible. The two parties bandied about slogans as decreasing productivity, challenges to American hegemony in the world economy, structural unemployment, and the outflow of capital undermined both of them.

By 1968, a substantial gap between economic and political realities had begun to appear. Lyndon Johnson's Vietnam War and Great Society were premised upon economic conditions (like a growing surplus, controllable inflation, and American dominance of the world economy) that no longer existed. Unable to recognize the depths of the crisis, Hubert Humphrey ran for president in that year, pledged to policies that the electorate, instinctively, knew would fail. It seemed, especially after the stunning Republican victory of 1972, that the Democrats would be in severe political trouble.

Eight years of Republican rule between 1968 and 1976, however, made it clear that the Republicans were not much of an alternative. If the Democrats could not develop an economics to match their politics, the Republicans were incapable of developing a politics to match their economics. Nixon, unlike Johnson or Humphrey, was aware of the depths of the economic crisis, and some of his policies—such as the imposition of wage-and-price controls, the decision to change the role of the dollar as an international currency exchange, the encouragement of trade with Communist-bloc countries, and the tendency toward protectionism—were more economically realistic than the utopian incantations of growth invoked by his opponents. But Nixon had an insufficient political base from which to pursue these changes. The Democrats still dominated Congress. Nixon made few efforts to revitalize the Republican party and even tried to undermine it from time to time. A policy based upon periodic recessions could not be bent to win overwhelming popular support. Nixon, and then Ford, were popular in business and conservative circles but, when they left, the Republicans were still a minority party.

By the time that Jimmy Carter became president, the United States had reached an impasse, with neither an economic policy nor a political coalition that could govern the country effectively. Economically the situation was quite distressing. During the Nixon–Ford years unemployment had crept to dangerously high levels, yet, in violation of the then popular economic theory, prices did not go down. As stagflation deepened, the United States continued to lose trade and capital investment to other countries, watching hopelessly as its former wards achieved higher rates of growth and lower rates of inflation. Finally, in 1973, OPEC drastically increased its price on the single most important commodity affecting the American economy and thereby brought about public recognition of the limits to unrestrained growth. The economic picture, in a word, called for some radical departures in public policy.

As was the case in 1946, politics would not permit what economics demanded. New policies implied a political coalition that could pursue them, yet the same stalemate that prevented Harry Truman from moving had reappeared once the rapid economic growth of the postwar period stopped. The policy elites were in disarray, arguing over the fallout from Vietnam and divided between free traders and protectionists. The labor movement, in the past a crucial source of support for the Democratic party, was shrinking as fast as the attacks on it were increasing. A conservative coalition that would win a majority in 1980 had not yet shown its strength. As the inability of either major party or ideological grouping in America to fashion a coherent response to the economic problems facing the country became more widely acknowledged, participation in politics reached an all-time low. Together the lack of dynamism in the economy and the paucity of options thrown up by the party system reenforced the impasse, and, as a result, the optimism so characteristic of American life was turning into despair and resignation.

This was the situation that greeted Jimmy Carter as he assumed the presidency in 1977. The new president faced a conundrum from the start. If he tried to bring about structural reforms in the economy to slow inflation or to increase employment, he would necessarily confront an entire generation's commitment to pro-growth policies, and the interest groups that had been spawned in their wake. Economic improvement, in other words, meant political confrontation with the corporations, military lobbyists, planners, unions, and powerbrokers that skimmed self-interest off of government programs. Yet, if Carter opted to play it safe by trying to win the political support of such powerful interest groups, he necessarily would be forced to follow economic policies that would exacerbate inflation and subsidize unemployment. The history of Carter's one term is the story of how, at first slowly and then rapidly, the administration chose the latter course. Yet, even though Carter backtracked from economic necessity in order to win political popularity, he was too late; the more the president tried to balance economics and politics, the more vulnerable he became, and the public's repudiation of him was overwhelming.

Before turning to the specifics of Carter's choice, and the consequences that followed from it, it is worth noting that his administration understood full well what needed to be done. In his first year as president, Carter threatened to veto expensive and inflationary boondoggles, upset the overseas expansionists by talking about cuts in the military budget, recognized the depths of America's problems in the world economy, and endorsed, even if backhandedly, a full-employment bill. Yet it is even clearer that in every significant area of public policy, the administration backed away from its own understanding whenever the winds of controversy began to blow. When he retreated from even trying to govern, Carter was praised for finally coming to his senses. In fairness to Carter, it must be stressed that many of the initiatives for which he was damned were admirable, and most of the reasons for which he was acknowledged as realistic and pragmatic were dangerous.

Carter's conundrum is worthy of close examination, for his presidency illustrates what happens to liberalism when political and economic conditions run in opposite directions. (Reagan's presidency offers a case study of what happens to conservatism under the same circumstances, but more on that in the next chapter.) The degree to which America's impasse deepened under Carter can be determined by examining the five policy areas discussed in this book: counter-Keynesianism; urban growth dynamics; overseas expansion; nationalistic internationalism; and aid to the Third World. In each area, the Carter administration reluctantly chose a course that, because of its political advisability, was an economic disaster.

## II

JIMMY CARTER's macroeconomic policy was marked above all else by an attempt to cure economic troubles through recession. One would be hard pressed to find a more socially harmful method for curbing economic dislocations. Yet the reason Carter put himself into a position where the only options open to him were old-fashioned Republican ones was an outgrowth of the compromises in postwar economic policy that enabled Keynesians to come to power, but only on condition that they divest themselves of Keynesian ideas.

Thirty years of encouraging business to invest as a means of producing a fiscal dividend for the voting constituents of the Democratic party had brought about ingratitude on both sides: an increasingly conservative and aggressive business class and a deeply unhappy Democratic electorate. Not only that, but the economic fallout from counter-Keynesianism was as substantial as the political difficulties: timid macroeconomic policy produced the worst of the private sector (unemployment) and the worst of the public sector (inflation) at the same time. Yet, if the problems were obvious, so was the difficulty of fashioning an alternative: business would resist controls even more strenuously in 1976 than it did in 1946. Given the continued business opposition to Keynesianism, Carter, dependent on business, had little choice but to pursue counter-Keynesianism even while knowing that it would fail. To work economically, a policy would necessarily court opposition from those who profit from poor economic performance; contrariwise, any proposals that were capable of sailing through Congress with business support could do so only if their economic ineffectiveness were guaranteed in advance. Thus, economic policymaking under Carter became an elaborate charade in which the president proposed remedies that everyone knew would be ineffective while proclaiming his opposition to any programs that might work.

In pursuing a centrist strategy, Carter learned that in an age of austerity the center shifts to the right. Policies made acceptable to business in the 1980s were far more conservative than those made acceptable to business in the 1960s. How Carter moved to the right while trying to stay in the center can be illustrated by each of the five compromises that embodied the heart and soul of counter-Keynesianism: demand management over supply-side intervention; ineffective government coordination between monetary and fiscal policy; a passive role for organized labor; the choice of free-trade policies that undermined the domestic planning capacity; and reliance on the military for economic stimulation.

Carter faced a situation in which the manipulation of aggregate demand no longer had much of an effect on overall economic growth. True, a sudden influx of demand stimulated by government purchases might revive a slow economy for a time. And a tax cut—which had become the Republican formula for manipulating demand—might similarly induce a short wave of spending. But either method would leave intact all the features of the economy that had brought about unemployment and slow growth in the first place: monopolistic concentration; capital-intensive industry; the export of jobs overseas; a preference for tight credit controls to hold down inflation; indebtedness to the world economy; inflationary monopoly pricing; subsidies for inefficient and unproductive industries; and an unwieldy defense sector. Tinkering, in other words, had just about reached its limits as a solution to economic troubles.

The president tinkered. Carter foreclosed any alternative to the manipulation of aggregate demand on the grounds that such changes would be too politically controversial. One relatively minor step, for example, would have been that form of supply-side intervention known as wage-and-price controls. It is considered axiomatic in most capitalist societies that the government should possess the power to control prices for emergency inflationary conditions. For reasons known only to Carter, he consistently announced, even when unprovoked, that he was opposed to an effective incomes policy (doing so as inflation went over the top in early 1980). Moreover, Carter maintained his opposition when the AFL suggested that the idea might not be so bad, thereby giving him the nucleus of a coalition for the policy had he been inclined to consider it. Unwilling to contemplate supply-side intervention, but facing a wage–price spiral, the administration tried a new compromise. It advanced a scheme that offered tax breaks to companies that made wage settlements within presidential guidelines. Aside from the dubious legality of the plan (the courts made its administration impossible), the most striking feature of a "tax-based incomes policy" was its political cowardice.[1] Proposing such a plan was a clear signal to corporate interests that this administration would take no meaningful steps to curb their pricing policy; indeed, in areas like energy, the administration was committed to having corporations raise their prices as high as they dared.

Carter's approach to those aspects of the counter-Keynesian compromise that dealt with monetary and fiscal policy was similar. It may be recalled that economic planning was dealt a devastating blow by the "liberation of monetary policy" that took place in 1951. When the Federal Reserve was permitted to make economic policy independent of the rest of the government, a contradiction was built into the heart of the counter-Keynesian compromise. Whenever activists on the Council of Economic Advisers got suspicious ideas about encouraging full employment, bankers in the Federal Reserve could restrain their unorthodoxy by raising the prime rate a point or two. The two directions would cancel each other out—not very sensible economically, but politically brilliant in that each wing of the coalition had something to take home.

Carter tried hard to keep this harmonious world intact. As a Democrat, he had to be concerned with holding unemployment within acceptable limits; and at least some of his programs—the increase in the military budget, a proposal to retain CETA jobs, and a jobs program in a 1980 welfare bill—were advanced on the grounds that work would be created. But whatever steps were taken to counter high rates of unemployment were undermined by the administration's approach to monetary policy. Not only did Carter refuse to try to bring the Federal Reserve System under the control of the government (Japan, for example, controls its own central bank), he went out of his way to inform Wall Street that he would not consider such a heretical act. When he appointed Paul Volcker to head the system, Carter took a step that neither Eisenhower nor Nixon had been willing to take: he put a hard-line monetarist in charge of the nation's money. (Both Republicans showed a propensity to appoint Arthur Burns to this position, and Burns was widely known for his pragmatism, not his monetarist orthodoxy.) Volcker's appointment, and his subsequent preference for credit controls to fight inflation, was the quintessential Carter approach to macroeconomic policy. Even as recessionary conditions persevered into the 1980 primaries, the Federal Reserve raised the discount rate to its highest point in postwar history. Carter was simply unable to pursue any economic policy independent of Wall Street.

Labor's role in the making of economic policy was a third area in which Carter tried to keep alive a counter-Keynesianism that was no longer viable. Many of those activists frustrated by the failure of the Employment Act of 1946 to provide new jobs banded together in the mid-1970s behind a new attempt to guarantee something resembling a full-employment economy. While a candidate, Carter was unable to resist the political appeal of the Humphrey-Hawkins bill among his constituents, and he reluctantly endorsed it. But he then devoted the full powers of his office to ensure that the bill would not contain any language that would result in a single new worker being guaranteed a job anywhere in the United States. The result was an escalation of impotence. In 1946, business opposed a *genuine* commitment to full employment on the grounds that it would exacerbate inflation; in 1980, conservatives argued that even a *symbolic* commitment to full employment would be inflationary. With even its rhetoric considered dangerous, Humphrey-Hawkins was gutted beyond recognition and then passed, one of the great nonevents of the Carter administration.[2]

Keynesianism, as I argued in chapter 3, had been premised on the notion that government could provide a certain insulation from the world economy, so that efforts to secure full employment would not be undermined by dogmatic free-trade commitments. Yet the economic planners of the postwar period, relying on the American hegemony over the world's economy, put their faith in free trade in the hopes that growth abroad would stimulate growth at home. For a considerable period of time, this aspect of the counter-Keynesian compromise worked, but by the late 1970s the solution fell apart. The expansion of American multinational corporations overseas, which had made possible an effort to reconcile national and international objectives, exacerbated domestic economic problems in a time of relative stagnation. Jimmy Carter faced a situation in which America was experiencing all the problems of an open world economy with few of the benefits of a closed one.

Under conditions roughly like these, Richard Nixon had flirted with a return to protectionism, but Carter had little taste for so explicit a repudiation of the counter-Keynesian compromise. The administration instead placed its hopes in the idea that a stimulation of the German and Japanese economies would rebound to the advantage of the United States. But those countries, worried about inflation, took few positive steps to expand, except to make promises to Carter that they had no intention of keeping. Carter's efforts to resurrect the growth coalition's international economic strategy were based on Trilateralism. Yet, as I will argue in more detail shortly, while Trilateral ideas might have worked in the 1940s under conditions of economic expansion, they were impossible to apply in the 1970s as austerity made itself felt. Unable to rely on growth in the world economy to solve his domestic problems, but unwilling to tackle those problems directly, Carter was paralyzed. He could not postpone the problem—as Kennedy and Johnson had done—but he could not solve it either.

The fifth aspect of the counter-Keynesian compromise was the decision to rely on nonredistributive forms of government spending, such as the military budget, in order to spur economic growth. Quick spurts of military construction still work to stimulate particular areas of the country and are of obvious benefit to the companies and unions involved; the MX missile, for example, will be helpful to the economy of Southern California. But the overall results of military spending are now recognized to be inflation, negative balances of payments, structural unemployment, and unproductive uses of capital.[3] Considering that an expenditure of the same amount of money on education or health would produce more jobs and growth than would spending on defense, reliance on the military budget makes less economic sense.

Carter initially seemed to understand the limits of using the military budget as an economic tool, but once he confronted the realities of American politics he backed off. Here, more than in any other area, a change in existing patterns of doing business required a full-scale confrontation with vested interests. Given his refusal to tamper with the less explosive aspects of the counter-Keynesian compromise, Carter was hardly likely to touch this one. He instead first endorsed higher military spending in order to win support for SALT II, then promised the MX missile (the greatest boondoggle in the history of a department given to cost overruns and waste), and finally, in response to the seizure of the American embassy in Tehran and the Soviet invasion of Afghanistan, allowed Congress essentially to write its own military budget, with considerable help from the Pentagon. Carter simply abdicated when it came to controlling the military–industrial complex.

In every area of macroeconomic policy, then, Carter tried to keep alive counter-Keynesianism, but at a time when the economic conditions that had made such an approach feasible in the past no longer existed. Such compromises, workable as the economy expands, have devastating consequences as it contracts. Whatever the economic problem—inflation, unemployment, dependence on the world economy, inefficiency, low productivity, the fall of the dollar, or even slow growth itself—the situation worsened the more Carter tried to improve it. And the more he tried to improve it, the more he became dependent on the political power of the very interest groups responsible for economic malperformance. In order to continue to cultivate the support of business and the military, both of which moved to the right as expansion at home and abroad contracted, Carter necessarily had to move to the right as well. Thus, even though counter-Keynesianism had been a centrist course in a time of general prosperity, the same policies shifted rightward in a period of austerity. By 1980, Carter's economic philosophy and his approach to economic problems were indistinguishable from traditional Republican rhetoric, enabling his Republican challenger to adopt, uncontested, the rhetoric of Franklin Roosevelt and John Kennedy in a successful bid for working-class votes. For thirty years, Democrats had been conceding authority in order to hold on to political power. Jimmy Carter learned, to his dismay, that there was no authority left to concede.

## III

ONE SHOULD NOT CONCLUDE from the preceding discussion that indecisiveness was in all cases the response of the Carter administration. In one area—the pursuit of growth policies while trying to help the poor—Carter was firm: he would sacrifice the needs of the poor.

Architects of postwar domestic policy were unwilling to drop a concern with equality and social justice even while pursuing practices of great benefit to vested interests. In areas like housing and health, grand majorities were fashioned around a pro-growth coalition, which promised a better life to the poor and protection to the middle class. Programs like the Housing Act of 1949 or Medicare in 1965, in order to meet these contradictory goals, became expensive, inflationary, and very popular. Unfortunately, not only did they fail to bring about social justice—in some cases they actually made conditions for the poor worse—they also undermined the fiscal stability of the state. The pro-growth juggernaut was on a

collision course with reality, and at some point it would clearly
have to be brought to a halt if economic sanity were to prevail.

As the fiscal crisis of the state placed restraints on how many
federal dollars could be poured into urban renewal and public
works projects, Carter's first response was straightforward. He
began by denying public funds to growth-oriented vested interests
in the Western states. (This attempt, one of the more admirable
acts of the administration, also revealed its understanding of the
economic necessity of curbing the development-at-any-cost mentality.) When the expected counterattack came, Carter's reaction was
to backtrack to the degree that any particular vested interest had
enough political power to make his life uncomfortable and his
reelection prospects dubious. In other words, Carter's initial attack
on the growth network was based on economics, and his retreat
was based on politics.

Unfortunately for Carter, the political power of organized interest groups increased in the latter half of the 1970s. As a result,
Carter, despite his economic understanding, became one of the
most growth-oriented presidents in the postwar period, measured
by the amount of money proposed for construction projects. Carter
approved the MX missile, for example, the cost of which would
exceed *all* the federal monies spent on *all* urban renewal projects
between 1949 and 1968. (Indeed, if the MX is divided between
Utah and New Mexico and some other part of the country, its
construction costs will be higher.) In addition, Carter accepted a
public works appropriation in the 1980 budget designed to counter
an emerging recession, even while conceding that because of construction delays the money would not be spent until the recession
passed. (When asked about this, an administration spokesman said
that one had to be realistic when it came to public works.) Finally,
this self-described fiscal conservative asked Congress to pass a
program for energy self-sufficiency that, in its quest for synthetic
fuels, would tear up most of the land in America that had managed
to escape the grasp of Robert Moses. (Signing the "synfuels" bill
on the last day of June 1980, Carter seemed to forget what its
ostensible purpose was. Noting that the new law would create
70,000 jobs, the president claimed that the effort to develop synthetic fuels "will dwarf the combined programs that led us to the
moon and built our interstate highway system.")[4] The building
frenzy that characterized the Kennedy years had overtaken Washington once again.

This time, though, construction was taking place under depress-
ing economic circumstances, thereby changing the nature of the
pro-growth coalition. In the 1960s, prosperity ensured that the
space program, new weapons, and downtown office plazas could
be built while still leaving programs for the poor. But, without
rapid economic expansion, growth programs could only be followed if the poor were excused from the gravy train. Fighting
inflation through reduced federal expenditures was a privilege
reserved exclusively for the underprivileged in the Carter years.
There were budgetary cutbacks, many of them severe, but, with an
uncanny knack for anticipating the political power of affected
groups, they seemed to affect most those who did not have the
clout of energy corporations or the Pentagon. Thus, the administration announced that since America's love affair with the auto could
not be stopped mass transit would suffer, in spite of the energy
crisis. Housing, health care, and public employment funds were
cut by this administration. Carter even tried to reduce social security payments—although through bipartisan agreement social
security had been outside of legislative controversy for a generation. The whole approach, in the words of Carter domestic adviser
Stuart Eizenstat, was to help the Democratic party shed its "historical mission" of helping the poor.[5] Carter's urban policy was the
creation of a development bank to make lending easier, and his
link to the New Deal was an inoffensive health care plan that he
never seriously tried to have passed. The degree to which one lived
in a condition of fiscal austerity under Carter depended upon the
amount of political power one had.

One hates to sound maudlin, particularly in a cynical age, but
Carter's administration was needlessly heartless. His programs
made the conditions of life for the disadvantaged visibly worse;
compassion and decency counted for naught with this administration. That such a moral man could pursue such immoral policies,
though, made sense given the pattern of postwar politics. Pro-
growth policies, from the start, assumed organized constituencies.
Unlike reform from below, which demands the extension of public
power to help the dispossessed mobilize themselves against social
injustice, growth policies were linked to already organized political
constituencies. During periods of economic expansion, the number
of such organized groups inevitably increases, as new claimants to
the expanding pie make themselves heard; during the relatively
prosperous 1960s, for example, even welfare recipients had an

organization. One of the first things that the poor sacrifice during periods of hard times is their organizations. Unlike the better-off, who intensify their lobbying in times of recession, the poor find it hard to mobilize and make claims when more immediate considerations of getting through the day preoccupy them. To pursue a governing strategy of listening to organized constituents in rough proportion to their power, then, means to move to the right as economic conditions deteriorate. Carter, like Kennedy and Johnson, was more interested in growth than justice; unlike them, his pursuit of both goals during a time of austerity took him out of the center of the spectrum and moved him to the right.

Ironically, the decision to ignore claims of social justice did not help Carter politically. Following all the rules of sound politics— compromise everything and always move to the center—Carter found himself in increasing political trouble. Just as the economic programs of growth politics do not work without growth, neither do the political rules. For all his conservatism on domestic programs, Carter could only have done better politically if he had tried to be a traditional liberal. His social conservatism left him exposed to attack from within his party—a challenge he defeated, but at great cost. Then he was unable to rally the older industrial states in his reelection campaign, at least in part because his policies had given them so little, and last-minute contracts and grants seemed too blatant. Finally, without much sympathy for his programs among the poorer classes, and possessing no vision of what to do with the presidency, Carter was vulnerable to a Reagan coalition that was secure in its own constituency and clear enough about its own vision. Not even Jimmy Carter could be a better Republican than the Republicans.

# IV

Jimmy Carter became president with little experience in or understanding of world events. That was one of the more interesting things about him. Unbeholden to the strategic theorists' obsession with *Pax Americana*, Carter was the first Democratic president since Roosevelt who was in a position to reject, once and for all, his party's marriage to militarism and overseas expansion. To do so, however, required yet another confrontation with business-as-usual, and by the end of his one term Carter had become a cold warrior perfectly in the tradition established by Harry Truman and John Kennedy.

When Carter took office, overseas expansionists were, as I re-counted in chapter 5, divided into two groups, arguing among themselves about the significance of Vietnam. One faction had become more cautious about the use of American military power, urging restraint on the part of the United States and diplomatic initiatives as a substitute for automatic force. Its antagonists in organizations like the Committee on the Present Danger advocated instead that imperial expansion be carried out even more sys-tematically. As for Carter himself, he seemed, if he had any posi-tion at all, to lean toward the revisionists. Aside from his appointment of Zbigniew Brzezinski as his national security ad-viser, Carter brought into his administration nearly all of the prominent disaffected cold war liberals, including Anthony Lake, Leslie Gelb, Paul Warnke, and, as secretary of state, Cyrus Vance. Quite intentionally overlooked were the most vociferous advocates of military force, men like Paul Nitze and Eugene Rostow.

The spirit of the administration as these men assumed their positions was decidedly hostile to imperial doctrines, indeed to doctrines in general. Leslie Gelb described the new mood:

> The general approach of this Administration in the first four months was not to try and mass this disparate, diverse, and sometimes incomprehensible foreign policy universe into a new strategy. There is no Carter doctrine, or Vance doctrine, or Brown doctrine, because of a belief that the environment we are looking at is far too complex to be reduced to a doctrine in the tradition of post-World War II American foreign policy. Indeed, the Carter approach to foreign policy rests on a belief that not only is the world far too complex to be reduced to a doctrine, but that there is something inherently wrong with having a doctrine at all.[6]

It is precisely this determination to avoid the mistakes of the past that makes so fascinating Carter's eventual decision to make just about every one of them, symbolized by his announcement of a "Carter doctrine" in January 1980. Although the administration resisted the lure of global interventionism—there were no troops sent to Nicaragua and the incursion into Iran was half-hearted and a miserable failure—it could not resist the political appeals of

higher military budgets, new weapons systems, and increased
tensions with the Soviet Union. The political risks of moving away
from the cold war instincts of a Truman or a Kennedy were too
strong for a weak administration to consider.

The return of cold war sentiment followed a circuitous path.
Faced with a split in his own party, Carter at first sought the usual
middle ground. Two early expressions of his administration's approach to the world were indicative of this centrist course, and of
the impossibility of following it. One was a top-secret overview of
the state of the world drafted by the National Security Council and
approved by the president. Known as PRM-10, the document was
insufficiently coherent to have much of an impact. One section,
written to please the doves, called for "essential equivalence" with
the Soviet Union in strategic weapons. The other section, for the
hawks, was a call for a new commitment to conventional arms and
for the development of a capacity to intervene in the Third World.
Internally contradictory, PRM-10 fell into oblivion within a year.
By the end of Carter's presidency, no middle course existed. The
second half of PRM-10 had become the Rapid Deployment Force,
while the first part had given way to a new U.S. emphasis on the
doctrine of counterforce first proposed by James Schlesinger. First
the MX missile (a first-strike weapon) and later the pronounce-
ment of a new strategic doctrine emphasizing the need to prepare
for limited nuclear war indicated that Carter would shift to the
right as far as domestic politics would take him.

Similarly, Carter at first aimed at a middle course in his policy
toward the Soviet Union. He had his chief adviser on Soviet affairs,
political scientist Marshall Shulman, testify to the effect that the
United States's relations with the Russians were marked both by
competition and by cooperation.[7] Thus, Carter tried to conclude
the SALT II arms treaty with the Russians while building up new
arms against them, and to preserve détente while developing the
capacity to fight a war. Such a middle course made sense in
terms of bureaucratic infighting within the administration, divided
between its Vance and Brzezinski wings. (Recalling a major statement on Soviet–American relations, Carter speechwriter James
Fallows noted that "Carter then assembled the speech essentially
by stapling Vance's memo to Brzezinski's without examining the
tensions between them. . . . The speech . . . had an obvious break
in the middle, like the splice in a film.")[8] But in the country at
large, a middle course no longer made sense, for much the same

reason that centrist policies were not possible in domestic affairs.

At home, austere economic conditions intensified the movement of big business to the right, demanding that Carter also shift in a conservative direction if he desired to develop noncontroversial economic and social welfare policies. Austerity had much the same effect on the military. Upset at the decline of its privileged position during the Nixon administration, and determined to improve its standing in the face of an anticipated fiscal squeeze, the military and its political allies began to launch a new crusade for funds long before the Soviet invasion in Afghanistan. Ever kowtowing to the powerful, Carter had already begun to revive the passions of the cold war even while seeking détente. Afghanistan and Iran ultimately legitimated the new hard line, but in retrospect it is clear that the administration had decided to place new nuclear missiles in Europe and to arouse public fears of a Soviet missile brigade in Cuba even before the dual explosion in the Middle East. Campaigning for reelection, Carter had become a born-again Harry Truman, using a crisis in world affairs to undergird his popularity against an electoral challenge from the left.

Besides the cultivation of the Soviet threat, the cold war expansionism of John F. Kennedy and Lyndon Johnson was also characterized by increases in the military budget and a propensity to intervene in the affairs of other countries. On the former, as I have pointed out, Carter's capitulation was complete, while promising starts were made on the latter.

Since the late 1940s, the size of the military budget has had at least as much to do with domestic politics as it has with threats to American security.[9] Nothing in the Carter period changed that trend. Determined, at first, to have his SALT treaty ratified by the Senate, Carter committed himself in advance to raising the military budget as high as it need be to gain that result. (Carter treated senators the way he treated Egypt and Israel, promising them unlimited funds in order to gain political peace; what worked with the latter, however, failed with the former.) This made his administration different from, say, Eisenhower's, for in the past weapons were discussed and then their costs estimated, whereas under Carter the costs were first established and then the appropriate weapons found. By reversing the procedure, Carter, like Truman and Kennedy, put himself in the hands of conservatives, who could continually raise the price of their support for his goals. Unwilling to break out of the pattern of liberal administrations pursuing conservative goals by spending a fortune on growth-oriented projects, Carter oversaw the start of a new round of militarism in the United States. Yet, while earlier Democrats could, under expansionary conditions, commit themselves to the military and still have something left over for domestic spending, Carter could not. His increases in the military budget were pursued while slashing domestic spending in order to balance the budget. Under austere economic conditions, Carter could raise the military budget at expeditious rates and still be unable to win support. (The SALT II treaty was never approved.)

Carter, to his credit, held firmer on the question of military intervention, especially in Latin America. Yet, almost as if to prove to the Washington establishment that he could be as shortsighted as his predecessors, Carter took major steps to overcome the "Vietnam syndrome" and make intervention more possible in the future. For example, the decision to proceed with the MX missile was justified by many on the grounds that, by giving the United States a strategic advantage, it would enable America to intervene in the Third World without retaliation from the Soviet Union. Carter also built up conventional forces and sponsored the creation of a Rapid Deployment Force for use in the Middle East. As a reaction to the events of 1979–80, the administration increased its forces in the Indian Ocean, shored up a NATO-like defense structure in the Persian Gulf, lifted its ban on supplying arms and nuclear fuel to Third World countries, strengthened the CIA, supported chemical warfare, and successfully sponsored a bill to establish registration for a future draft. Even while limiting its intervention to a failed rescue mission in Iran, the Carter administration followed policies that would prepare the way for overseas military expansion by his successor.

By the end of the Carter administration, the middle course had evaporated in favor of a policy barely distinguishable from that of the conservative hard-liners in Washington: confrontation with the Soviet Union; higher military expenditures; new strategic weapons; an emphasis on conventional warfare; and the development of an interventionary capacity in the Third World. George Nash, writing about the 1960s, had the relationship correct even if he was mistaken on the direction. "Conservative foreign policy," he writes, "more and more came to resemble the old liberal policy of containment. . . . And so, on foreign policy . . . many conservatives found themselves defending what Arthur Schlesinger, Jr. once called the 'vital center.' "[10] The only problem with this formulation is that the conservatives were not in power, while the centrists were. In actuality, it was the politically proper pursuit of centrist principles that drew one Democratic administration after another further to the right. Carter, like John Kennedy, spent a considerable amount of time appeasing the military, but, unlike Kennedy, he had to shift ground more rapidly in order to do so.

The irony of the return to the cold war is that the administration that sponsored it never seemed to believe in it. Carter was unable to make a convincing case as to why the Soviet invasion of Afghanistan was such a great threat to peace, and neither America's allies nor the American people nor, indeed, Carter himself suspended politics as usual for the duration of the "threat." The incantation of Soviet misdeeds, rather, had simply become one of the laws of motion of American politics—common occurrence when a weak Democrat runs for reelection. Cold war expansionism was chosen by Carter, not because of its own virtues—it has very few, as most of the world understands—but because there was no existing coalition in the United States that could propose an alternative. The economic basis of cold war policies, in contrast to the Truman period, no longer existed. But their political base was firmer than ever. In 1980, as in 1950, America's political stalemate could be overcome only by invoking threats from abroad. By invoking the Soviet threat, Carter prepared the way for an administration that really believed in it.

## V

"THE INTERNATIONAL ORDER created after World War II is no longer adequate to new conditions and needs."[11] So began one report of the Trilateral Commission, an influential group that placed many of its key theorists in high policymaking positions in the Carter administration. In recognizing that the international order was no longer "adequate," the commission seemed to promise that Carter would move away from the centrist compromises that had plagued international economic policymaking in the postwar years. The postwar monetary and trading systems, as I argued in chapter 6, linked national and international needs into a creative synthesis that worked well so long as America was the dominant hegemonic power in the world economy. But to keep America on top, policymakers either had to suppress growth in the world economy, a self-destructive option for a growth coalition, or to channel it into American-based multinational corporations. The latter approach, which worked so long as domestic and international growth proceeded together, exacerbated problems at home in a time of economic stagnation. As the domestic consensus over nationalistic internationalism fell apart, the long-delayed choice between an open and closed economy would finally have to be made. Richard Nixon opted for national needs when he suspended American participation in the Bretton Woods Agreement, but domestic and international surprises prevented the Republicans from carrying their protectionism too far. Through the Trilateral Commission, Carter suggested that he would resolve the choice the other way, in favor of a return to free trade and an economy open to the world.

Two issues dominated foreign economic policy discussions during the Carter years: free trade versus fair; and the reform of the international monetary system. In both areas, America's privileged position in the world economy no longer existed, demanding a new approach, yet America's domestic political stalemate still existed, preventing a new approach. Facing this impasse, the Carter administration began an international course, but eventually settled on more nationalistic policies. Trilateralism, which became an attempt to resurrect the Bretton Woods system in a new form, simply could not work without a global economy that had the dynamism of the earlier period.

The Trilateralists, like most other policymakers in the postwar period, were unwilling to abandon a commitment to free trade:

> A proliferation of controls on trade and capital movements would damage not only the direct participants, but third parties as well. . . . We do not see the danger of a major depression. Modern governments are too sensitive to unemployment to allow that to happen. What we do fear is a widespread use of controls on international transactions precisely to assure the autonomy governments may feel necessary to preserve national unemployment.[12]

Free trade, since World War II, had been for the Democratic centrists an alternative to restructuring the world economy; once the reforms of Keynes and White proved politically impossible, then growth in the world economy could, indeed, only occur when the most efficient producers of a commodity are free to sell wherever they can find buyers. Carter's commitment to Trilateralism and to free trade was thus in keeping with the postwar pattern of politics, but with one major difference. Previous presidents, like Kennedy, were advocating free trade when industries in *other* countries would be most harmed by the lack of protection. Could the centrist commitment be maintained when it was *American* firms that were less efficient? Whatever his ideological sympathies for free trade, in other words, Carter faced domestic political pressures in favor of protection that would be difficult to ignore.

The steel industry was the best example of Carter's problems. Steel was once a symbol of American economic know-how, but throughout the postwar period the industry was in a state of decline. By 1973, Americans were importing 13 percent of their steel; this jumped to 20 percent by 1977.[13] The obvious reason was that foreign steel, particularly from Germany, Japan, and Brazil, was cheaper. Controversy will also exist about why: steel companies laid the blame on everyone but themselves, first on environmental controls and then on "dumping," the alleged Japanese practice of deliberately selling steel abroad at less than the cost of production in order to open up new markets. But there was obviously more to it than this. The steel industry suffered from the distortions of postwar prosperity: the export of jobs, reliance on guaranteed government purchases for military needs; economic concentration and its resulting lack of innovation; diseconomies of scale; and the encouragement of business unionism. Complacent to an extreme, management relied on "open hearth" methods, ignoring American-invented oxygen production techniques that increased productivity in Japan. Steel was one of the most politically powerful American industries, a major reason for its economic decline.

Steel is also made in Ohio, a bellwether state in America, one impossible for any national politician to ignore. Carter had little choice but to seek protection for the American steel industry, whatever its inefficiencies. He directed his under secretary of the treasury, Anthony Solomon (later to replace Paul Volcker as head of the New York Federal Reserve Bank), to find some correspondence between Trilateralist economic views and Ohio political realities. With the wisdom of his namesake, Solomon came up with a proposal to set a "trigger price" for steel imports, meaning that if Japanese steel came into the country under the set price, it could be taxed so that it would sell at the established price. Meanwhile, federal tax policy would be used to stimulate modernization in the

American industry and aid would be provided to communities hard hit by unemployment. Steel executives liked the plan. "Taken all together," George A. Stinson of the National Steel Corporation noted, "the plan is a very welcome confirmation that the administration is dedicated to a program of effective assistance to the steel industry."[14] The union agreed. In his first significant test, Carter moved away from a reflexive free-trade policy. (Not that it helped all that much. American steel companies continued to go out of business, Youngstown lost huge numbers of jobs in 1979, and Solomon's formula had collapsed by 1980.)

The steel situation was indicative of the conundrum facing Carter. Because his administration was unwilling to consider far-reaching reforms in its relations with the poorer countries of the world (see next section for details), it needed to rely on the kind of economic growth induced by free trade. But since domestic political realities prevented the administration from committing itself to free trade, it was deprived of its own alternative. Therefore, for all the Trilateral talk of a new trading order, the administration simply had no policy on this crucial question. When industries with little clout (such as shoe manufacturers) were involved, a free-trade policy could be carried out, but, when it mattered, the administration was forced to retreat. The almost comical goal announced by Robert Strauss, Carter's free-trade negotiator in 1977, was "free trade, but fair,"[15] a policy that can be pursued with all the ease of being half-pregnant. Carter tried hard to find the centrist path, but to his dismay one no longer existed.

The possible reconstruction of the international monetary system was an additional item on Carter's agenda. Since 1971, when Nixon suspended the convertibility of the dollar, the major countries allowed their exchange rates to vary according to supply and demand—"free floating," in the terminology of economists. While such a situation had its strong defenders, particularly on the right-wing end of the spectrum, there were serious dislocations caused by all the unwanted American dollars floating over Europe, uncontrollable by any government. The lack of a fixed currency standard also brought about a sharp rise in speculation, especially in gold, which increased in price from its pegged rate of $30 an ounce before 1971 to over $800 an ounce in late 1979. Moreover, without an international standard the decline of the dollar intensified, and few holders of that unfortunate currency—including OPEC—found their investments safe from deterioration. Since the increasing importance of the multinational corporation had made international trade more common than ever, the lack of a fixed currency standard was as intolerable as it had become inevitable.

Many of these problems had been anticipated by the Trilateral Commission theorists who staffed the Carter administration. "The task before us," the commission had written as early as 1973, "is to renovate the monetary system so that it can do as well in the next two decades as it did in the two decades following the Second World War, recognizing that the underlying conditions at present are very different than they were in the late 1940s."[16] Expressed in that one sentence was the major dilemma facing Carter. From the late 1940s to the late 1960s, there was an international monetary system that worked, but it had been based on the strength of one national currency, the dollar. When that "underlying condition" changed, any workable solution had to change as well. Either a new hegemonic currency would have to be selected again to dominate the world economy—the dollar once more, or the yen, maybe the mark—or steps would have to be taken in the direction of genuine international cooperation. As it happened, the first option was economically impossible, for no one national economy dominated the world economy, and the second was politically implausible, for it required that America give up some of its autonomy. Nothing, therefore, was done, at least by the United States.

During the 1970s, the dollar became seriously overvalued. Financial institutions and countries that held surpluses were uninterested in dollars because they would lose relative to other currencies. Periodic efforts had been made at a series of meetings to realign the world's currencies based on a devalued dollar, but the problem seemed out of control. At least two reasons for increased financial instability were present. For one thing, speculation was no longer a matter for amateurs. Multinational corporations were rapidly shifting funds from one account to another in the hopes of making quick profits—good business practice from the point of view of the firm but unstable for the world economy as a whole. In addition, huge numbers of dollars in Europe gave rise to a speculative free-for-all, as each Eurodollar could be invested many times over. Attempts at reform undertaken by the Committee of Twenty [finance ministers] of the IMF were unable to win lasting agreements, in part because any major change in the Eurodollar market would be resisted by the multinationals and any change toward greater internationalization, for example by increasing the role of Special Drawing Rights, would be fought by the United States if national autonomy would be diminished. As intractable as international monetary problems were, workable reforms seemed more offensive to American interests, and some, like Robert Solomon, argued that America should simply learn to live with floating exchange rates.[17] After some activity, Carter came to accept that advice, Trilateral reforms disappeared from view, and inaction, as it had under Nixon, became the quintessential form of American action. A global system was perpetuated that, in the words of Valéry Giscard d'Estaing, "reveals a profound disorganization of the monetary community and marks a step back into anarchy and irresponsibility."[18]

Recognizing that Europe could no longer look to the United States for financial leadership, the French and Germans led the way toward the creation of a European Monetary Union, a regional effort toward monetary stability. Whether it ultimately succeeds or fails, this attempt by Europe to solve its own problems indicated how far events had come since Bretton Woods. Then, the United States incorporated Europe into its own hegemonic sphere, thereby pursuing its national goals in an international guise. Now Europe, with Japan, was the most powerful capitalistic power in the world, and it was determined to protect its own emerging hegemony. In addition, just as the loss of political power weakens a country's ability to organize the world economy, Europe's financial independence hastened political assertiveness. West Germany encouraged trade with the Soviet Union, tried to find a middle position between the two superpowers on cruise missiles, and cut back its defense spending, while France's Giscard, in 1980, proclaimed that the World War II era was over and that France and Germany together would become a "community of destiny" that would return Europe "to its power and influence in the world."[19]

At the start of Carter's presidency, Trilateral ideas seemed like the wave of the future. America would join with its friends in Europe and Japan to reorganize the world's wealth and power. By the end of Carter's term in office, the various plans and programs of the Trilateral Commission were as much in demand as used Studebakers. Trilateralism was an attempt to recreate the atmosphere at Bretton Woods, only this time, instead of America dominating the system, the three great areas of Western capitalism would do it together. More internationalist than the nationalism of

Bretton Woods, Trilateralism simply could not work when the world economy was stagnant. On the one hand, America's capitalistic partners were suspicious of the nationalism that America had incorporated into its internationalism and were unwilling to go along unless the United States indicated its willingness to agree to international rules. But on the other hand, any attempt to modify American national prerogatives would be attacked at home as a giveaway. In no other country in the world could a program invented by multinational corporations and bankers be attacked as world government—a theme sounded by Ronald Reagan in the 1980 primaries. (Reagan's vice-president was a trilateralist.) Trilateralism was a program to unify the American people in a cooperative venture with Europe and Japan; the only problem with it was that in a declining economy neither party wanted the marriage.

On both trade and currency issues, then, the Carter administration first opted toward more internationalistic solutions but was forced to back off from them given the domestic political stalemate. As Carter moved closer to protectionism for industries like steel and further away from international cooperation over currency matters, he solidified his political base, but he intensified all the economic problems inherent in nationalistic internationalism. At the start of the postwar era, the reformist ideas of Keynes and White were found to be too radically internationalist for the American Congress; by 1980, even Trilateralism, a far more conservative set of ideas, was looked upon suspiciously. Knowing what had to be done, Carter was prevented from doing it. America was still committed to nationalistic internationalism, even as the rest of the world searched for a more sensible solution.

# VI

IN 1973, a biting critique of American foreign aid efforts appeared in the journal *Foreign Policy.* "The United States is the least responsive to Third World needs of any industrialized country at this time," it argued.

U.S. help is small in quantity, and getting smaller. Its quality is declining. It often runs directly counter to the central objectives of the LDCs [less developed countries]. . . . It lags far behind the policies of Europe and Japan. The United States

regards developing countries both large and small . . . solely
as pawns on the chessboard of global power politics. . . . U.S.
development aid, as a percentage of GNP, is now next-to-last
among all industrialized countries.[20]

These were not the words of some Third World socialist brimming
with righteous anger toward Yankee imperialism, but of C. Fred
Bergsten, who would become assistant secretary of the treasury in
the Carter administration and play the major role in shaping the
administration's stance toward the Third World.

Bergsten repudiated the Nixon administration's approach to the
less developed countries. Nixon and Kissinger, while willing to
negotiate with basic commodity producers on some issues, were in
general both ignorant of and unsympathetic to questions involving
development. They presided over the collapse of the United
States's attempt to reconcile the goals of economic development
with the privileges of multinational corporations, lending agencies,
and the military. Convinced of the need to keep American power
in the Third World intact, the Nixon administration was not
attracted to an emphasis on growth as a substitute for political
change in the world's balance of power. Bergsten's article seemed
to suggest that when Carter came to power the new administration
would attempt to find a strategy for making the concerns of Third
World exporting countries part of the policymaking process in the
United States.

Good judgment foreshadowed such a course. Transformations
taking place around the globe, particularly the oil boycott of 1973,
had demonstrated that one ignored Third World sensibilities only
at one's own risk. Bergsten was expressing a position that had strong
support among the American political elite. The 1980s Project of
the Council on Foreign Relations, for example, made the reduction
of global inequalities a high-priority item and endorsed, in its own
fashion, some of the principles of the New International Economic
Order.[21] The Overseas Development Council took the lead in
sponsoring a variety of alternative approaches to development
assistance designed to avoid the failures of the previous thirty
years: labor-intensive agricultural reforms, production for domestic
markets, an emphasis on human resources development, and attempts to stabilize the world's population were some of the methods suggested.[22] At the World Bank a strategy that emphasized
basic human needs was worked out, seeking the abolition of abso-

lute poverty within twenty-five years.[23] Even the Trilateral Commission, of which Bergsten was a member, spoke of rejecting a "rich man's club" and wanted to be "responsive to growing demands for welfare and justice."[24] There seemed to be more policy recommendations than a new administration would know how to handle.

Given the outpouring of new ideas and proposals, the Carter administration was in a strong position to reject the realpolitik of Kennedy and Johnson's approach to economic development. Nixon's parochialism made a moral overture politically attractive, and the new president's concern for human rights could easily be broadened to include economic rights—such as the right not to die of starvation. The world atmosphere during the aftershocks of 1973 —reflected in the call by the eminently conservative *Economist* of London for "aid, not trade" and a Marshall Plan for the Third World[25]—was conducive to the formulation of new policies toward basic commodity producers. Unfortunately, the rest of the world may have understood the need for new policies, but America did not. At home, public sentiment turned against foreign aid on the grounds that America's efforts had been unappreciated in the Third World. Feelings toward foreign aid were roughly like feelings toward welfare. Not understanding that centrist compromises transformed aid from a humanitarian gesture into a preoccupation with American security that other countries rightly understood as an imperial intervention into their own affairs, the American people rejected conservative policies on the grounds that they were too liberal. As a result, congressional opposition to foreign aid was as strong in the late 1970s as it had been in the late 1940s. Third World militancy may have demanded some policy, but the domestic political stalemate would ensure that none would be forthcoming.

At first, the Carter administration seemed willing to try. The new treasury secretary, Michael Blumenthal, endorsed the idea of stabilized export earnings, through a multilateral mechanism if need be, a sharp break from previous American policy. In addition, Carter did not specifically reject the "common fund," an idea that had been put forward at the 1976 UNCTAD meetings in Nairobi to develop a $6 billion effort to deal with supplies, prices, and the income of producer countries.[26] (The Common Fund had been offered by the moderate Group of 77 as an alternative to a more radical solidarity fund proposed by the nonaligned bloc.) When

compared to the self-righteous fulminations of Daniel Patrick
Moynihan at the United Nations, Carter's appointment of Andrew
Young seemed reassuring to the Third World. Here was the one
area where the administration offered the most complete possibility of a political breakthrough.

How surprising, then, was the swiftness of the retreat. Within
the new administration's first *month*, Fred Bergsten, that blunt
critic of previous administrations, told *The New York Times* that
Carter's approach to the Third World would be consistent with
that of his predecessors.[27] Soon thereafter Bergsten announced his
support for "direct assistance," a device by which the United States
would retain control over the uses to which aid would be put.
(Direct assistance was actually a step backward from Nixon's approach.) Richard Cooper, another Trilateralist Carter adviser, suggested that all foreign aid should be based on some kind of
"performance criteria," so that, if it was shown not to be "working,"
it should not be given. With a cynicism rivaling Moynihan's, Trilateralist Richard Gardner—who had been the American author of
the commission's seemingly favorable report on foreign aid—
announced that "the people of the United States are not interested
in transferring wealth from the poor people in the rich countries to
the rich people in the poor countries."[28] Carter's new approach to
the Third World climaxed in August 1979 when Andrew Young
had to resign because of his close contacts with the Palestine Liberation Organization, a symbol for much of the Third World of
its powerlessness. By 1980, the Carter administration's policies toward the Third World rivaled Nixon's in their enlightenment and
generosity.

What happened? For one thing, Carter faced the same problem
that confronted every Democratic administration since Truman's.
Presidents may come to understand that global poverty and social
injustice in the long run work to harm America's interests, but
policies are made in the short run and need congressional and
popular approval. Had Carter tried to carry out his initial rhetoric,
he would have faced relentless opposition from every vested interest that made profits from global poverty and on top of that
would have had to take a position counter to the increasingly
parochial concern of the ordinary voter facing a recession. Like
previous Democrats, then, Carter chose to compromise his own
understanding in order to achieve a modicum of political security.
But whereas Kennedy and Johnson were able, through com-

promise, to win political support for overseas aid, even if distorted in form, Carter was not. Foreign aid looked different through the lenses of austerity than through those of prosperity. In periods of growth, Third World commodity producers are more militant, and their threats, whether to move closer to the Russians or to raise prices, seem serious enough to smooth the way toward foreign aid. In this sense, the 1973 oil boycott was the last gasp of a prosperous world economy, for by 1980 the world had gone into a sustained recession, and as growth declined, so did the "threat" from the Third World. As militancy decreased, so did the chance for policy toward development.

Although OPEC and demands for a New International Economic Order seemed to indicate growing unity in the Third World, the slowdown of the postwar economic boom pointed in an opposite direction. In the last half of the 1970s, Third World countries lost their earlier militancy. Oil boycotts did not occur, and a satisfactory relationship between OPEC and the energy conglomerates was worked out. At the Jamaica meetings of the International Monetary Fund in 1976, Third World countries slowly backed off from their desire to reorganize the world economy and instead humbly asked for loans. The Nairobi UNCTAD meetings not only rejected the idea of a solidarity fund, but also rejected "indexation" plans that would have tied commodity prices to rising inflation. (Indexation was the linchpin of the Shah of Iran's program, and he was hardly a radical.) Worldwide recessionary conditions, in short, did more to curb militancy in the Third World than all the policing and military programs of the United States. Economic conditions left the poor countries no choice but to turn "back to the policy of patching up the old system which they rejected as inadequate in 1975," as Geoffrey Barraclough wrote.[29]

When it became aware of the Third World's retreat from militancy, the Carter administration, not needing votes in Africa, backed away from its earlier proposals on development. Thus in one final area did austerity mean that the center had shifted to the right. For so long as what Bergsten called the "threat" from the Third World seemed real, and it could only seem real when economic conditions expanded, a centrist course offered at least some development assistance surrounded by vast amounts of military aid. By the time of the Carter administration, stagnation in the world economy obviated the United States from developing any policies at all. At home, the administration's approach was to cut back funds to the groups that needed them the most; abroad, it's approach was much the same—countries whose only claim for assistance was their poverty would have to find it from some place other than America.

Under Carter, appropriations for foreign aid reached their lowest point in postwar American history. Between 1960 and 1963, foreign aid as a percentage of the GNP averaged 0.5 percent, decreasing to 0.25 percent in the years 1973–78. By 1979, the figure had shrunk to 0.17 percent, the lowest aid appropriation among all the industrial democracies except Italy.[30] The country that prided itself on its generous spirit was the most chintzy foreign aid provider among the richer countries. With characteristic bad timing, these cuts in foreign aid came just as a new wave of Third World revolutions began. Hard times may encourage economic acquiescence, but they also support political desperation. In Nicaragua, the Sandanistas expelled their American-supported dictator, and insurgency increased in El Salvador. (Carter did try to propose foreign aid to Nicaragua, but Congress was not so disposed.) Meanwhile, Iranians held hostage, not just a group of Americans, but the entire interventionist approach to the Third World that had characterized the postwar period. Carter's reaction was perfectly in keeping with other policy areas. Sending Secretary of State Muskie to the Foreign Policy Association in July 1980, the administration called for a vast new aid effort, not on the basis of human need, but as a counterweight to communist expansion. Muskie's speech was a transcript from the days of John Kennedy and Walt Rostow. After twenty years, American aid assistance was back to where it began.

# VII

FOR FOUR YEARS Jimmy Carter held tenaciously to his position in the center of the political spectrum as the space occupied by the center became smaller. The administration was on a moving sidewalk; by standing perfectly still, it managed to move backward. Carter's macroeconomic policy became indistinguishable from the recommendations of the Republican party. He resolved the contradiction between growth and social justice by giving up on the latter. Promising starts toward avoiding the imperial temptation were dropped when they proved to be politically troublesome. No significant steps were made to curb the appetites of American nationalism. Policies toward the world's majority—the poor—were nonexistent. The Carter administration, in a word, retreated from the demands that economic conditions imposed upon it, while ever conscious of the political realities it faced; yet, for all its adherence to the rules of proper politics, the administration was one of the most politically inept in the annals of American politics.

Yet it was not, when all is said and done, Carter's incompetence that cost him the office. Carter proved that a growth-oriented liberalism has no political base without the growth to sustain it. Carter had an economic understanding of what needed to be done, but no political base to pursue it. Carter's conundrum, in short, was America's. It was not the president who failed but the pursuit of growth politics in a no-growth economy. It is possible to win support from vested interests like business and the military. It is also possible to lead. It was not possible, as Carter learned, to do both in the late 1970s. No other man would have done a much better job, and some may do worse. So long as the economy insists on pulling the political system down to its level, a conundrum like Carter's becomes inescapable.

# IX

## America After Reagan

G ROWTH, per se, is a worthwhile objective. Economies should develop and prosper; wealth, as Sophie Tucker once said, is better than poverty; and the poor and disadvantaged do better when the economy is booming than when it is still. America's impasse was caused, not by growth, but by the political price that was paid to achieve it. Growth did not come free. In the face of extraordinary growth at home, passion and controversy were held to be ungrateful. In the face of imperial growth abroad, they were held to be unconstitutional. In order to bring about economic and imperial expansion, America sacrificed political vitality. The capacity of either major party or dominant set of ideas to establish goals and an agenda for reaching them was undermined by the fixation on economic and imperial conquest.

First to pay the costs demanded by growth were liberals and Democrats. A generation or so ago, American liberalism existed as a coherent outlook on the world. Liberals, overwhelmed by depression and war, developed a program for controlling both. Depressions, caused by business irresponsibility, would be eliminated by planning and programs of income redistribution. War, caused by the greediness of nation states, would be limited through international cooperation and efforts at global humanitarianism. Unable to achieve these goals due to the deep political stalemate that had existed in the United States since 1938, liberals sublimated them into the quest for an expanding economy at home and a protective umbrella for the world at large. Since the first objective could only be obtained by winning business confidence and the second by courting the support of the national security establishment, American liberalism became dependent on the two forces that it needed to control in order to realize its program. Instead of eliminating depression and controlling war, the Democrats became the party of induced recession and cold war hostility. With the exception of a two-year period during the Johnson administration, the greater the power exercised by liberal Democrats in the postwar years, the further from the New Deal agenda America wandered. By the time of the Carter debacle, liberalism had turned into its opposite. With little save growth to hold it together, yet at a time when the economy simply would not deliver the growth that was needed, the Democratic party had little of coherence to say about America's malaise, and the people turned to the Republican alternative.

If liberalism was destroyed by its faith in growth, the transformation of American conservatism—and thereby the Republican party—was even more startling. Before its love affair with expansion, America contained a conservative tradition that put its faith in localism at home and isolationism abroad. Domestic policy, it was argued, was best carried out at the state and local level, where particular conditions would not be overrun by national uniformity. Inflation, conservatives suggested, was the great enemy of society, and the best check against inflation was small government on the one hand and vigorous economic competition on the other. Low taxes, the heart of the Republican program, implied few expensive ventures abroad, which sat well with the isolationism of the Republican heartland. America would not bail out the world's poor, nor would it finance the world's money; at the same time, such postwar innovations as a peacetime draft, foreign troops, a professional spy network, and a permanent and expensive military establishment were all held to violate conservative principles. Embodied in the outlook of a man like Robert Taft, such a conservative program seems as antique in the 1980s as the liberal humanitarianism of Chester Bowles or Henry Wallace.

American conservatism was destroyed by the same political stalemate that vitiated American liberalism. In their hearts Americans may have longed for fiscal restraint, low taxes, and periodic deflations, but the business of making money during the postwar boom convinced them to open the public pocketbook. Similarly, there was something virtuous about Taft's opposition to military adventures abroad, but virtue seemed redundant to the postwar power grab that passed for international relations. Taft, in other words, was as far from the White House as Wallace. Americans voted for conservatives to represent them in Congress, but no conservative ever could, as a conservative, win control of the presidency. If American liberals lacked respectability among the elite, American conservatives had little popularity among the masses. Hampered by this stalemate, liberal Democrats repudiated their principles and brought to power pragmatic advocates of growth politics. So, after a time, did conservatives. The Republican party shifted into the hands of men like Eisenhower and Nixon, both of whom accepted the necessity for big government at home and foreign involvement abroad. Under their leadership, the Republicans eventually committed themselves to growth politics, if at a slower pace and with slightly different means than the Democrats.

Heirs to growth priorities, the "conservatives" who came to power with Ronald Reagan, like the "liberals" who worked for Jimmy Carter, have come to stand for notions wildly antagonistic to their roots. No longer admiring small government, American conservatives put their faith in a huge military apparatus and an interventionist foreign policy. In the name of traditional virtue, such conservatives would give a free hand to business practices that destroy neighborhoods, separate families, promote hedonism, encourage mobility, and plan obsolence. Speaking on behalf of localism and community, the Republican party upholds the automobile, opposes energy conservation, prefers nuclear to solar power, undermines efforts at local planning, opposes attempts by communities to prevent factory closings, and sets off region against region in a search for new sources of power. Claiming to represent a "moral majority," the Republicans call for a de-emphasis on human rights and encourage immoral dictators in the Third World. Supposedly "pro-life," they support programs—from lifting regulations on smoking to removing pollution controls—that will produce an increase in death. Constitutionalists, the Republicans have become a party advocating the use of any and all means in the furtherance of what is proclaimed to be the national interest. Conservatives who will not conserve, the men who came to power in 1980 are as replete with contradictions as those they were so determined to replace. It took liberals a generation to discredit themselves. Now that everything happens faster, it should take conservatives a decade.

Four contradictions, in particular, will bedevil the Republicans once they attempt to carry out their program. Insofar as the Republican vision can be boiled down to its essentials, it consists of the following interrelated prescriptions: greater freedom for the private sector; a preference for state and local governments over the federal government when public intervention cannot be avoided; the passage of legislation such as tax cuts designed to be of direct benefit to corporations in order to stimulate the economy; and an intensified campaign to give the United States strategic superiority over the Soviet Union. As the Reagan administration seeks to implement these objectives, it will discover that each principle contradicts another. Understanding these inconsistencies, the Republicans, like the Democrats, have turned to growth and expansion as a substitute.

Laissez-faire economics underwent a remarkable intellectual revival at the end of the 1970s, cresting in the deification of Milton Friedman. Yet, in spite of an evident public sympathy for taking government off of the backs of the economy, there is not much lifting that can be done. America has one of the lowest rates of government intervention in any of the advanced capitalist societies. A conservative administration would be able to repeal health and safety legislation and to make it easier for polluters to pollute and cancer-causers to cause cancer, but the idea that reducing the role of government would lead to sudden spurts of productivity and an end to stagflation is hard to take seriously, except during an election campaign. Friedmanism, wonderful stuff for appealing to frustration and anger, is hardly a guide for economic conduct in a society where profits and markets are secured by an active state. A Republican party linked to companies that need government is not likely to engage those companies in a bloody battle. The Republican party enters the 1980s divided between genuine Friedmanites and conservative nationalists who would, in the name of national security, *increase* the role of government. It is not hard to imagine the latter gaining the upper hand as austerity makes itself felt.

Similarly, the conservative preference for state and local government, often expressed in theory, is too easily violated in practice. Long ago, American conservatives learned that world power and localism were incompatible. Seeking to strengthen America's industrial might, President Reagan will inevitably be attracted to vast schemes involving the federal government. To be sure, land, resources, and brains will be turned over to the private sector, but the idea that a state or community will be able to control a corporation of vastly greater size is difficult to imagine. When a commitment to increased military expenditure is added to the formula, the prospects for localism dim even more. Ronald Reagan may like to bemoan the fact that Washington has grown too big, but his own program is devoted to making it bigger. He who wants a powerful America must accept a big national government.

Reagan's first major legislative proposal was his February 1981 economic policy emphasizing budget and tax cuts designed to favor business expansion. Aside from the fact that corporate taxes plumeted during the Democratic years, there is every indication that further tax cuts will not produce substantial economic stimulation. Republican economists like Arthur Laffer maintain that lower taxes would actually increase government revenue, for they would create such a favorable climate for investment that more firms would make more money, expanding the federal treasury. Thus, Laffer happily concludes, tax cuts would not only stimulate private investment but would also finance new government programs, should they be needed. If the economy were as competitive as Laffer's models, he might be right. But the reality is that large corporations choose to invest their funds in safe places, and, if past experience is any guide, corporations would take their windfall and, when not using it to buy other companies, would invest it overseas where the rate of return is higher. Lafferism is a subsidy for *dis*investment. Soon after cutting taxes, President Reagan would have to give up his plans for military superiority or seek an increase in taxes to pay for it.

The final, and least conservative, idea in the conservative program is the call for strategic superiority over the Soviet Union. Aside from the probability that the Soviet Union would meet every attempt by the United States to destabilize parity, or that an attempt by the United States to escalate the arms race would court strong opposition in Western Europe, there is the further problem that Reagan's military program would bankrupt the American economy. One can, in an era of limits, have a strong dollar or a strong military, but not both. Spending unlimited sums on capital-intensive, energy-guzzling, inflation-producing, and unproductive boondoggles is not likely to encourage confidence in the dollar abroad. Remilitarization in an age of austerity is a program headed for disaster.

There was a time when liberals faced contradictions as divisive as these. Planners who lacked the authority to plan; advocates of social justice who rewarded the beneficiaries of injustice; peaceful men who fought a war to prove it; internationalists wrapped in parochial garb; and global humanitarians who offered counterrevolution to the world's poor—American liberals necessarily threw themselves into the pursuit of economic growth out of the manifest contradictions in their vision. Now that power has shifted to the right, so have the inconsistencies of growth politics. Localists seeking national and world power; fiscal conservatives sponsoring expensive government programs; tax-cutters who want to waste public funds; and isolationists seeking to recreate a world in their image—American conservatives have already begun to mimick the liberal quest for economic and imperial expansion as the solution to their equally paralyzing absurdities. The 1980 election was something of a great transformation, but it was a realignment over economic means, not political ends. Growth politics is as popular as ever, but its center of gravity is in the process of shifting from one party to the other.

For liberals, economic growth became a mechanism by which they could offer benefits to their working-class and minority constituents while creating public policies beneficial to business. As such programs became counterproductive and inflationary, public sentiment would turn to the Republicans, who offered fiscal relief. Yet the cautiously deflationary monetarist policies of the Republicans, if practiced, would rekindle unrest, for they would increase unemployment and produce generally lower profits. Unable to win political popularity through such a program, the Republicans would adopt growth programs in spite of themselves, increasing their popularity while decreasing their ideological consistency. The Republican choice was one of honoring their traditions, and thereby dooming themselves to perpetual minority status, or seeking to become a majority ("moral" or otherwise) and repudiating their historical program. The closer the Republicans came to power, the greater the severity of this dilemma, culminating in 1980 with a serious internal split in the party between a pro-growth faction and the traditional Republicans of Wall Street.

Ronald Reagan was able to win the 1980 election by repudiating his own party's traditions and by adopting the pro-growth mantle that had, in the past, been proudly worn by liberals. His platform, written by the pro-growth faction of his party, was the most unembarrassed call for economic and overseas expansion since John F. Kennedy's ringing declarations of 1960. Here is what the Republicans said about economic growth in 1980:

> The Republican Party believes nothing is more important to our nation's defense and social well-being than economic growth. . . . With this kind of economic growth, incomes would be substantially higher and jobs would be plentiful. Federal revenues would be high enough to provide for a balanced

budget; adequate funding of health, education, and social spending; and unquestioned military preeminence, with enough left over to reduce payroll and income taxes of American workers and retirees. Economic growth would generate price stability as the expanding economy eliminated budget deficits and avoided pressure on the Federal Reserve to create more money. And the social gains from economic growth would be enormous.[1]

The spirit of Leon Keyserling, adviser to so many Democratic presidents, lives on. Pro-growth liberals like Keyserling thought that growth would enable the Democrats to offer programs to the poor and disenfranchised while winning the support of business. Pro-growth conservatives like the authors of this platform, learning nothing and forgetting nothing, offer growth as a way of balancing the budget and increasing military spending at the same time.

Not only are the domestic sections of the 1980 Republican platform a paraphrase of John F. Kennedy, but so are the foreign policy appeals. Talk of the "administration's neglect of America's defense posture in the face of overwhelming evidence of a threatening military build-up,"[2] as the 1980 Republican platform expresses it, is not new talk, but these are the kind of words that were, from NSC-68 to the Gaither Report, leveled at Republicans, not by them. Once advocates of restraint, the Republicans are becoming the party of empire. A week after the 1980 election, Ronald Reagan's foreign policy advisers presented to him a report arguing that "no area of the world is beyond the scope of America's interest,"[3] thereby bringing the spirit of Maxwell Taylor into a party that already had incorporated the wisdom of Leon Keyserling. From now on, it will be Republican conservatives, no longer Democratic liberals, who will develop a utopian foreign policy designed to reconcile all objectives (and, in the process, obtain none of them). The notion that diplomacy and foreign policy involve choice, lost when the Democrats dominated the state, is in danger of going into hiding when the Republicans do. Growth at home and empire abroad, compared to the impossibility of exercising political choice, are too attractive for an unsteady coalition to ignore.

Whoever inherits power in America inherits as well the contradictions of growth politics. During the long boom that began in 1945 and crested in 1968, liberal Democrats, unable to unify themselves, chose growth as a substitute for programs that contained internal consistency. Similarly, in the downswing of the postwar long wave, American politics will be dominated by splits within conservative ranks over the proper course of economic management. Growth, which became for liberals a magic formula for overcoming the suspicion in elite circles that they were too radical, enables Republicans to overcome the suspicion among the voters that they are too reactionary. Only by invoking the spirit of Franklin Roosevelt and by practicing growth politics more than the Democrats were willing to do could Ronald Reagan gain power in 1980.

There are only two issues at work in American politics most of the time: economic growth and military strength. When the Democrats, as in 1960, were able to convince the electorate that they could best achieve these objectives, they were the dominant party. In the 1980s, the Republicans have made the more compelling case, and they are becoming the dominant party. In the upswing of the postwar growth wave, liberals believed in expansion and conservatives urged caution; in the downswing, conservatives talk of unleashing the economy and liberals worry about the cost. Nothing illustrates the political bankruptcy of American society better than this reversal of roles. Liberalism and conservativism have been stripped of political vision, as both, in their day, sought in growth and expansion an easy alternative to political choice and controversy. Rather than pose the hard options needed to take America out of its impasse, both parties and dominant sets of ideas engage in an increasingly bitter and futile debate over how best to achieve objectives that can no longer, in the world that actually exists, be achieved.

This is not to argue that there are no differences between liberals and conservatives, Republicans and Democrats. It is one thing to follow growth politics when there is growth, another thing entirely to do so when there is austerity. Expanding the economy and the empire when the economy and empire were expanding was a recipe for irrelevance. Trying to expand the economy and empire when the constraints are so high is a formula for disaster. From the viewpoint of a sensible fit between economics and politics, the triumph of Reaganism is a stupendous setback, not because the Reagan administration will be rigidly ideological (it will not be), but because the pursuit of its goals at a time when its goals are more utopian than ever is bound to produce fear, scapegoating, and ugliness when the goals are not achieved. The impasse that hems in Reagan is the same impasse that constricted liberal Democrats; the consequences of the impasse will not be the same at all.

The so-called conservative transformation of American politics begun in 1980, therefore, is more properly understood as another chapter in a long-running saga of seduction and betrayal. Now it will be Republicans who will suffer the pain of being torn between a political system that demands growth to function and an economy that can no longer provide it. Unless the Republican party restructures the economy and cuts back military spending—and there is little evidence that it would ever contemplate either move —America's impasse will deepen as the effort to resolve it intensifies. America is free, if it chooses, to seek greater freedom for its private sector in an effort to spur growth once more. It can try to reconstitute its military empire and to intervene in the affairs of other countries. Nothing can prevent the United States from building more highways while allowing its cities to deteriorate, to spend vast sums and destroy the West in order to find fuel, to increase the risks of cancer, to poison its citizens in the name of economic health, or to build missiles that run on race tracks in the name of security. If America wants to reject international monetary cooperation, the world will have little choice but to proceed without it. The Third World would be unable to prevent the United States from taking its resources by force. In other words, the United States still has the power to do many things, including the power to forget. But to think that such conservative programs would work America out of its impasse is, if anything, more utopian than the liberal illusion that one can stop depression through recession or win the peace by preparing for war. America needs, not a gross expansion of an already flawed economic system, but a rebuilding of its rapidly deteriorating political life.

Growth was a wonderful thing while it lasted, making possible all kinds of miracles (among them, the fact that the author of this book, a carpenter's son, became the author of this book). Yet, having distorted the economy beyond recognition, uncontrolled growth now threatens to warp the political system as well. For all the talk of a conservative mandate in 1980, Ronald Reagan received a smaller proportion of the eligible vote in that year than Jimmy Carter did in 1976. If trends continue at their present rate, the largest political grouping in America will soon be the nonpolitical. A system that cannot make political choice cannot command political allegiance. Americans who live with an economy that must throw people out of work in order to control inflation should not be surprised that they have a political system that must disenfranchise its citizens in order to choose its leaders. Much talk is heard in the 1980s of the need for a program of economic revitalization. Yet, as was true also in the 1940s, economic direction must come from the political system, and American politics is stagnant. America needs a program of political revitalization before its economy will begin to work again.

## II

EVEN THOUGH ITS ECONOMY was in shambles, America had a real politics during the Great Depression. Liberals believed in social justice and equality, while conservatives defended business liberty. Passions were exercised, loyalties tested, sentiments mobilized. At root, the New Deal period was an attempt to answer three questions: should the economic system be based on the market or the state? should government be coordinated and national, or local and decentralized? to what degree should public policies be addressed to the needs of a particular class? Under the imperatives of postwar growth politics, these questions, unable to be discussed directly, were addressed through drift and resolved with confusion. For Americans to engage in political revitalization, all three need to be asked once more, this time deliberately and with an appreciation of the consequences of one decision over another.

States and markets are the two dominant ways of organizing a modern political economy. All systems will combine elements of both, since capitalist societies long ago discovered some advantages to planning and planned economies found themselves in need of markets. But every political system must also decide which is the ultimate authority, for the state and the market are organized by contrasting imperatives. Markets are based on the maximization of *self-interest*, either the interest of the businessman to make a profit or the interest of the nation state to seek its autonomy in a world of nation states. Market principles imply that businessmen must be allowed to sell where they please; that trade between one country and another be permitted to take place without regard to domestic fallout; and that, as the Republican party platform of 1980 states, government should not interfere with the right the people have to drive their cars at any speed they choose. Defenders of the market claim that it maximizes freedom, a difficult claim to substantiate since to do so requires an economic conception of freedom so restrictive that it not only ignores, but violates, the freedom of a community to establish collective goals for itself. More properly put, market societies maximize the self-interest of those who benefit from the operations of the market; the size of that group depends on how broadly the market works.

If markets justify themselves through the principle of self-interest, states manifest a particular concern with *security*. The two dominant themes of state intervention in the modern world have been social security at home and national security abroad, each offering protection against—the pursuit of self-interest. Most citizens concluded that the free operation of self-interest caused the Depression, requiring state intervention to guarantee security. Similarly, the pursuit of the self-interest of all nation states seems to lead directly to war, forcing countries to search for foreign policies premised upon conceptions of security against war. At the present moment, the pursuit of self-interest at home produces inflation, while self-interest abroad suggests an endless arms race. Maximizing self-interest, in short, implies a tolerance for insecurity; ensuring security can only be done by limiting self-interest.

One of the most striking features of growth politics was the paucity of serious discussion of relative advantages of states and markets (and one of the most striking signs of the end of the postwar growth wave is the reemergence of interest in these questions).[4] It was as if this thorny problem had simply disappeared from intellectual consideration. Liberal advocates of growth, for example, lost sight of the objectives toward which growth was directed. Postwar liberals had no desire to repudiate the emphasis on security and welfare that was embodied in Rooseveltian rhetoric, but, dependent on an expansion of the economic surplus to finance this security, they were unwilling to tamper with the self-interest of business. Arguing that they were not anti-business, but were capable of managing a capitalist economy better than businessmen could, postwar liberals fudged the distinction between self-interest and security, speaking of these contrasting objectives as complementary. (*Planning for Freedom* was the title of a representative book by Eugene V. Rostow,[5] an articulate postwar liberal advocate of growth who recognized the transformation of American politics and supported Ronald Reagan—the new growth advocate—in 1980.)

Self-interest and security were equally incompatible in the international system, though few were willing to recognize the point. America committed itself, again under liberal urging, to a vast program of national security, but it did so in a contradictory way. Nation states are most secure when they do *not* feel free to do whatever they choose in the international system, for the simple reason that other nation states also exist, each also trying to maximize its self-interest. Peace is kept and security affirmed when nations enter into diplomacy to resolve disputes and when they join together to limit and contain economic controversies. For one nation state to proclaim that it will be free to pursue its self-interest while no other nation state will be permitted to do so—this was the first premise of both America's foreign policy and its international economic policy in the postwar years—is to negate the diplomacy and internationalism that make security possible. Never understanding that self-interest and security were different objectives, the United States pursued the former to obtain the latter, only to find that the harder it worked, the further away its goal seemed to be. The growth of empire and the reliance on hegemony to organize the world economy prevented the United States from recognizing that the pursuit of its self-interest was undermining the world's security.

Ronald Reagan's election in 1980 gave conservatives the hope that once again self-interest will triumph. The market, the new president maintains, should be allowed to dominate the state, and America will no longer be ashamed to assert its interests in a hostile world. Yet, one obstacle stands like a massive roadblock over a major shift toward the assertion of self-interest: reality. In the real world of political economy, actions by private corporations independent of a coordinating mechanism like the state are impossible to contemplate. In the real world of international affairs, total freedom of action at a time of fractured hegemony—and given the existence of nuclear weapons—is a pipe dream. The Reagan administration, any administration, once it starts to deal with the world as it is, will find that there are no answers along the road of self-interest; concentrations of monopoly power at home and a multiplicity of national powers abroad have eliminated the theoretical beauty of market-based models. Unable to base programs on a self-interest that no longer can be realized, conservatives, like liberals, may shift back in the direction of security, advocating government intervention at home to control inflation (wage-and price-controls? tariffs?) and periodic diplomacy overseas to gain security (SALT III?). Life for the average American will be more difficult under the Republicans, but for the managers of the economy conditions will be as close to the ideals of a self-regulating market as they were under the Democrats. It might, therefore, make more sense to think directly about the maximization of security as an alternative, the subject of the next section of this chapter.

A second set of questions never fully articulated during the period of the popularity of growth politics involves the degree of public authority. Should public power be located in agencies that have sufficient authority to make their decisions stick, or should it be flexible, working to gain the cooperation of the vested interests that resist the imposition of governmental power? In a society dominated by vested interests, creating effective public authority requires strenuous effort. Rare is the established interest that, used to its privileges, will support the creation of a public agency that can compel it to cease doing what has so profitably occupied its time. Resistance to authority is an American trait so ingrained that it would make an anarchist blush. Those who fight and lose in the legislative struggle generally carry their battles to the administrative process, seemingly forever. To control the destiny of any community, government must possess a mechanism for overcoming this resistance in the public interest. Confronting what Franz Schurmann has called the realm of interests[6]—that vast array of private bodies, regulatory agencies, congressional committees, and lobbyists whose function is to prevent the exercise of effective public authority—should be a major objective of public policy.

Despite the fact that the question of public authority was one of the most widely discussed topics of the New Deal, there was almost no serious attempt made to grapple with the problem during the heyday of growth politics. Liberal planners were aware of the problem, and the creation of agencies like the Council of Economic Advisers was supposed to help the state assemble authority. Yet, to hold *power*, liberals were forced to sacrifice *authority*. Thus, counter-Keynesianism opposed direct intervention in the economy, preferring less authoritative but more politically acceptable intervention on the demand-side. Public housing, to take another example, was doomed once the Truman and Kennedy administrations chose not to fight for a centralized authority with the power to confront the real-estate lobby. Negative, obstructionist, and petty complaints of private interests to the public good were a constant feature of postwar politics, yet, while understanding that such complaints would undermine the ability to plan and make policy, liberals had little choice but to heed them, given their dependence on business for growth and the military for security. Designed to manage, the public agencies created by growth politics lacked sufficient authority to make management possible. Government was called in to put out the fires, but its hoses were taken away. Just enough public authority was exercised to discredit the use of the state, but not enough to enable it to achieve its objectives. As a result, the public policies pursued by liberals in the postwar years were not public, and they were not policies.

To achieve the effective use of public authority in the global system, some contravention of the realm of national interest was necessary. In spite of the fact that the postwar period began with liberal dreams of international authority—both the United Nations and the International Monetary Fund were premised on such a vision—the United States was unwilling to sacrifice sufficient national sovereignty to make international authority possible. Rejecting the advice of liberals like Harry Dexter White and John Maynard Keynes, the United States, to its horrendous disadvantage over time, suppressed international liquidity to keep itself on top of the world economy. Similarly, the imperatives of a cold war foreign policy downplayed international cooperation in favor of a crude interpretation of the national interest. American national power became a substitute for the lack of international power in the world system, but, when slow growth undermined the ability of the United States to play the role of world governor, the system was left without effective ability to counter the self-interest of its most important participants.

Conservatives in America have generally proclaimed themselves in favor of weak public authority, except for the police. Indeed, the Republican party for a century has been little more than an aggregate of self-interests. The election of a conservative majority in 1980, therefore, represents no significant shift in the postwar approach to the question of public authority. Both domestically and in the international system, liberal desires to exercise competent authority were so fractured by solicitations of vested interests at home and the national interest abroad that in neither area did the exercise of legitimate authority actually take place. Conservatives claim that since the accumulation of authority proved impossible, one should give up on the objective. Ronald Reagan's administration seems determined to ferret out what few traces of working public authority exist and to eliminate them. When the next round of energy crises, declining public morale, or international anarchy compels the public to pay attention to this age-old problem, believers in political revitalization should be prepared with some thoughts about how the exercise of effective public authority can be facilitated.

Third, there was a question of social class to be addressed, but the pattern of growth politics in the postwar period prevented it from being considered intelligently. Social class disparity is the dirty laundry of American politics, the out-of-sight reality that tells more about the condition of the house than what is on display. Political coalitions need to tie themselves to a social class in order to have a purpose, even while trying to broaden their base to other classes in order to win elections. The Republican party has generally understood this, tying its fortunes to those of business. During the New Deal, the Democrats began to understand it as well, allying their party with the working class in a way that began to resemble the European experience with social democracy. Without a firm base in a social class, a political party has little upon which to rely when matters get rough, as, in politics, they often do.

When the New Deal was transformed into a quest for growth, the class character of American politics was proclaimed to be irrelevant, if not subversive. From Truman to Carter, liberal advocates of growth sought the support of organized labor, but followed policies designed to encourage organized business. Thinking they had resolved the class struggle through the ballot box, growth politicians relied on domestic and imperial expansion to avoid making choices among social groups. Rejecting the direct incorporation of labor into the policymaking process, pro-growth liberals offered the labor movement the benefits of output rather than the prerogatives of input. Labor would be given higher wages, cost-of-living adjustments, ever-expanding commodities; all the labor movement had to give up in return was control over the work place and direct access to political power. Meanwhile businessmen, treated as pariahs during the Great Depression, would no longer be treated as economic royalists if they agreed to be "responsible." Growth priorities dictated that policymakers delude themselves into thinking that consensus was the purpose of politics, when, as

Lyndon Johnson discovered, the search for consensus in a divided society destroys the instrument that undertakes it.

In the world at large, social class was as ignored as it was in the United States. Growth advocates, as I argued in chapter 7, had a choice between responding to the needs of the world's poor or ignoring them. Under the imperatives of growth politics, both—hence neither—were done. Liberal programs like Point Four and the Peace Corps seemed to call for the elimination of poverty, while conservative financial policies and the instincts of the military and the CIA perpetuated dependence. Growth politics worked at obvious cross-purposes. Neither liberal nor conservative, the emphasis upon development sought from the world's poorest classes both love and fear. A society that could not recognize the reality of class divisions at home had even more difficulty acknowledging their existence abroad.

Class disparity does not disappear because policymakers (and pro-growth intellectuals) proclaim that it has. Postwar liberals failed because they were unable to keep the support of the working class while unable to gain the support of business. The conservative Republican administration that came to power in 1980 will seek to answer the question of social class explicitly in favor of those at the top (though pro-growth leaders of the Republican party, such as Congressman Jack Kemp, urge the Reagan administration not to repeal the spirit of Franklin Roosevelt and John Kennedy). On this question, the Reagan administration has already committed itself to a thoroughly pro-business orientation, for supply-side economics, as practiced under current conditions, is little more than the trickle-down theory of prosperity once so popular in the Republican party. When the full consequences of a pro-business program become evident, the great majority of Americans who do not own companies may search for an alternative, at which point a program of political revitalization based upon another set of answers to these questions will, it is hoped, be considered.

To summarize, three of the most important questions in modern politics deal with the organization of the economy, the degree of public authority, and social class. American liberalism, due to its dependence on growth, was unable to develop effective answers to any of these questions. American conservatism now has its chance. Yet there is substantial evidence that conservatives either will not be able to put their preferred ideological notions into practice, or,

if they are, the social costs would be so great that public repudiation, assuming the continued existence of democracy, would be
only a matter of time. Postwar liberalism, seduced by growth,
failed; postwar conservatism, being seduced by growth, will fail.
Can anything work? A positive answer may be found by formulating answers to the three crucial questions being discussed in this
chapter in the absence of the allurement of uncontrolled growth at
home and empire abroad.

# III

POLITICAL REVITALIZATION—a path out of America's impasse—is
possible, *if* it is based on three propositions. First, the American
people must take whatever steps are necessary to guarantee their
security: against inflation and unemployment at home and against
the possibility of nuclear war and an uncontrolled arms race abroad.
Second, Americans must create for themselves a public authority
that will help them achieve this security, which requires both a
strong government at home capable of planning and intervening in
the public interest and a strong international authority capable of
countering the self-interest of nation states. Third, the majority of
the American people must recognize that they have in common a
class position and they must be as willing to use government to
support that position as business, in the past, has been willing to
use government to support its position.

Such a program clearly leads in the direction of what has been
called socialism, but with a major difference. Though it is beyond
the scope of this book to argue this point, postwar socialism has also
been a product of growth politics, certainly in state socialist societies like the Soviet Union, but also in social democratic countries
like Sweden.[7] The United States, which has lagged so much
behind the rest of the world along the path to socialism, ironically
could leap ahead if it were able to formulate a popular program
based on the principle of balanced and democratically controlled
growth. It will not be easy; unrestrained growth and popular
democracy in America are generally held to be synonymous.
Merely to suggest the possibility is to tar oneself with the anti-
growth brush, almost as taboo in America as subversion. Yet there
is a sign of hope, even if a perverse one. America's political system
deteriorated when its economy was booming. Now that its economy is failing to deliver both the goods and its promises, perhaps
its political system can be made to work.

I am not advocating austerity. My argument is that the political costs of uncontrolled growth have been so great that reduced rates of growth and a shrunken imperial apparatus offer the American people the possibility of lowering the costs. Given the fact that the Third World insists on some control over its resources, and that other capitalist countries have gained economically, America will be accepting a small proportion of the world's product.[8] With its tax base declining, there will be less revenue available to finance public programs, meaning that choices will have to be made. The major question on the political agenda is whether the American people will have their public policies dictated to them in the name of fiscal austerity or creatively fashioned by them in the name of revitalized democracy.[9] The only alternative to an economic austerity program, as economist Lenny Goldberg has pointed out, is to raise *political* issues: who benefits from particular programs and why?[10] Less economics, in a word, suggests the possibility of more politics; for every aspect of uncontrolled growth brought under popular control, political capacity expands.

In the world that currently exists, those who offer the American people the vision of growth as it was—whether in the form of Reaganism, traditional cold war liberalism, or social democracy—offer, not only the human and social bankruptcy that comes with it, but an illusion that will undermine public faith in those who make the promise. Growth in community and an expansion of people's capacities seem more realistic objectives than a mad and divisive scramble over increasingly fewer crumbs. Rather than austerity, which is increasingly the practice of dominant coalitions if not yet their ideology, I am calling for a commitment to human and social growth with all the zeal that Americans once displayed for an expansion of the gross national product. Americans, in a word, should recognize the fantastic opportunity that has been presented to them by the collapse of expansion and empire and use the opportunity to rebuild their depleted social existence. Less satiated consumers, they may find themselves more satisfied citizens.

In what follows, I will return to the areas where postwar economic and imperial expansion obviated the need for political choice—that is, to the case studies examined in chapters 3–7—and try to pose recommendations that offer a possibility of political revitalization. My purposes are twofold. First, rather than offering a comprehensive plan of what could be done, I have a less ambitious scheme in mind. All I hope to show is that the possibilities are enormous once the need to win the confidence of the military and business no longer acts as a constraint on the political intellect and imagination. What follows, then, is not a blueprint but some statements of possibility. Second, as much as possible I will present policy alternatives that have already been developed by other people: activists, planners, intellectuals, even dissenting policy-makers. The ideas discussed here are already in the currency of the realm, even if they remain generally unnoticed in Washington.

1. *Macroeconomic policy*. The great accomplishment of the Republican party under Ronald Reagan is the rediscovery of the supply-side. To their credit, conservatives began to understand that tinkering with aggregate demand had accomplished just about everything it could in postwar America, a lesson that Jimmy Carter could never absorb. Yet, like a cave dweller who discovers fire but burns down the forest instead of cooking his meat, the Republicans urge, not that the supply-side be brought under public control, but that the collective will and intelligence be ever banished from it. For political revitalization to take place, "supply-side economics" is a necessity, but it should be directed toward one objective: securing the economic and political health of the American people.

The first premise of an economic policy must be a full-employment program, for every other policy area to be discussed hinges upon it. Insecurity of employment has made citizenship impossible in the United States. So long as the possibility of losing one's job exists, the impossibility of being a social person remains. We cannot call free a person who must support a bloated military apparatus in order to hold onto his or her job in a company dependent on military contracts. We cannot call healthy and secure a country that punishes certain regions or cities because jobs have left for other regions or cities. The social costs of insecure employment are as high as the costs of unemployment; both erode the capacity of the political system to respond to evident needs in rational ways. To guarantee every American a job is to establish the precondition for a system of economic planning that would enable a human community to bring its maximal intelligence to bear on the solution to economic problems. The fear of losing jobs consigns a political system to the dead end of suppressing imagination to preserve what already exists.

Just as destructive to the potentiality of political life as insecure

employment is an insecure income, especially one eroded by inflation. As every historian knows, inflation is insidious to community.
Rapid increases in prices repudiate promises, destroy trust, and
undermine faith. As every unit of self-interest seeks to turn itself
from a loser to a winner in the battle against inflation, Adam
Smith's invisible hand reverses itself, ensuring that the sum total of
all private acts is to cheapen and worsen public ones. For a revitalized political system to function, the insecurity bred by inflation must either be eliminated or, failing that, brought under
democratic control.

There is no question that a program of full employment and
price stability can work; the only question is how much needs to be
sacrificed in order to obtain it. Throughout the postwar period,
growth advocates claimed that wage-and-price controls or full-
employment guarantees would undermine productivity, destroy
business confidence, and produce sluggish economic performance.
Whether they were right or wrong is now irrelevant; a program
without controls and planning has produced declining productivity
and disinvestment. With a stroke, much of the presumed cost of
moving toward full employment has been abolished. Conservatives
also argued that government intervention into the economy would
reduce the scope of human freedom, but subjects who are effectively blackmailed into supporting policies that harm the community in order to preserve their jobs are hardly free. Americans
were told that if they put their faith in growth the other things
would take care of themselves. The other things did not. Americans must now put their faith in full employment and income
security and let growth follow from that.

Full employment and a stable incomes policy must be combined with a program of reindustrialization. Numerous ideas for
revitalizing the economy are floating around the economics profession. Lester Thurow, for example, has proposed that public policy
be directed toward the encouragement of "sunrise" industries
(semiconductors, genetic engineering), while easing the death of
"sunset" industries (shoes, automobiles, steel).[11] Yet, one of the
major obstacles facing a commitment to the expansion of newer,
more productive industries is the conservatism bred by job insecurity. Traditional industries in the United States have declined
due both to managerial complacency and to union practices. Between them, management and labor in the declining industries are
powerful enough to win subsidies and protection; they continue to

practice growth politics in a no-growth economy. If America had a jobs-and-income program, in other words, it would be in a position to develop an industrial policy as well, for there would be less of an incentive to keep a declining industry in existence to protect jobs if alternative jobs were guaranteed.

Economies have changed and developed since the beginning of time, and a public policy that seeks to plan and control those changes makes greater sense than one that tries to pick up the pieces after the changes have taken place. Current programs for reindustrialization in the United States have confused cause and effect. Gigantic subsidies to encourage the production of synthetic fuels, for example, accept an energy-intensive economy as a fact of life and then seek to make it work. Meanwhile, the number of American firms capable of making mass-transit cars has been reduced to one. Reindustrializing the status quo, which both parties essentially advocate, would not revitalize very much. So long as growth politics dominate the state, government will be unable to develop what Ronald Müller calls the "breathing space" necessary "to help crack the supply-side vicious circle of the economy— sagging investor confidence and investment, which contribute to declining productivity growth that brings even lower investment, which further diminishes productivity and is a basis of faltering trade competitiveness, an unstable dollar and inflation itself."[12]

A creative reindustrialization policy, once jobs and income were secure, would use effective public power to develop sunrise industries that promote the common interests of society. Mass transit, for example, could be made a profitable sunrise industry if public support for it existed, while the sun should set on the MX missile and the Trident submarine. The point of having a new industry is not just to increase the gross national product but to correct imbalances between the energy available and the energy expended or between the need for defense and the weapons available to fill the need. *Industrialization for what* ranks with *industrialization for whom* as the kind of question that needs to be addressed by a program of economic and political revitalization.

The elements of a macroeconomic policy for political revitalization already exist and include:

• a commitment to full employment and the creation of a government agency that would guarantee it by subsidizing the movement of workers into jobs in productive, community-determined sunrise industries. A full-employment program without authority—such as the 1946 act or the Humphrey-Hawkins bill—is no longer worth passing. If a program with teeth cannot be gotten through Congress, advocates of the idea should try to build massive support for it outside the legislative halls.

• price controls. The details of a program to control inflation in the necessities has been worked out by Gar Alperovitz and his associates at the National Center for Economic Alternatives.[13] Prices are too important to be left to those who raise them.

• reindustrialization. The federal government must be given the authority to encourage balanced growth in highly productive new industries that serve social needs. As capital formation becomes democratized, the possibility of political revitalization expands. Productivity can be encouraged by convincing workers to support new technologies in return for democratic control over how to use them. Managerial complacency has been a significant cause of declining productivity. In industries like automobiles and consumer electronics, management has forfeited its right to manage. A reindustrialization program based on shop-floor participation, at this stage in history, is more compatible with increasing productivity than one based on self-serving deals between conservative union bureaucrats and even more conservative managers.

2. *Domestic policy.* As America enters the 1980s, the poor are being punished for a crime they did not commit. Cutbacks in social services are urged with bipartisan self-righteousness, while opposition to the achievement of greater equality manifests itself in every region and among every ethnic group. America seems to have abandoned its historical ideals without much of a struggle, for the efforts to help the poor—now judged to have failed—were minimal at best. Liberals long ago transformed their humanitarianism into a race toward growth, and conservatives were never very humanitarian to begin with. What failed were reforms that lacked the authority to reform.

Political revitalization and a new approach to domestic policy go hand in hand. Voting turnout in poor and minority communities is so low that a significant portion of the American population can no longer be said to be citizens in even the most minimal sense of

the term. One wonders who is fooling whom. It is obviously possible in a middle-class democracy for a national consensus to develop that will punish the poor; by themselves, the poor are unable
to obtain benefits through the legislative process. Yet the social
costs of a policy of middle-class self-interest are incalculable. The
fear of crime, like the fear of inflation, undermines the possibility
of trust that makes social life possible. The losses in productivity
suffered because of the existence of a permanent underclass hurt
everyone. No country can aspire to world leadership, as America
insists on doing, when it is incapable of maximizing the energy and
intelligence of its entire citizenry. Can America move beyond a
politics of middle-class self-interest to develop a program that
would rebuild its domestic spirit? Only, in my view, if the whole
question of class is reintroduced into American political discourse
and, in the process, redefined.

Growth politics in postwar America were premised on the assumption that the working class would slowly be transformed into
middle-class citizens, an assumption that held up so long as the
growth took place. Consequently, domestic programs were
couched in universal language; instead of being targeted specifically at the poor, they became part of a general quest for a better
life for all. (In the process, such programs also became open-
ended, inflationary, and self-contradictory.) When the very poor
were left behind by such programs, the middle class was encouraged to believe that its interests lay with those at the top of
society, further isolating those at the bottom and making possible a
shift to the political right. America's middle class, all the while
thinking that it was helping the poor, financed out of its tax dollars
the costs of urban development and pro-growth reconstruction.
Now that the growth has stopped, the demands of growth politics
compel the middle class to put the blame on the poor for higher
taxes and domestic programs that could not, from the start, reach
their objectives. The result is a politics of resentment that feeds
conservative fury.

Yet in a slow-growth economy, middle- and lower-income Americans begin to have more in common economically, even if they are
driven further apart ideologically.[14] Stagflation increases the size
of the working class by undermining middle-class security. No displaced middle-class person wishes to be informed that he or she is
now once again a member of the working class, yet the major hope
for political revitalization in America rests on the notion that all

those who work for a living in an insecure economy have in common an interest in guaranteeing their economic security. A revitalization of class politics would make possible the notions that work can be honorable, that all should be entitled to it, and that domestic policy as a result should have the limited objective of helping people in those temporary periods when work is not available or when people cannot perform it. Fiscal responsibility and political clarity in social policy can be reclaimed when domestic programs are no longer an excuse for tearing down homes or building hospitals and highways. A domestic program for economic and political revitalization should contain elements like the following:

• job training. The first priority of social policy should be to train those who need skills for the jobs they will have if an industrial policy is created premised upon full employment.
• alternative delivery modes. Under the imperatives of growth politics, the middle class paid taxes to support the delivery of services more than the services themselves. Huge bureaucracies, cost-plus contracts, and unsound financial practices lay behind housing and health policies. Domestic policy can be made to respond to social needs if it encourages delivery systems that have political and fiscal integrity. Rehabilitating existing housing stock; providing community-based day-care centers and self-help medical care; eliminating the welfare bureaucracy; and banning the construction of new urban highways—these kinds of programs would prevent the hostiliy and resentment that were the inevitable result of using the rhetoric of helping the poor to line the pockets of the rich.

3. *Foreign policy.* For a political culture said to be materialistic and practical, Americans have sacrificed financially to support an empire that rewards them psychically and symbolically. As the conservative consensus of the 1980s seeks to recreate the imperial apparatus shattered during Vietnam, the costs will increase. Americans will not only sacrifice their cities, stable prices, social trust, and their future to build up their military forces in a futile search for security, they will also destroy any possibility of revitalizing their political system. For empire and a healthy politics are incompatible. As Norman Birnbaum has noted:

Every American President since John Kennedy has been sacrificed as one of the costs of empire. (And perhaps Kennedy too. . . . Vietnam defeated Lyndon Johnson. Richard Nixon's deployment against the Democrats of the agencies and techniques that Johnson mobilized against the antiwar movement terminated his presidency. Gerald Ford's interregnum ended when the Republican right decided that, in foreign policy, he and the "traitor" Kissinger were indistinguishable from the Democrats. The Ayatollah Khomeini, in the end, defeated Jimmy Carter. . . .[15]

National security was a major theme that led to the conservative victory in 1980. Yet so bereft of imagination did America become during its flirtation with expansion that people naturally assume that security and a large military budget are synonymous. The Reagan administration, if it carries out its program to restore the empire, will prove otherwise. A sharp increase in military spending is a recipe for insecurity, a sure-fire method to eliminate the diplomacy that can make Americans secure in a polycentric world. Every attempt made by the United States in the postwar world to strengthen unilaterally its military apparatus has led to another hysterical round of insecurity. In its quest to make itself secure, the United States has tried everything except the one approach that might work: a careful examination of its national interest and a deliberate shedding of what is not essential to that interest.

The national interest of the United States should reduce itself to one principle: to protect the security of the American people. The greatest threats to that security are posed by the way that America has treated its relations with the Soviet Union and by the continued American itch to deal with the rest of the world by force.

Nothing is more threatening to security than the possibility of nuclear war, although the prospect of an unrestricted arms race with the Russians comes close. In both cases, current doctrine is premised upon a course designed to maximize insecurity. We are told that America must prepare to fight a nuclear war in order to avoid one and that America's arsenal needs to be strengthened in order to control the arms race. Yet deterrence theory, which made little sense when the number of nuclear weapons was minimal, makes even less when the superpowers approach what Nigel Calder has called a surplus economy with respect to nuclear weapons.[16] Claiming that deterrence had become passé, the

Carter administration, in Presidential Directive 59, moved toward a strategic policy of preparing for a limited nuclear war, a strategy that advisers to Ronald Reagan not only endorse but even originated. From this point forward, each nuclear superpower has little choice but to move its doctrines ever closer to actually fighting a nuclear war in order to convince the other side not to start one first. Like the logic behind SALT—one must be free to reach very high limits on weapons in order to make arms talks acceptable to both sides—nuclear diplomacy is being practiced in a way fraught with danger.

Resurgent imperial inclinations lay behind the feeling of dependence on strategic raw materials from the Third World, especially the Middle East. Fear of running out translates directly into popular support for the Rapid Deployment Force and other mobile offensive-weapons systems. It is often said that Americans have a short historical memory, but this is not precise. Americans do remember Vietnam; that is why they have to work so hard at suppressing its lessons. The world is unstable, and it makes perfect sense for Americans to worry about their insecurity when change is so evident. But to think that an interventionary deployment of force would solve the insecurity of energy supply better than domestic conservation betrays a staggering lack of political capacity. As the Reagan administration's preoccupation with El Salvador testifies, the temptation to reestablish an empire premised upon military force seems irresistible. Yet empires have historically been undermined by the illusion that a country can be strong abroad while starving itself at home in a futile attempt to perpetuate that strength. A truly strong country would allow a weak one like El Salvador to choose its own government.

Once imperial instincts are factored out of foreign policy, diplomacy becomes possible. Proposals for a noninterventionist foreign policy have been advanced by many writers, both by those on the left as well as by those who consider themselves libertarians.[17] Specifics, by definition, await specific situations, but it does seem to me that a post-imperial foreign policy would seek to reject the need for a first-strike strategic policy, take the lead in urging the creation of international agencies charged with the authority to negotiate disputes, and pledge nonintervention into the affairs of other countries. Rather than trying to mimick whatever it perceives the Russians to be doing, thereby making its foreign policy as unsuccessful as its antagonist's, the United States should be dealing with the world as it will be, not as it was in 1945.

4. *Foreign economic policy.* Should the United States restrict the entry of Datsuns into the United States in order to protect Chrysler? Should American firms be free to invest anywhere around the world in order to maximize profits? Should foreign firms willing to establish plants inside the United States be welcomed? Few questions are harder to answer given the age-old rivalry between free-traders and protectionists. In an era of decline, sympathy for protectionism grows. Yet, generally unasked in the debate are two crucial questions: protection of what? protection for whom?

The objective of foreign economic policy, in my opinion, should be the protection of the economic security of the American people. There are times when that security can be accomplished through open economic relations with other countries. There are other times when restrictions on free trade may have to be imposed. The foreign economic policy of the United States should not be allowed to destroy the livelihood, security, and stable economic expectations of the American people, or else democracy becomes impossible.

A foolish policy is one that tries to limit the entry of more efficient and less expensive products because America cannot match them. If the Japanese learn to build better cars than Detroit, they should be rewarded with a large American market. However, such a statement presupposes a full-employment program in the United States. Indeed, full employment makes possible a serious commitment to free trade, for once jobs and income are protected the danger of foreign competition is lessened—and conceivably turned into an advantage, since a country that has been falling behind can learn from the leader's mistakes.

Moreover, the United States might decide as a matter of economic policy to maintain some industries that are no longer competitive in the world economy for the purpose of ensuring supply. Under such conditions, the Youngstown plan developed by church, labor, and community leaders to reopen closed steel plants on the basis of increased worker output makes considerable sense. As the Youngstown example shows, American ingenuity can be considerable, although in this case the Carter administration chose not to put up the funds for the experiment.

To ensure economic security, it may be necessary to impose

restrictions on the freedom of business to move whenever and wherever it wants. Disinvestment by business in American communities has become a serious matter requiring effective public policy, and in this area, as in so many, articulate and workable policies have been proposed, in this case by Barry Bluestone and Bennett Harrison.[18] Local communities in the United States have invested considerable resources in making their environments attractive to business: tax abatements, the provision of public services, and the forfeiture of clean air and water, for example. For business to disinvest in the hopes of making greater profit in other countries, or in other parts of this country, is to break a social contract and undermine the possibility of an effective political community. As Bluestone and Harrison suggest in much greater detail than can be provided here, legislation can be developed that would control the impact of plant closings if the will exists to make economic security a higher priority than growth at any price. (Similarly, people in a community have the right to demand of foreign investors conditions that would not permit them to disinvest at will.)

America also needs a policy to help reorganize the world's monetary and trading systems. Bretton Woods became an attempt to have the dollar play the twin role of domestic currency and international standard, but when American hegemony collapsed, so did the dollar. Since at least 1971, Eurodollar speculation, uncertain commodity prices, and rapid shifts in exchange rates have led other countries to begin the process of working out regional solutions, like the European Monetary Union. Yet, while this occurs, the Reagan administration is captivated by dreams of American nationalism; its refusal to endorse the Law of the Sea treaty was a perfect example. America is in danger of imposing isolation on itself unless it becomes willing to participate in international economic negotiations that would establish trade and currency rules premised upon the needs of all the participants, not just one.

To strengthen economic security, the United States should take the following steps with respect to international economics:

- create a full-employment policy at home so that foreign competition would be welcomed, discouraging tariffs and import quotas;
- place mandatory controls on the outflow of American capital to other countries;

• take the lead in convening another conference—have it at Bretton Woods again if need be—that would transform the International Monetary Fund and World Bank back to the original purpose and would recreate the terms of the International Trade Organization Treaty that the United States rejected in 1947. As the world economy is mired in stagflation, the need for international liquidity and increased trade between nation states is greater than ever. The United States would benefit in the long run if it could overcome its blind adherence to restrictive and self-serving policies toward the other economies of the world.

5. *Policies toward the Third World.* Of the five policy areas discussed in this book, the least compelling, as America enters the 1980s, is the relationship between the United States and the countries of the Third World. For some time, Congress has not been interested in the question of foreign aid, except as a military measure. During the Carter administration, as a result, the United States became the second least-generous country in the industrialized North in its response to the needs of the South. With the election of a budget-cutting Ronald Reagan as president, prospects for a reversal of this trend seem nonexistent. One of the very first acts of the Reagan administration was to threaten a full-scale reduction in foreign aid, although the global realities facing Secretary of State Haig compelled some modifications of the domestic realities that preoccupied budget director Stockman. At the same time, the Reagan administration is committed to strengthening the CIA and to firming up its links with police-state dictators in Asia and Latin America. It would be difficult to conjecture less likely conditions for thinking in new ways about America's relations with the world's poor.

Yet the issue never dies. In 1980, a U.N. commission chaired by Willy Brandt of West Germany proposed a new agenda for North–South relations.[19] Outside the United States, particularly in Northern Europe, programs for foreign aid still win a wide hearing. Even a conservative like Margaret Thatcher discovered, once in office, that a mature settlement in Zimbabwe made more sense than conservative longings for a colonial empire. The reason the issue does not die is obvious: the world is explosive, as revolutions in Iran never fails to serve as a reminder, and a country that treats the world with contempt will be so treated in return.

Taking place in the world is a process that neither the United States nor the Soviet Union wishes to acknowledge: the breakdown of bipolar hegemony.[20] For most of the postwar period, the United States and the Soviet Union organized the rest of the world around the magnets of their respective power. A pervasive mood has been introduced into the United States to the effect that America is losing power, which is true, and that the Soviets as a result are gaining it, which is false. Both magnetic fields are losing strength. There are four obvious indications of the deterioration of bipolar hegemony: the increasing independence of Western Europe from the United States; the inability of the Soviet Union to impose automatically its will on Eastern Europe and countries like Poland; the rise of China to potential superpower status; and the increasing autonomy of the Third World as symbolized by OPEC and other commodity-producing organizations. One of the most important questions that the United States will at some point have to confront is what it plans to do about the multipolarized world that is coming into existence.

From the standpoint of maximizing the security of the American people, it makes far more sense to recognize what is taking place in the world and to plan for it rather than to insist on conditions that can no longer be restored. If the United States continues to rely on its military and intelligence apparatus to protect its interests in the Third World, it will find itself facing more Iranian revolutions. As America loses greater influence in the Third World due to its misguided determination to preserve it, the American people will be asked to support ever more repressive and vicious policies that will undermine that influence further. There is no future for the American people along the avenue chosen by imperial ambition. The United States should instead devote itself to a realistic strategy toward the Third World based on the forces that are already in motion. Such a strategy would include:

- an endorsement of the Brandt Commission report and a concerted effort to provide foreign aid through international agencies not committed to strategic and capitalist interests;
- the repudiation of covert operations by intelligence agencies in the Third World. If the Soviets want to spy on people and win their hatred and distrust (as they have done on nearly every continent), that is their affair.
- restrictions on the actions of the military and multinational

corporations operating in the Third World. When as conservative and pro-capitalist a regime as Brazil's finds it necessary to
impose limits on U.S. multinational corporations, the question
becomes: who will take the lead in regulating the unregulated?
A policy under which the United States showed some sensitivity to the conduct of its own agencies in the Third World—
instead of the currently popular idea of lifting all limits on such
conduct to promote profits—would go further in protecting
the American people against the resentment of the rest of the
world than a policy of waiting for the host government to take
the same steps.

In the America of the 1980s, ideas and proposals for public
policy abound as never before. The number of magazines, conferences, and tendencies is truly remarkable. In every region of the
United States, community-based groups are talking about alternative energy plans and thinking about new ways of collecting
garbage and directing traffic.[21] The slowing of the economy and
the limits of empire have already given rise to a flourishing of
alternatives; yet, in Washington, neither political party is in a position to listen to them. Growth politics still operates at the national
level, even if the economy is in a no-growth state. Both dominant
parties must first win the approval of business for any domestic
policy, thereby ensuring that any such policy will fail. Each party
outdoes the other in seeking to win the confidence of the military
and the national security apparatus in foreign policy, thereby
dooming international programs to repeat the mistakes of the past.
It used to be that the problem in America was the lack of an
alternative. Now the problem is the lack of political capacity to
realize the multitude of alternatives that are being developed.
To keep alive the faint hopes of business expansion and the resumption of empire, America is forced to sacrifice, through a collective suicide ritual, whatever chances it has to develop a match
between its political capacity and its economic potential.

# IV

WITH BOTH POLITICAL PARTIES in the United States practicing growth
politics in a no-growth economy, the American political system has
become highly unstable. Public opinion is fickle, political parties

are unable to organize stable coalitions, and policies are proposed only to be repudiated shortly thereafter. Under these circumstances, the public mood that made possible Ronald Reagan's victory in 1980 will soon tire, preparing the groundwork for yet another futile attempt to resolve the impasse. Unless the next shift is even further to the right than Reaganism, the forthcoming phase in the political cycle will be a return to the liberal ideas of old. Americans who are now attracted to business freedom and military power as abstract ideas will, when they pay for the costs of those programs, rediscover the appeal of social justice and global cooperation. Yet, to return to a discredited liberalism would be no more a solution than to flirt with a faddish conservatism, for the economic conditions that support both no longer exist. The United States no longer has a liberal tradition, nor does it possess a conservative one. Since 1946, politics in America has been about growth, and when there is no growth there are no politics.

Growth politics in a no-growth economy produces the conditions for its own perpetuation. Those claiming to have a magic formula for restoring prosperity win a hearing, no matter how blatantly contradictory their nostrums. (Indeed, the New Right economics of men like Arthur Laffer and George Gilder is about as scientifically grounded as the New Right attempt to make a case for divine creation.) Meanwhile, the liberal alternative, if Felix Rohatyn is any example, is to put forward a modern version of Malthus, urging people to lower their political vision in order to bring it in line with a reduced set of economic expectations.[22] The path out of America's impasse lies neither in the search for a Holy Grail of prosperity nor along the road of eliminating citizenship as the price to pay for continued business investment. In an age of austerity, economics seems more relevant than politics, as people are told to sacrifice their security, their neighborhoods, their regions, and their ideals for the sake of an increasing rate of return. The irony is that, under conditions of austerity, politics *must* be made to triumph over economics, for only through a revitalization of the collective energy of all the people can an effort be made to find a way out of the impasse. America, as its citizens prove every day, does have the capacity to make itself whole again, but it can only do so by taking advantage of the social ideals of all, not the economic appetites of a few.

# ACKNOWLEDGMENTS, NOTES AND INDEX

# Acknowledgments

M Y STRONGEST DEBT is to David Gold. We began this book as a collaborative project, and the first draft of chapter 3 was jointly written with him. Circumstances did not allow us to finish the book together, but without his help it would never have been begun. Three other chapters were inspired by the research and writing of good friends. The idea behind chapter 4 came from John Mollenkopf, whose forthcoming book on the rise and fall of growth coalitions in American cities will be the definitive work on the subject. Conversations and collaborations with Michael Klare and Jerry Sanders shaped chapter 5. The writing of chapter 6 was guided by the work of Fred Block.

Jeff Frieden, Paul Blumberg, David Plotke, Ray Franklin, and John Judis read the entire manuscript and offered positive encouragement and, in Jeff's case, a major reformulation. Norman Birnbaum intervened at a crucial moment with just the right words to keep the project alive. Charles Noble, Mark Kesselman, and Ira Katznelson were instrumental at an early stage in the writing. Members of the San Francisco Bay Area *Kapitalistate* Group, in particular Jens Christiansen, Les Guliasi, James Hamley, Clarence Lo, Patricia Morgan, Brian Murphy, and Patrick O'Donnell, offered support, criticism, and comradeship. Victor Navasky, Kai Bird, Richard Lingeman, and the staff of *The Nation* helped me improve the readability of these ideas.

*America's Impasse* originated at the Childhood and Government Project of the University of California, Berkeley. My thanks go to Will Riggan for insisting that no adequate treatment of the postwar experience in foreign and domestic policy existed. Troy Duster, the director of the Institute for the Study of Social Change at the University of California, Berkeley, was instrumental in the completion of this work, providing me with office space, a self-correcting typewriter, and franking privileges. When Troy was on leave, W. Russell Ellis kept the support alive. Connie Price protected me from the world when the need arose and kept my spirits buoyant. Others at the institute, especially David Matza and David Wellman, were helpful at all stages of the project. Financial help that enabled me to continue writing and thinking was generously provided by Bruce Seivers and the California Council for the Humanities in Public Policy, Richard Parker and the Seed Fund, and Carol and W. H. Ferry.

Pantheon Books offered me, for the first time, something close to my image of what a publisher should be. In particular, Phil Pochoda, my editor, had the grace to be harsh, seeing the project through to completion even at difficult times. Donna Bass, Don Guttenplan, and Doug Stumpf helped in numerous ways, and William Golightly, my copyeditor, improved the prose. Gail Satler completed the index.

This book is dedicated to my parents, who have so often given me support when I needed it. For the past three years, AnnaLee Saxenian has been part of my life, and her commitment, her strength, and her optimism have improved both this book and, I venture to say, the person who wrote it.

—Alan Wolfe
Brooklyn, New York
January 1981

# Notes

## I: An Uncertain Mandate

1. Quoted in *The New York Times*, November 6, 1980, p. A24.
2. Quoted in Tom Wicker, "Reagan's Real Test," *The New York Times*, November 7, 1980, p. A27.
3. *Business Week*, June 30, 1980, p. 86.
4. The *Business Week* Team, *The Decline of American Power and What We Can Do About It* (Boston: Houghton Mifflin, 1980), pp. 13, 227–228.
5. Quoted in Wicker, "Reagan's Real Test."
6. Idem.

## II: The Rise and Fall of Growth Politics

1. Figures from *Economic Report of the President, 1978* (Washington: Government Printing Office, 1978), p. 257.
2. Robert J. Donovan, *Conflict and Crisis: The Presidency of Harry S Truman* (New York: Norton, 1977), p. 108.
3. Gabriel Kolko, *Main Currents in Modern American History* (New York: Harper and Row, 1976), p. 312.
4. Craufurd D. Goodwin and R. Stanley Herren, "The Truman Administration: Problems and Policies Unfold," in *Exhortation and Controls: The Search for a Wage-Price Policy, 1945–1971*, ed. Craufurd D. Goodwin (Washington: Brookings Institution, 1975), p. 9.
5. Kolko, *Main Currents*, p. 317.
6. Herbert Stein, *The Fiscal Revolution in America* (Chicago: University of Chicago Press, 1969), pp. 242–44.
7. Godfrey Hodgson, *America in Our Time* (Garden City, New York: Doubleday, 1976), p. 19.
8. Michael Hudson, *Global Fracture* (New York: Harper and Row, 1977), p. 13.
9. A fascinating account of the way in which American policy affected domestic options within Europe is contained in Charles S. Maier,

"The Politics of Productivity: Foundations of American International Economic Policy After World War II," in *Between Power and Plenty*, ed. Peter J. Katzenstein (Madison, WI: University of Wisconsin Press, 1977), pp. 23–49.

10. Cited in Alonzo L. Hamby, *Beyond the New Deal: Harry S. Truman and American Liberalism* (New York: Columbia University Press, 1973), p. 6.

11. Kolko, *Main Currents*, p. 312.

12. Eric F. Goldman, *The Crucial Decade and After: America, 1945–1960* (New York: Vintage, 1960), p. 14.

13. Samuel Lubell, *The Future of American Politics*, 3rd ed. rev. (New York: Colophon Books, 1965), pp. 27, 39.

14. Donovan, *Conflict and Crisis*, p. 109.

15. Ibid., p. 184.

16. I. F. Stone, *The Truman Era* (New York: Vintage, 1973), p. 122.

17. This quotation, and all the ones that follow from the Clifford memo, are from "Memorandum for the President, November 19, 1947," Clifford Papers, Truman Library.

18. Mary Sperling McAuliffe, *Crisis on the Left: Cold War Politics and American Liberals, 1947–1954* (Amherst, MA: University of Massachusetts Press, 1978).

19. Bert Cochran, *Labor and Communism: The Conflict that Shaped American Unions* (Princeton: Princeton University Press, 1977), p. 260.

20. Idem.

21. Arthur Schlesinger, Jr., *The Vital Center* (Boston: Houghton Mifflin, 1948).

22. Ibid.

23. Hodgson, *America in Our Time*. See also Marc Weiss and Martin Gellen, "The Rise and Fall of the Cold War Consensus," in *A House Divided*, eds. Judith Carnoy and Marc Weiss (Boston: Little, Brown, 1973).

24. Edward R. Tufte, *Political Control of the Economy* (Princeton: Princeton University Press, 1978).

25. All of my figures on the GNP and industrial production after 1945 come from the very helpful statistical appendix in Goodwin, *Exhortation and Controls*, pp. 407–420.

26. For figures, see Block, pp. 141–160.

27. Herbert Parmet, *The Democrats* (New York: Oxford University Press, 1970), pp. 151–161.

28. John M. Blair, *Economic Concentration* (New York: Harcourt Brace Jovanovich, 1972), pp. 64, 331.

29. Ernest Mandel, *Late Capitalism* (Atlantic Highlands, NJ: Humanities Press, 1975), p. 487.

30. Cited in Jim F. Heath, *Decade of Disillusionment* (Bloomington: University of Indiana Press, 1975), p. 107.

31. Mandel, *Late Capitalism*, p. 142.

32. Rostow, p. 286.

33. George L. Perry, "Stabilization Policy and Inflation," in *Setting National Priorities: The Next Ten Years*, eds. Henry Owen and Charles L. Schultze (Washington: Brookings Institution, 1976), p. 271.

34. Samuel Bowles and Herbert Gintis, "The Crisis of Liberal Democratic Capitalism," unpublished paper, February 1980, pp. 26–27.

35. These figures are from Manuel Castels, *The Economic Crisis and American Society* (Princeton: Princeton University Press), pp. 114–123.

36. Ibid., p. 107.

37. Charles Schultze, *The Public Use of Private Interest* (Washington: Brookings Institution, 1977).

38. I have examined the positions of these men much more carefully in "The Rise and Fall of Trilateralism," in *Trilateralism: Elite Planning for World Management*, ed. Holly Sklar (Boston: South End Books, 1980) and in "Resurgent Cold War Ideology: The Case of the Committee on the Present Danger," in *Capital and the State in U.S.–Latin American Relations*, ed. Richard Fagen (Stanford: Stanford University Press, 1979), pp. 41–75.

39. *The New York Times*, February 19, 1981, p. B8.

## III: Counter-Keynesianism

1. Arthur Schlesinger, Jr., *A Thousand Days* (Greenwich, CT: Fawcett, 1965), p. 134.

2. *Business Week*, June 30, 1980, p. 66.

3. *The General Theory of Employment, Interest, and Money* (New York: Harcourt, Brace & World, 1936), p. 378. Emphasis added.

4. For a more detailed argument on this point, see Andrew Martin, *The Politics of Economic Policy in the United States: A Tentative View from a Comparative Perspective* (Beverly Hills: Sage Publications, 1973).

5. *General Theory*, p. 376.

6. John Maynard Keynes, "National Self-Sufficiency," *The Yale Review* 22 (Summer 1933): 758. Cited in Stephên Hymer, "International Politics and International Economics," in *Stress and Contradiction in Modern Capitalism*, eds. Leon N. Lindberg et al. (Lexington, MA: Lexington Books, 1975), p. 358.

7. Seymour E. Harris, ed., *Saving American Capitalism* (New York: Knopf, 1948), p. 4.

8. Stephen Kemp Bailey, *Congress Makes a Law* (New York: Columbia University Press, 1950), pp. 57–59.

9. Cited in Karl Schriftgiesser, *Business Comes of Age* (New York: Harper & Brothers, 1960), p. 148.

10. Charles Lindblom, *Politics and Markets* (New York: Basic Books, 1977), p. 170.

11. Grant McConnell, *Private Power and American Democracy* (New York: Knopf, 1966).

12. Joan Robinson, *Economic Philosophy* (Garden City, NY: Anchor Books, 1964), pp. 99–100.

13. Herbert Stein, *The Fiscal Revolution in America* (Chicago: University of Chicago Press, 1969), pp. 241–280.

14. Richard Child Hill, "At the Cross Roads: The Political Economy of Postwar Detroit" (Paper delivered at a conference on Urban Political Economy at the University of California, Santa Cruz, April 8–10, 1977), pp. 11–12.

15. Barton Bernstein, "Economic Policies," in *The Truman Period as a Research Field*, ed. Richard S. Kirkendall (Columbia, MO: University of Missouri Press, 1967), pp. 121, 122.

16. Daniel Yergin, *Shattered Peace* (Boston: Houghton Mifflin, 1977), p. 398.

17. Cited in Schriftgiesser, *Business Comes of Age*, p. 186.

18. Fred L. Block, *The Origins of International Economic Disorder* (Berkeley and Los Angeles: University of California Press, 1977), p. 103.

19. Stein, *The Fiscal Revolution in America*, p. 240.

20. Cited in ibid., p. 363.

21. Arthur Schlesinger, Jr., *Robert Kennedy and His Times* (Boston: Houghton Mifflin, 1978), p. 407.

22. Cited in Ronald Frederick King, "The Politics of Regressive Taxation Changes: The Investment Tax Credit of 1962 as a Hegemonic Public Policy" (Paper prepared for delivery at the 1977 annual meeting of the Midwest Political Science Association), p. 12.

23. Herbert Parmet, *The Democrats* (New York: Oxford University Press, 1970), pp. 151–161.

24. Stein, *The Fiscal Revolution in America*, p. 421.

25. See Robert S. McIntyre, "Credit Where Credit Is Due," *The New Republic*, April 22, 1978, p. 17.

26. Godfrey Hodgson, *America in Our Time* (Garden City, NY: Doubleday, 1976), p. 225.

27. Arthur M. Okun, *The Political Economy of Prosperity* (New York: Norton, 1970), p. 33.

28. Reprinted from George L. Perry, "Stabilization Policy and Inflation," in *Setting National Priorities: The Next Ten Years*, eds.

Henry Owen and Charles L. Schultze (Washington: Brookings Institution, 1976), p. 300.

29. Okun, *The Political Economy of Prosperity*, p. 75.

30. Warren L. Smith, "Monetary and Fiscal Policies for Economic Growth," in *Perspectives on Economic Growth*, ed. Walter W. Heller (New York: Vintage Books, 1968), p. 56.

31. An excellent account of the rise in the rate of unemployment that is generally accepted as "full" is presented by Richard DuBoff, "Full Employment: The History of a Receding Target," *Politics and Society* 7 (1977): 1–25.

32. Cited in Otis L. Graham, Jr., *Toward a Planned Economy* (New York: Oxford University Press, 1976), p. 256.

33. One place in which these words are quoted is Leonard Silk, *Nixonomics* (New York: Praeger, 1973), p. 57.

34. On Nixon's anger, see William Safire, *Before the Fall* (Garden City, NY: Doubleday, 1975), p. 491.

35. Cited in Graham, *Toward a Planned Economy*, p. 218.

36. Nixon's plans to reorganize the government are discussed in Richard P. Nathan, *The Plot That Failed* (New York: Wiley, 1975).

37. Calculated from the *Economic Report of the President, 1978* (Washington: Government Printing Office, 1978), p. 257.

38. Graham, *Toward a Planned Economy*, p. 264.

## IV: Reform Without Reform

1. For an early statement of this feeling, see Arthur Okun, *Equality and Efficiency: The Great Trade-off* (Washington: Brookings Institution, 1975).

2. Quoted in Mark I. Gelfand, *A Nation of Cities: The Federal Government and Urban America, 1933–1965* (New York: Oxford University Press, 1975), p. 140.

3. Cited in Richard O. Davies, *Housing Reform During the Truman Administration* (Columbia, MO: University of Missouri Press, 1966), pp. 18, 20.

4. Davies, *Housing Reform*, p. 109.

5. Ibid., p. 113.

6. Barton J. Bernstein, "Reluctance and Resistance: Wilson Wyatt and Veterans' Housing in the Truman Administration," *The Register of the Kentucky Historical Society* 65 (January 1967): 47–66.

7. James Duffy, *Domestic Affairs* (New York: Simon and Schuster, 1978), p. 43.

8. Davies, *Housing Reform*, p. 43.

9. Ibid., p. 105.

10. Quoted in ibid., p. 136.

11. Ibid., p. 108.

12. Quoted in ibid., p. 102.

13. Rosemary Stevens, *American Medicine and the Public Interest* (New Haven and London: Yale University Press, 1971), p. 275.

14. See *Building America's Health: A Report to the President by the President's Commission on the Health Needs of the Nation*, vols. 1–4 (Washington: Government Printing Office, 1952, 1953).

15. Cited in Robert J. Donovan, *Conflict and Crisis: The Presidency of Harry S. Truman* (New York: Norton, 1977), p. 125.

16. Cited in Dan M. Feshbach, "Allocative Politics in the Hill-Burton Hospital and Survey Construction Act" (Department of City and Regional Planning, University of California, Berkeley, 1977) p. 16.

17. Ibid., p. 1.

18. Barry Ensminger, *The $8 Billion Hospital Bed Overrun* (Washington: Health Research Group, 1975), p. 5.

19. For the notion of a pro-growth coalition I am indebted to John Mollenkopf. See his article, "The Postwar Politics of Urban Development," in *Marx and the Metropolis*, eds. William K. Tabb and Larry Sawyers (New York: Oxford University Press, 1978), pp. 117–152.

20. Edward S. Flash, Jr., *Economic Advice and Presidential Leadership* (New York: Columbia University Press, 1965), p. 129.

21. Cited in Gelfand, *A Nation of Cities*, p. 290.

22. Ibid., p. 296.

23. Ibid., p. 337.

24. Mollenkopf, "Postwar Politics," p. 126.

25. Ibid., p. 140.

26. Roger Friedland, "Class Power and the Central City" (Ph.D. dissertation, Department of Sociology, University of Wisconsin, 1976).

27. Robert Caro, *The Power Broker* (New York: Knopf, 1974).

28. Cited in Marc Weiss and Martin Gellen, "The Rise and Fall of the Cold War Consensus," in *A House Divided*, eds. Judith Carnoy and Marc Weiss (Boston: Little, Brown, 1973), p. 32.

29. Barry Checkoway, "The Politics of Postwar Suburban Development" (Working Paper no. 13, Childhood and Government Project, University of California, Berkeley, 1977). See also Patrick J. Ashton, "The Political Economy of Suburban Development," in Tabb and Sawyers, *Marx and the Metropolis*, pp. 64–89.

30. Duffy, *Domestic Affairs*, p. 52.

31. Martin Anderson, *The Federal Bulldozer* (Cambridge, MA: MIT Press, 1964); James Q. Wilson, ed., *Urban Renewal: The Record and the Controversy* (Cambridge, MA: MIT Press, 1969); Robert Goodman, *After the Planners* (New York: Simon and Schuster, 1971).

32. Chester Hartman et al., *Yerba Buena* (San Francisco: Glide Publications, 1974) and Chester Hartman and Rob Kessler, "The Illusion

and Reality of Urban Renewal," in Tabb and Sawyers, *Marx and the Metropolis*, pp. 153–178.

33. For details, see Caro, *The Power Broker, passim.*

34. Theodore Lowi, *The End of Liberalism* (New York: Norton, 1969).

35. Cited in Checkoway, "Postwar Suburban Development," p. 29.

36. Ibid., p. 30.

37. Raymond Wolfinger, *The Politics of Progress* (Englewood Cliffs, NJ: Prentice-Hall, 1974).

38. Gelfand, *A Nation of Cities*, pp. 208, 209, 215.

39. Lowi, *The End of Liberalism*, pp. 250–283.

40. See J. R. Lave and L. B. Lave, *The Hospital Construction Act* (Washington: American Enterprise Institute for Public Policy Research, 1974).

41. Melvin Webber, "The BART Experience: What We Have Learned," *The Public Interest* 45 (Fall 1976): 79–108.

42. Frances Fox Piven and Richard Cloward, *Poor People's Movements* (New York: Vintage Books, 1979), p. 14.

43. Here, I am following the argument of Bernard J. Frieden and Marshall Kaplan, *The Politics of Neglect: Urban Aid from Model Cities to Revenue Sharing* (Cambridge, MA: MIT Press, 1975).

44. Cited in ibid., p. 61.

45. Ibid., p. 59.

46. Cited in Michael Harrington, *Decade of Decision* (New York: Simon and Schuster, 1980), pp. 211–212.

47. Theodore R. Marmor, *The Politics of Medicare* (Chicago: Aldine, 1970), p. 23.

48. Robert Stevens and Rosemary Stevens, *Welfare Medicine in America: A Case Study of Medicaid* (New York: The Free Press, 1974), p. 47.

49. Marmor, *The Politics of Medicare*, p. 86.

50. *The Los Angeles Times*, January 22, 1979, p. 1.

51. Henry Aaron, *Politics and the Professors: The Great Society in Perspective* (Washington: Brookings Institution, 1978), p. 12. Also cited in Harrington, *Decade of Decision*, p. 242.

52. Karen Davis and Cathy Schoen, *Health and the War on Poverty: A Ten-Year Appraisal* (Washington: Brookings Institution, 1978).

53. Frances Fox Piven and Richard Cloward, *Regulating the Poor* (New York: Vintage, 1971), pp. 248–284.

54. Sar A. Levitan and Robert Taggart, *The Promise of Greatness* (Cambridge, MA: Harvard University Press, 1976), p. 102.

55. Ibid., pp. 119–149.

56. Ibid., pp. 3, 4.

57. Frieden and Kaplan, *Politics of Neglect*, pp. 198–202.

58. Quoted in Louis Fisher, *Presidential Spending Power* (Princeton: Princeton University Press, 1974), p. 195.

59. Vincent J. and Vee Burke, *Nixon's Good Deed: Welfare Reform* (New York: Columbia University Press, 1974); Daniel Patrick Moynihan, *The Politics of a Guaranteed Income* (New York: Vintage, 1973).

60. Richard P. Nathan, *The Plot That Failed* (New York: Wiley, 1975).

## V: Paying an Imperial Price

1. Ronald Radosh, *Prophets on the Right* (New York: Simon and Schuster, 1975).

2. Joseph Schumpeter, *Imperialism and Social Classes* (Cleveland: World, 1968).

3. Daniel Yergin, *Shattered Peace* (Boston: Houghton Mifflin, 1977).

4. This story is well told in Richard M. Freeland, *The Truman Doctrine and the Origins of McCarthyism* (New York: Schocken Books, 1974), pp. 47–69, 151–200.

5. Alan Wolfe, *The Rise and Fall of the "Soviet Threat"* (Washington: Institute for Policy Studies, 1979).

6. Acheson, in his autobiography, tells how he sought a statement of the Soviet threat that would be "clearer than truth." Dean Acheson, *Present at the Creation* (New York: Norton, 1969), p. 375. Nitze informed an analyst of NSC–68 of the need to sharpen the language in order to win the bureaucratic battle. Paul Y. Hammond, "NSC–68: Prologue to Rearmament," in *Strategy, Politics, and Defense Budgets*, ed. Warner Schilling (New York: Columbia University Press, 1962), p. 309.

7. Edward S. Flash, *Economic Advice and Presidential Leadership* (New York: Columbia University Press, 1965), p. 38.

8. "NSC–68: A Report to the National Security Council, by the Executive Secretary on United States Objectives and Programs for National Security," in Thomas H. Etzold and John Lewis Gaddis, *Containment* (New York: Columbia University Press, 1978), pp. 385–442.

9. Fred L. Block, *The Origins of International Economic Disorder* (Berkeley and Los Angeles: University of California Press, 1977).

10. John Bartlow Martin, *Adlai Stevenson of Illinois* (Garden City, NY: Doubleday, 1976), p. 705.

11. Samuel P. Huntington, *The Common Defense* (New York: Columbia University Press, 1961), p. 87.

12. Maxwell Taylor, *The Uncertain Trumpet* (New York: Harper & Row, 1960), p. 11.

13. U.S. Congress, Joint Committee on Defense Production, *Deter-

rence and Survival in the Nuclear Age (The "Gaither Report" of 1957) (Washington: Government Printing Office, 1976), p. 23.

14. Taylor, *The Uncertain Trumpet*, p. 34.

15. Henry A. Kissinger, *Nuclear Weapons and Foreign Policy* (New York: Harper & Brothers, 1956), p. 55.

16. *The "Gaither Report" of 1957*, p. 23.

17. Kissinger, *Nuclear Weapons*, p. 412.

18. Arthur Schlesinger, Jr., *A Thousand Days* (Greenwich, CT: Fawcett, 1965), p. 296.

19. Alain C. Enthoven and K. Wayne Smith, *How Much Is Enough?* (New York: Harper & Row, 1971), p. 11.

20. Schlesinger, *A Thousand Days*, p. 297.

21. Ibid., p. 311.

22. Maxwell Taylor, "The Lessons of Vietnam," *U.S. News and World Report*, November 27, 1972, pp. 22–26; Raymond Barrett, "Graduated Response and the Lessons of Vietnam," *Military Review* (May 1972): 80–91; Leslie Gelb, "Six Lessons We Should Have Learned in Vietnam," *Washington Post*, June 14, 1972, p. A-26; and Clark Clifford, "A Vietnam Reappraisal," *Foreign Affairs* 47 (July 1969): 601–622. For a different view, see Leslie Gelb and Richard Betts, *The Irony of Vietnam* (Washington: Brookings Institution, 1979).

23. Quoted in Godfrey Hodgson, *America in Our Time* (Garden City, NY: Doubleday, 1967), p. 229.

24. Idem.

25. Richard N. Cooper, "U.S. Economic Growth and World Leadership," in *Perspectives in Economic Growth*, ed. Walter W. Heller (New York: Vintage, 1968), p. 117.

26. In 1966, Heller said: "This country, with its prodigious productive capacity, faces no runaway inflation. . . ." Walter Heller, *New Dimensions of Political Economy* (Cambridge, MA: Harvard University Press, 1966), p. 84.

27. A good review of these economic difficulties is contained in Herbert Y. Schandler, *The Unmaking of a President* (Princeton: Princeton University Press, 1977), p. 225–228.

28. Schandler, *The Unmaking of a President*, p. 195.

29. Ibid., p. 120.

30. Ibid., p. 141.

31. Ibid., p. 259.

32. Tad Szulc, *The Illusion of Peace* (New York: Viking, 1978); William Shawcross, *Sideshow* (New York: Simon and Schuster, 1979).

33. Henry A. Kissinger, *American Foreign Policy*, 3rd ed. (New York: Norton, 1977), p. 150.

34. Ibid., p. 161.

35. On Kissinger's difficulties with the cold warriors see Roger Morris, *Uncertain Greatness* (New York: Harper & Row, 1977), p. 212.

On the SALT talks in general, see John Newhouse, *Cold Dawn* (New York: Holt, Rinehart and Winston, 1973).

36. U.S. Congress, Senate, Committee on Foreign Relations, *Warnke Nomination* (Washington: Government Printing Office, 1977), p. 5.

37. *Warnke Nomination*, p. 5.

38. *Warnke Nomination*, p. 145.

39. Statement on Foreign and Defense Policy, by Eugene V. Rostow (Prepared for delivery before the Platform Committee of the Democratic National Convention, May 19, 1976), p. 6.

40. Gelb, "Six Lessons We Should Have Learned in Vietnam," in *Washington Post*.

41. United States Committee on the United Nations, *Controlling the Conventional Arms Race* (New York: U.S.C.U.N., 1976).

42. Anthony Lake, *The "Tar Baby" Option: American Policy Toward Southern Rhodesia* (New York: Columbia University Press, 1973).

43. For greater detail on this point see Alan Wolfe and Jerry Sanders, "Resurgent Cold War Ideology: The Case of the Committee on the Present Danger," in *Capital and the State in U.S.–Latin American Relations*, ed. Richard Fagen (Stanford: Stanford University Press, 1979), pp. 41–75.

## VI: Nationalistic Internationalism

1. Quoted in Alfred C. Eckes, *A Search for Solvency* (Austin: University of Texas Press, 1975), p. 52.

2. Ibid., p. 56.

3. Richard N. Gardner, *Sterling–Dollar Diplomacy in Current Perspective*, rev. and enl. ed. (New York: Columbia University Press, 1980), p. 76.

4. Eckes, *Search for Solvency*, p. 117.

5. Gardner, *Diplomacy in Current Perspective*, p. 98.

6. Ibid., p. 81.

7. Eckes, *Search for Solvency*, p. 157.

8. Ibid., p. 86.

9. Gardner, *Sterling–Dollar Diplomacy*, pp. 130, 131.

10. Ibid., p. 99.

11. Ibid., p. 134.

12. Karl Schriftgiesser, *Business Comes of Age* (New York: Harper & Brothers, 1960).

13. Statement of the War Writer's Board, in Gardner, *Sterling–Dollar Diplomacy*, p. 141.

14. Ibid., p. 259.

15. Roy Harrod, cited in ibid., p. 268.

16. David P. Calleo and Benjamin M. Rowland, *America and the*

*World Political Economy* (Bloomington: Indiana University Press, 1973), p. 64.

17. Fred L. Block, *The Origins of International Economic Disorder* (Berkeley and Los Angeles: University of California Press, 1977), p. 143.

18. Eckes, *Search for Solvency*, p. 242.

19. Ibid., pp. 238–239.

20. Robert Solomon, *The International Monetary System, 1945–1976* (New York: Harper & Row, 1977), p. 33.

21. Richard N. Cooper, *The Economics of Interdependence* (New York: McGraw-Hill, 1968), p. 5.

22. Block, *International Economic Disorder*, pp. 112–113.

23. Quoted in Arthur Schlesinger, Jr., *A Thousand Days* (Greenwich, CT: Fawcett, 1965), pp. 129–130.

24. Gardner, *Sterling–Dollar Diplomacy*, pp. xxxiv–xxxv.

25. Eckes, *Search for Solvency*, p. 243.

26. Robert V. Roosa, *The Dollar and World Liquidity* (New York: Random House, 1967), p. 145.

27. Martin Mayer, *The Fate of the Dollar* (New York: Times Books, 1980), p. 118.

28. Michael Hudson, *Global Fracture* (New York: Harper & Row, 1977), p. 49.

29. James P. Hawley, "U.S. Restrictions of Export of Capital, 1961–71" (Ph.D dissertation, McGill University, Montreal, Canada, 1976).

30. Quoted in Mayer, *Fate of the Dollar*, p. 138.

31. Robert Gilpin, *U.S. Power and the Multinational Corporation* (New York: Basic Books, 1975), p. 14.

32. Ibid., p. 152.

33. Ibid., p. 161.

34. Richard Barnet and Ronald Müller, *Global Reach* (New York: Simon and Schuster, 1974).

35. This chart is reprinted from Edward R. Fried and Philip H. Trezise, "The United States in the World Economy," in *Setting National Priorities: The Next Ten Years*, eds. Henry Owen and Charles L. Schultze (Washington: Brookings Institution, 1976), p. 170.

36. Mary Kaldor, *The Disintegrating West* (New York: Hill and Wang, 1978).

37. C. Fred Bergsten, *The Dilemmas of the Dollar* (New York: New York University Press, 1975), p. 112.

38. Gottfried Haberler and Thomas D. Willet, *A Strategy for U.S. Balance of Payments Policy* (Washington: American Enterprise Institute, 1971); Lawrence B. Krause, *Sequel to Bretton Woods: A Proposal to Reform the World Monetary System* (Washington: Brookings Institution, 1971).

39. Roger Morris, *Uncertain Greatness* (New York: Harper & Row, 1977), p. 102.

40. Hudson, *Global Fracture*, p. 59.

41. Gardner, *Sterling–Dollar Diplomacy*, p. xxxv.

42. Motoo Kaji, Richard N. Cooper, and Claudio Segré, *Toward a Renovated World Monetary System* (1973), in *Trilateral Commission Task Force Reports, 1–7* (New York: New York University Press, 1977), pp. 1–31.

## VII: Developing Development

1. Quoted in David A. Baldwin, *Economic Development and American Foreign Policy, 1943–62* (Chicago: University of Chicago Press, 1966), pp. 72–73.

2. Ibid., p. 74.

3. Ibid., p. 142.

4. Ibid., p. 29.

5. Cheryl Payer, *The Debt Trap: The IMF and the Third World* (New York: Monthly Review Press, 1974), p. 25.

6. Alfred C. Eckes, *A Search for Solvency* (Austin: University of Texas Press, 1975).

7. *Report to the President on Foreign Economic Policies* (Washington: Government Printing Office, 1950).

8. International Development Advisory Board, *Partners in Progress* (New York: IDAB, 1951).

9. Committee for Economic Development, *Economic Development Assistance* (New York: CED, 1957).

10. Arthur Schlesinger, Jr., *A Thousand Days* (Greenwich, CT: Fawcett, 1965), p. 540.

11. W. W. Rostow, *The Stages of Economic Growth*, 2nd ed. (New York: Cambridge University Press, 1971), p. 163.

12. Quoted in Schlesinger, *Thousand Days*, p. 541.

13. Cited in Baldwin, *Economic Development*, p. 180.

14. Robert A. Packenham, *Liberal America and the Third World* (Princeton: Princeton University Press, 1973).

15. Ibid., p. 63.

16. Cited in ibid., pp. 114–115.

17. Cited in Baldwin, *Economic Development*, pp. 174–175.

18. Schlesinger, *Thousand Days*, p. 503.

19. For the story of Bowles's treatment, see David Halberstam, *The Best and the Brightest* (Greenwich, CT: Fawcett, 1973), pp. 87–90.

20. Schlesinger, *Thousand Days*, pp. 183–184.

21. The officials are Gustav Ranis and Joan Nelson. See Teresa Hayter, *Aid as Imperialism* (Baltimore: Penguin Books, 1971), p. 88.

22. Hayter, *Aid as Imperialism*, p. 91.

23. Payer, *Debt Trap*, pp. 143–165.

24. Joan M. Nelson, *Aid, Influence, and Foreign Policy* (New York: Macmillan, 1968), p. 38.

25. Cited in Orlando Letelier and Michael Moffitt, *The International Economic Order* (Washington: Transnational Institute, 1977), p. 22.

26. A. W. Singham, ed., *The Non-Aligned Movement in World Politics* (Westport, CT: Lawrence Hill, 1977).

27. Richard R. Fagen, "Equality in the South in the Context of North–South Relations," in Albert Fishlow et al., *Rich and Poor Nations in the World Economy* (New York: McGraw-Hill, 1978), p. 207.

28. M. Ahluwalia, "Income Inequality: Some Dimensions of the Problem," in Hollis Chenery et al., *Redistribution with Growth* (New York: Oxford University Press, 1974), p. 12.

29. Lester B. Pearson, *Partners in Development: Report of the Commission on International Development* (New York: Praeger, 1969).

30. Gunnar Myrdal, *The Challenge of World Poverty* (New York: Vintage, 1970).

31. Overseas Development Council, *The United States and the Developing World: Agenda for Action.* Published yearly since 1973 by Praeger. See also Guy Erb and Valeriana Kallab, eds., *Beyond Dependency: The Developing World Speaks Out* (New York: Praeger, 1975).

32. Joan Edelman Spiro, *The Politics of International Economic Relations* (New York: St. Martin's Press, 1977), p. 228.

33. Cited in Letelier and Moffitt, *International Economic Order*, p. 40.

34. Michael Harrington, *The Vast Majority* (New York: Simon and Schuster, 1977), p. 232.

35. Daniel Patrick Moynihan, "The United States in Opposition," *Commentary* 59 (March 1975): 31–44.

36. A good summary of the argument is P. T. Bauer, "Western Guilt and Third World Poverty," *Commentary* 61 (January 1976): 31–38.

37. *The Rockefeller Report on the Americas* (Chicago: Quadrangle, 1969).

38. For an overview, see Samuel L. Baily, *The United States and the Development of South America, 1945–1975* (New York: New Viewpoints, 1976), pp. 117–128.

39. ". . . in almost every known instance where United States authorities had the opportunity to make policy-relevant choices between a Southern regime with socialist implications and some other regime—no matter how repressive and anti-equity—the choice has almost always been for the latter. What the Chilean case did was pose the choices and the alternatives most dramatically of all, but the logic employed in making the choices was no different than it would have been had the alternatives been murkier and the values in conflict more problematic." Fagen,

"Equality in the South," p. 204. It remains to be seen whether Nicaragua will constitute an exception.

# VIII: Carter's Conundrum

1. For an analysis of the shortcomings of such tax-based incomes policies, see Sam Rosenberg, "Incomes Policy: The 'Tip' of the Iceberg," in R. Cornwall and M. Claudon, *New Approaches to Fighting Inflation* (New York: Academic Press, forthcoming).

2. See Richard Child Hill, "Left with the Democrats? The Rise and Demise of a Full-Employment Bill," in *U.S. Capitalism in Crisis* (New York: Union for a Radical Political Economics, 1978), pp. 275–283.

3. Seymour Melman, *The Permanent War Economy* (New York: Simon and Schuster, 1974).

4. *The San Francisco Chronicle*, July 1, 1980, p. 10.

5. *The New York Times*, January 5, 1979, p. 1.

6. Leslie Gelb, "National Security and the New Foreign Policy," *Parameters* (journal of the U.S. Army War College), November 8, 1978, p. 10-F.

7. Marshall D. Shulman, testimony before the House Subcommittee on Europe and the Middle East, October 26, 1977.

8. James Fallows, "The Passionless Presidency," *Atlantic*, May 1979, p. 43.

9. Alan Wolfe, *The Rise and Fall of the "Soviet Threat"* (Washington: Institute for Policy Studies, 1979).

10. George H. Nash, *The Conservative Intellectual Movement in America* (New York: Basic Books, 1976), p. 323.

11. Richard N. Cooper, Karl Keiser, and Mastake Kosaka, *Toward a Reconstructed International System* (New York: The Trilateral Commission, 1977).

12. Motoo Kaji, Richard N. Cooper, and Claudio Segré, *Toward a Renovated World Monetary System* (1973), in *Trilateral Commission Task Force Reports, 1–7* (New York: New York University Press, 1977), p. 24.

13. On some of these problems, see U.S. Congress, Senate, Subcommittee on Anti-Trust and Monopoly of the Committee on the Judiciary, *Hearings on Economic Concentration*, 90th Cong., 2nd sess., 1968, p. 3446.

14. *The New York Times*, December 7, 1977, p. 73.

15. *The New York Times*, June 13, 1977, p. 1.

16. Kaji, Cooper, and Segré, *Renovated World Monetary System*, p. 4.

17. Robert Solomon, *The International Monetary System* (New York: Harper & Row, 1976), pp. 267–289.

18. Quoted in Mary Kaldor, *The Disintegrating West* (New York: Hill and Wang, 1978), p. 87.

19. John Vinocur, "The Bonhomie in Bonn," *The New York Times*, July 11, 1980, p. A3.

20. C. Fred Bergsten, "The Threat from the Third World," *Foreign Policy* 11 (Summer 1973): 104–105.

21. Albert Fishlow et al., *Rich Nations and Poor Nations in the World Economy* (New York: McGraw-Hill, 1978), and W. Howard Wriggins and Gunnar Adler-Karlsson, *Reducing Global Inequalities* (New York: McGraw-Hill, 1978).

22. Roger Hansen, "Major U.S. Options on North–South Relations: A Letter to President Carter," in *The United States and World Development: Agenda 1977*, eds. John W. Sewell et al. (New York: Praeger, 1977).

23. Mahbub ul Haq, *The Poverty Curtain* (New York: Columbia University Press, 1976), and Hollis Chenery et al., *Redistribution with Growth* (New York: Oxford University Press, 1974).

24. Richard N. Gardner, Saburo Okita, and B. J. Udink, "A Turning Point in North–South Economic Relations," in *Trilateral Commission Task Force Reports, 1–7* (New York: New York University Press, 1977), p. 59.

25. Michael Harrington, *The Vast Majority* (New York: Simon and Schuster, 1977), p. 243.

26. Orlando Letelier and Michael Moffitt, *The New International Economic Order* (Washington: Transnational Institute, 1977), p. 41.

27. *The New York Times*, February 11, 1977.

28. Cited in Geoffrey Barraclough, "Waiting for the New Order," *The New York Review of Books 25* (October 26, 1978): 52.

29. Ibid., p. 49.

30. Figures cited from an editorial in *The New York Times*, July 15, 1980.

# IX: America After Reagan

1. *Republican Platform*, proposed by the Committee on Resolutions to the Republican National Convention, July 14, 1980, p. 26.

2. Ibid., p. 51.

3. Richard Burt, "Reagan Team Says U.S. Must Deal with Any Threat," *The New York Times*, November 13, 1980, p. A8.

4. For example, see Charles Lindblom, *Politics and Markets* (New York: Basic Books, 1977), and Milton and Rose Friedman, *Free to Choose* (New York: Harcourt Brace Jovanovich, 1980).

5. Eugene V. Rostow, *Planning for Freedom* (New Haven: Yale University Press, 1959).

6. Franz Schurmann, *The Logic of World Power* (New York: Pantheon Books, 1974).

7. I have argued this point, with respect to social democracy, at much greater length in "Has Social Democracy a Future?" *Comparative Politics* 11 (October 1978): 100–125.

8. For a fuller statement, see Richard Barnet, *The Lean Years* (New York: Simon and Schuster, 1980).

9. An answer along the lines of fiscal austerity is provided in Felix Rohatyn, "The Coming Emergency and What Can Be Done About It," *The New York Review of Books*, December 4, 1980, p. 20.

10. Lenny Goldberg, "Surviving the Politics of Austerity," *Working Papers* 7 (November–December 1980): 40.

11. Lester Thurow, *The Zero-Sum Society* (New York: Basic Books, 1980).

12. Ronald E. Müller, *Revitalizing Amercia* (New York: Simon and Schuster, 1980), p. 279.

13. Gar Alperovitz and Jeff Faux, *Rebuilding America* (New York: Simon and Schuster, 1981).

14. See Paul Blumberg, *Inequality in an Age of Decline* (New York: Oxford University Press, 1980).

15. Norman Birnbaum, editorial in *The Nation*, November 22, 1980, p. 535.

16. Nigel Calder, *Nuclear Nightmares* (New York: Viking Press, 1980).

17. Earl C. Ravenel, *Never Again: Learning from America's Foreign Policy Failures* (Philadelphia: Temple University Press, 1978).

18. Barry Bluestone and Bennett Harrison, *Capital and Communities* (Washington: The Progressive Alliance, 1980).

19. Willy Brandt and Anthony Sampson, eds., *North–South: A Program for Survival* (Cambridge, MA: MIT Press, 1980).

20. This is the theme of Mary Kaldor, *The Disintegrating West* (New York: Hill and Wang, 1978).

21. Rohatyn, "The Coming Emergency," p. 20.

# Index

## About the Author

Alan Wolfe is professor of sociology at Queens College and the Graduate Center of the City University of New York. He is the author of *The Rise and Fall of the "Soviet Threat," The Limits of Legitimacy,* and *The Seamy Side of Democracy*, which was nominated for the Pulitzer Prize in 1973.